Subject
to Reality

WOMEN AND FILM HISTORY INTERNATIONAL

Series Editors
Kay Armatage, Jane M. Gaines, and Christine Gledhill

A new generation of motion picture historians is rediscovering the vital and diverse contributions of women to world film history whether as producers, actors, or spectators. Taking advantage of new print material and moving picture archival discoveries as well as the benefits of digital access and storage, this series investigates the significance of gender in the cinema.

A list of books in the series appears at the end of this book.

,

Subject
to Reality

Women and Documentary Film

SHILYH WARREN

UNIVERSITY OF ILLINOIS PRESS

Urbana, Chicago, and Springfield

Library of Congress Cataloging-in-Publication Data
Names: Warren, Shilyh J., 1974– author.
Title: Subject to reality : women and documentary film / Shilyh
    Warren.
Description: Urbana : University of Illinois Press, 2019. |
    Series: Women and film history international | Includes
    bibliographical references and index.
Identifiers: LCCN 2018049780| ISBN 9780252042539 (hardcover :
    alk. paper) | ISBN 9780252084348 (pbk. : alk. paper)
Subjects: LCSH: Documentary films—United States—History—
    20th century. | Women motion picture producers and
    directors—United States. | Feminism and motion pictures. |
    Motion pictures and women.
Classification: LCC PN1995.9.D6 W37 2019 | DDC 070.1/8—dc23
    LC record available at https://lccn.loc.gov/2018049780

Ebook ISBN 9780252051371

I watch how desperately we need political memory, so that we are not always imagining ourselves the ever-inventors of our revolution; so that we are humbled by the valiant efforts of our foremothers; and so, with humility and a firm foothold in history, we can enter upon an informed and re-envisioned strategy for social/political change in decades ahead.

—Cherríe Moraga[1]

Contents

Acknowledgments

This book emerged out of more than a decade of thinking, researching, teaching, and movie watching. The seed was first planted when I was a student in the Duke University Graduate Program in Literature, where complex models of feminist thinking inspired field-changing thought experiments in classrooms, living rooms, office hours, and conferences.

I'm grateful for the tough love and generous support I received from brilliant feminist faculty at Duke, especially Ranjana Khanna, Negar Mottahedeh, Robyn Wiegman, and Jane Gaines in Literature. Fellow travelers through graduate school in that place we came to love with such uncommon devotion, you were all part of this, too.

I benefited enormously from talented librarians across Duke University (and especially at Lilly Library), and the archival mavens at the Sallie Bingham Center for Women's History and Culture. Financial support from Duke University allowed me to travel to the New York Public Library, where I first watched on 16mm most of the films from the 1970s that generated the questions at the heart of this book. At the Donnell Media Center, Elena Rossi-Snook and Johnny Gore made all kinds of miracles happen for me and continue to do so for all of us who are dedicated to the preservation and exhibition of independent documentary filmmaking.

At North Carolina State University, I had invaluable support from students and faculty, especially the stunning example of scholarly generosity that is Maria

Pramaggiore, as well as the opportunity to teach courses that directly informed my ideas about documentary and the history of women in cinema.

My colleagues at the University of Texas at Dallas guided me through the thick writing of this project, both intellectually and emotionally. I'm especially grateful to my writing group: Ashley Barnes, Charles Hatfield, Annelise Heinz, Natalie Ring, Eric Schlereth, and Daniel Wickberg, who read practically every chapter of this manuscript, engaged in vigorous debate, and consistently helped me make sense of my ideas and passions. My gratitude also extends to numerous current and former colleagues and students who expressed consistent support and encouragement throughout the years when I was writing and teaching to the anxious rhythm of the tenure clock.

As this project began to take form as a book, several other readers came to my rescue, especially Beatriz Balanta, Amy Freund, Amelie Hastie, and Kimberly Lamm, whose insightful interlocution inspired the most significant and revelatory revisions. My talented research assistant Amal Shafek also deserves special mention for her careful work reading and editing the full manuscript.

My reviewers at the University of Illinois Press offered generous responses and crucial feedback, especially Alexandra Juhasz and Sophie Mayer, inimitable feminist writers who pushed my thinking profoundly. My editor, Daniel Nasset, gracefully shepherded this project and connected me to the brightest thinkers in my field.

To my friends as well as the strangers who told me they were looking forward to reading this book: thank you. To Janelle Ellis, a constant source of support and inspiration and my favorite person to see movies with: thank you. To my family, those of you both near and far, who kept asking me how the book was going: thank you. And to Daniel, Lucas, and Zev, thank you, because you had to bear the brunt of it all for years and years and years.

I am also grateful for the generous guidance and attention I received from curators and archivists at the Library of Congress, including Rosemary Hanes and Mutahara Mobashar, and the Martin and Osa Johnson Safari Museum, especially Conrad Froehlich and Jacquelyn Borgeson Zimmer.

Finally, to the filmmakers at the heart of this book, those who sent me work and answered my phone calls and emails, those I've met in person, as well as the many more I will never know: thank you for making cinema the instrument of your desire and political commitments. May you inspire many more of us for ages to come.

Subject
to Reality

Introduction

Two Real Moments

Question: What is a revolutionary aesthetic?
Answer: What is revolution?
—Barbara Martineau[1]

This book reconsiders the history and study of women's documentary film-making in the United States during two key periods—1920 to 1940, and the long 1970s—when significant transformations in cinematic technologies coincided with major transformations in sociopolitical discourses surrounding gender and race. The decades between 1920 and 1940 saw not only modern technological innovations, including synchronous sound recording in cinema, and social transformation in the rise of the "New Woman,"[2] but also ethnocentric waves of passion for the fetishized Other, the popularization of eugenics, the back-lash against women's right to vote, and the reign of Jim Crow in the South. At the beginning of the long 1970s, cameras became portable and film stock and recording equipment more versatile at the same time that the revolutionary thinking of disenfranchised populations forced massive social and political upheavals, including radical antiwar and anticapitalist demonstrations and the pursuit of expanded rights and freedoms for women, gays and lesbians, and people of color. Straddling these decades, *Subject to Reality* seeks out the surprisingly entwined political, social, and discursive threads that wound their way into documentary filmmaking during these periods, focusing intently on gender, race, and class politics throughout.

The discovery that most influenced the claims I make throughout *Subject to Reality* struck me as I was thinking and writing about women's documentary production of the 1970s. I began to wonder what past cinematic influences women filmmakers of the 1970s had drawn from. In one of the earliest studies of women's filmmaking of the 1970s, Jan Rosenberg notes that women in the sixties and seventies who aspired to "make movies" sometimes gained industry experience working on documentary film crews, where they were most likely employed as "sound girls" by male directors.[3] Alternatively, women with economic advantages also began attending newly established film schools and/or studied film as part of their undergraduate educations. Thanks to Kristen Fallica's institutional history of the feminist media organization Women Make Movies, which was founded in the early 1970s, we also know that women picked up 16mm cameras and began learning from and with each other and more experienced partners and friends as an expression of their feminist politics.[4] However, I was especially curious to know if and how women left their mark on documentary filmmaking in the decades prior to and leading up to the 1970s.

I was stunned to find limited research devoted to the long history of women in documentary. Of course, women have been making documentaries since the emergence of cinema in the late nineteenth century, and many of these, though by no means all, have focused feminist concerns. Surprisingly, however, a comprehensive historical survey of women's contributions to documentary filmmaking has yet to be written. *Subject to Reality* anticipates that momentous project but pursues an alternative ambition. Rather than comprehensive, my approach is passionately transhistorical, setting women's cultural expression during these two explosive periods into conversation, and thereby provoking a reconsideration of a number of key debates about subjectivity, feminism, realism, and documentary that have had lasting epistemological and material consequences for film and feminist studies.

Within the archives of scholarship and production, I discovered that early women documentarians tended toward ethnographic and anthropological films. This realization transformed my thinking about the trajectory of women's documentary film production in the twentieth century. Broadly speaking, this lineage could claim global filmmakers as diverse as Katherine Dunham, Helen Levitt, Shirley Clarke, Jane Belo, Maya Deren, Forough Farrokhzad, Chick Strand, Ateyyat El Abnoudy, Barbara Myerhoff, Mona Hatoum, and Trinh Minh-ha—women who have consistently used cameras to read and represent cultures, both foreign and familiar, that beckoned them. In *Subject to Reality* I focus on the United States, situating women documentarians, such as Osa Johnson, Frances Flaherty, Zora Neale Hurston, Margaret Mead, Joyce Chopra, Amalie Rothschild, Martha Coolidge, Madeline Anderson, Christine Choy, and others, in the sociopolitical contexts specific to American life in these two tumultuous periods. Hence, *Subject to Reality*'s dual objective is to uncover a lost ethnographic history of women's documentary production and investigate the political and aesthetic legacy of this early history in the later, more deliberately feminist and yet equally misremembered period of the 1970s.

The ethnographic strain, which in some historiographies begins with the success of Robert Flaherty's *Nanook of the North* (1922), has long been of interest to documentary scholars. Important attention to the ethnographic legacy and its political consequences and dilemmas abounds in the work of Paula Rabinowitz, Bill Nichols, Catherine Russell, Fatimah Tobing Rony, and Alison Griffiths. Close to my own work on the seventies, Rabinowitz's *They Must Be Represented: The Politics of Documentary* excavates the ethnographic twists and turns throughout the development of *cinéma vérite,* for example, which in the 1970s shifted from "the private exposure of public events and figures" to "the public display of private, even secret lives."[5] In films like *Grey Gardens* (1974) and the televised documentary series *An American Family* (1974) and *Roots* (1976), Rabinowitz noted that a "convergence" of new ways of thinking about the family, race, politics, documentary, and ethnography occurred in the 1970s.[6] Just as feminism politicized the domestic sphere and private life and America reconsidered its history of racial discrimination, "ethnography had 'moved in' to its own backyard, fieldwork being as much about self-inspection as travel to other cultures."[7] For Rabinowitz, however, the ethnographic turn inward to personal territory marked an "invasion" that in *An American Family,* especially, was "firmly lodged within its imperialist legacy."[8] In *They Must Be Represented* ethnography represents the slippery logic of imperial desire and a dangerous collusion with the grammar of colonialism. For alternatives, Rabinowitz looks to the work of experimental filmmakers Chick Strand and Trinh Minh-ha, who boldly rejected and reconfigured realism and colonial tropes in their visual ethnographies of the 1980s and 1990s. Rabinowitz's eloquent attention to experimental feminist ethnographies thus replays a familiar script in feminist film studies that has tended to either reject or ignore more conventional and realist documentaries like the ones that interest me here.

In *Subject to Reality,* I seek an alternative formal path through the tangled histories of ethnography, feminism, and documentary. In particular I challenge the tendency to pass over realist documentaries, evident in Rabinowitz as well as throughout feminist film scholarship.[9] More pointedly, *Subject to Reality* asks how ethnographic thinking and seeing shaped the historical arc and aesthetic, ethical, and political commitments of women's realist documentaries throughout the twentieth century. In fact, the enmeshment between these discourses is profound and not merely a matter of formal and philosophical debates about the limits of realist aesthetics. When feminist film scholar Amelie Hastie calls herself an "anthropological cineaste of another future," in her article about 1970s film feminisms, she astutely places herself within this important lineage of women's production and feminist reception.[10] Similarly, it was anthropologist Helen Powdermaker who famously dubbed Hollywood the "dream factory" in her 1950 ethnographic study of the industry.[11] That is to say, the shared interests of women in anthropology, academic film studies, and political feminism have long shaped the production and reception of documentary in the United States. *Subject to Reality* explores the consequences of this cross-pollination as it has shaped women's documentaries, and especially the films that have been glossed over as "boring" "organizing tools" or merely "talking-head films" and, more skeptically, rejected as reactionary, bourgeois, colonialist, and naïve.

Without this history, the study of the *and* in "documentary and feminism"—catalyzed most recently by Diane Waldman and Janet Walker in *Feminism and Documentary* in 1999—lacks key historical and aesthetic links in the chain of events that comprise the entwined history of anthropology, cinema, postcolonial theory, and gender studies.[12] As Waldman and Walker indicate in their field-shifting introduction to the volume, feminism, ethnography, and documentary share a commitment to exploring and resisting the habitual dynamics of power between selves and others, filmmakers and filmed subjects, and subjects and objects.[13] The fact is that the films and filmmakers I discuss throughout this book have received precious little attention from fellow scholars, and by overlooking this work we have missed an important opportunity to explore cinematic responses to the uneven dynamics of power between filmmakers and filmed subjects that continue to shape the making of documentary films about gender, race, class, and sexuality.

Furthermore, setting these two periods of women's filmmaking into conversation creates a valuable through-line that prioritizes women's film *production* throughout the long history of women's documentary filmmaking. *Subject to Reality* argues that the neglect of women's documentary filmmaking is due in part to inflexible modes of thinking about political subjectivity (revolution) and cinematic realism (aesthetics). That documentaries are "subject to reality" because they take the real world as their starting point is undeniable. However, the way that documentary realism both represents and produces women as "subjects of reality" calls for a granular investigation of the formal and ethical complexities of women's practice. *Subject to Reality* insists that new analytical methods, aesthetic forms, and political subjects emerge when we reintegrate lost and sidelined work into the entwined historiographies of documentary, feminism, and film theory.

The First: 1920–1940

In the past decade, an impressive new wave of scholarship on women's global participation in early cinema has developed throughout feminist studies.[14] However, that body of work has focused almost exclusively on fictional film-making and filmmakers, and only recently have scholars granted attention to early women documentarians in particular.[15] Likewise, renewed interest in second-wave feminism has generated retrospective attention to 1970s feminist film theory, but material histories of women's film production, circulation, and reception remain scarce.[16] In North America, it turns out, numerous women made documentaries in the silent era and during the early years of talkies. Adriana and Dolores Ehlers were sisters from Mexico who studied documentary in the United States during World War II. Elizabeth Chevalier Pickett began her career by directing nonfictional films for the Red Cross in the late 1920s. Jenny Gilberston, who was born in Scotland in 1901, made films about Shetland life in the early 1930s and went on to work in Canada and London; in her sixties, Gilberston made a remarkable film about her travels to the Arctic, which was broadcast in the late 1970s on the CBC in Canada and the BBC in the UK.[17] However, even the most celebrated and productive filmmakers among them, Osa Johnson and Frances Flaherty for example, have rarely received attention from either documentary or feminist film scholars. Likewise, how strange it is that Zora Neale Hurston and Margaret Mead, two of the most well-known intellectual women in America, have yet to figure prominently in surveys of documentary filmmaking and thinking.

Each of these four women played a unique role in the long history I pursue in *Subject to Reality.* Furthermore, each sheds important light on the tangled histories of colonialism, cinema, and anthropology, which, as Ellen Strain explains, all share origins in what scholars refer to as the turn-of-the-century "frenzy of the visible" that came with the innovation of optical technologies like photography and cinema.[18] Ella Shohat and Robert Stam likewise point out that the emergence of cinema "coincided with the giddy heights of the imperial project"[19] and readily link the epistemological claims of imperialism and anthropology to the technological imperatives of cinema, particularly as these discourses constructed representations of "other territories and cultures."[20] Cinema, they explain, "lent indexical credibility to anthropology, arming it with visual evidence not only of the existence of 'others' but also of their actually existing otherness."[21] Cinema, in other words, mediated the relationship between selves and others in ways that consistently buttressed the sense of superiority of the West.

Documentary, perhaps even more than fictional filmmaking, has been en-tangled uniquely in this matrix of power, vision, and knowledge. While it may be true that colonialism, cinema, and anthropology all draw from a set of "domi-nant epistemologies, worldviews, and economic conditions of the early 20th century," documentary—as the purveyor of the truth image in cinema—ranks among the most powerful discourses through which Western subjects have as-serted possession and mastery over what Heidegger called "the world as picture" and especially as this world produces and regulates images of the Other.[22] In *Subject to Reality,* I ask how women filmmakers and filmmaking collaborators responded uniquely to the colonial desire to visualize, fix, and know otherness. I resist the totalizing assumption that anthropology, cinema, and colonialism yielded a one-size-fits-all imperial imaginary in early film production. Instead, I investigate the range of ways women filmmakers responded to the challenge of subjectivity, reality, and difference in two affectively charged moments of technological, social, and political transformation—moments when the ocular-centric sense of mastery granted to the white Western subject (in part through cinema) was deeply challenged by new modes of reproduction and the visual and political assertion of the racialized Other.

I insist on the ethnographic impulse of women's documentary filmmaking because I also want to prioritize matters of racial difference in women's docu-mentary filmmaking and emphasize how aesthetic choices (in this case real-ism) are driven by ethical and political commitments to the Other. I focus on the ways these cinematic conventions and debates anticipate feminist politics that strive to balance asymmetries of power and the ethical dilemmas inherent to projects where racial, sexual, and class differences shape the relationships between the filmmaker, her subjects, and the audience. Through close readings of films that have received little or no attention from scholars, I bring the early period of women's documentary filmmaking to light as a mode of filmmaking very much interested in the politics of difference and the ethics of representa-tion, which in turn opens a surprising counternarrative about the racial politics of the feminist 1970s.

My reconsideration of the origin stories of early ethnographic documentary filmmaking reveals a network of currents that surface and dive throughout this book: the ethical dilemmas inherent to projects about racialized others, the co-lonial legacies of anthropology and documentary, and the historical tendency to suppress the labor and presence of women. The opening chapter on Frances Flaherty and Osa Johnson initiates this new conversation about the history of women's contributions to documentary film. Both filmmakers worked collab-oratively with their husbands and devoted their careers to the representation of

Others. Their bodies of work, including letters, articles, interviews, and films, draw our attention to representational quandaries inherent to ethnographic documentary. In the slightly later ethnographic films of Zora Neale Hurston and Margaret Mead, we find commitments and strategies that anticipate the archive of the 1970s that I explore in the later chapters. In particular Hurston and Mead manifest the certainty that feminist knowledge is derived directly from the lived and observed experiences of diverse women, and especially through observational footage. In what Linda Williams calls feminist hindsight, Johnson, Flaherty, Hurston, and Mead emerge from the "wreckage" as central figures in the discursive and material histories of women, anthropology, and documentary.[23]

The Second: The Long 1970s

I found it especially curious that feminist film scholars of the 1970s did not pursue the recuperation of women's documentary production from earlier periods. So much of the intellectual force of feminism in the early 1970s focused on recovering women's silenced voices and artistic production from the past. In 1975, for example, novelist Alice Walker published a chronicle in *Ms.* magazine of her search for Zora Neale Hurston's grave.[24] At the time, few literary scholars were aware of Hurston's oeuvre; her unmarked grave remained buried in knee-high weeds in the "Garden of the Heavenly Rest" in south Florida. Walker's description of her search for Hurston pulses with grief and joy, resuscitating Hurston's ethnographic aesthetic for black feminist politics of the 1970s. Walker makes it clear that racial and gender discrimination colluded to obscure and neglect this towering figure, whom she dubs eternally, "A Genius of the South: Novelist, Folklorist, Anthropologist" on the gravestone she erects at Hurston's burial site. It was Walker's search and rescue mission that helped propel Hurston into the canons of ethnography, literature, feminism, and critical race studies, where she has enjoyed a steady revival ever since. Her surprising work as a filmmaker, however, has been noticed far less often.[25] In fact, Hurston made a number of revelatory ethnographic short films in the 1920s and '30s, which I discuss in chapter 2.

Like Walker's attention to Hurston's literary legacy, women curators and festival organizers of the 1970s excavated and directed attention to sidelined Hollywood directors, Dorothy Arzner and Ida Lupino, for example, and German directors Leontine Sagan and Leni Riefenstahl. At the inaugural Women's International Film Festival in New York City in 1972, where these and more than five hundred films by women were screened, almost half of the selections were contemporaneous short and feature-length documentary films by women—a staggering number, which one reviewer at the time remarked, "reflects a need on the part of women film-makers to fill the vacuum of information about real women."[26] The irony of this productive dual focus on neglected early filmmakers and contemporaneous documentary productions is that early women documentary filmmakers, like Johnson, Flaherty, Hurston, and Mead, slipped between the cracks and fell into relative obscurity for decades. Despite the feminist impulse that undergirded the festival, the demand that women's obscured work be known and seen left a number of crucial stones unturned. What could have been a powerful encounter between women documentary filmmakers throughout the cinema century instead became a missed opportunity for historical perspective. *Subject to Reality* attends to this omission more than four decades later, providing a retroactive map of paths not taken at the intersection of feminism, ethnography, and documentary.

The seeds of neglect of women's early documentary film production sown in the 1970s outside and inside the academy would grow rhizomatically through the decades, such that by the early 1980s, even women's documentary films of the 1970s—once heralded as the new bold language of feminism—had been dismissed as "false starts" for *cinefeminism* and relegated to the historical dustbin.[27] Poststructural skepticism about authorship, psychoanalytic interest in narrative and desire, and a reluctance to be more assertive about challenging the terms of emergent antirealist film theory, not to mention a long-standing reluctance to think about documentary filmmakers as artists, all contributed to sidelining women's documentary film production in feminist film studies as it coalesced in the mid-1970s. As a result, we are left with the realization that neglect is also part of the legacy of feminist film studies; that is, the neglect and often the outright rejection of women's film production, especially women's documentary, has long sustained the critical methodologies of feminist film theory.

In retrospect the 1970s constitute a vital period of U.S. women's documentary filmmaking. First, so many women activated by the revolutionary politics of the late 1960s and early 1970s turned to aesthetics, and filmmaking in particular, to explore their feminist awakening and desires for change, solidarity, political recognition, and economic redistribution. Second, this surge in the United States in the 1970s constituted perhaps the greatest and most sudden explosion of women's work in documentary. As Susan Kleckner, who with Kate Millett co-directed *Three Lives* (1971)—an interview-based triptych of three white women who narrate their personal biographies—remembers, "In 1970 women making a documentary about women was a revolutionary idea."[28] To understand the genealogy of the category "feminist documentary" in contemporary U.S. academic and popular discourse, I think it is important to revisit the genre's history, its pioneers and innovators, its trends and its sticking points, especially leading up to and including the 1970s.

Women's documentary films made in the United States during the feminist seventies drew on a broad range of realist documentary practices, including personal voice-over narration, filmed interviews, and archival and observational footage (also called vérite). Through this realist lens, women focused on newly identified "women's issues," such as media representation, women's health, sexuality, motherhood, marriage, and domestic labor; other films also centered on forgotten luminaries in women's history, women's participation in labor struggles, and the legacies of racial and economic discrimination. These include films I discuss in this book, such as *Joyce at 34*; *Nana, Mom and Me*; *Old Fashioned Woman*; *I Am Somebody*; *From Spikes to Spindles*; *Inside Women Inside*; and others.

As much as they are different from one another, women's realist documentaries share a commitment to the lived experiences and political desires of women and manifest what Joan Wallach Scott calls "a feminist methodology" in their attention to self, other, and the power relations that determine being, thinking, and knowing within the social fabric.[29] In the seventies, filmmakers took advantage of the new possibilities created by portable 16mm cameras and synchronous sound technologies and put other women in front of the camera to showcase the struggles they faced *as women,* as subjects of the reality of gender inequality. The reverberations of these cinematic interventions, as revolutionary as they were aesthetic, echoed throughout film festivals, college campuses, feminist publications, and consciousness-raising sessions around the United States.

Only a handful of books and scholarly articles have focused intensely on this period of women's documentary filmmaking. In the mid- and late-1990s, Alexandra Juhasz, Walker and Waldman, and Jane Gaines all published essays that reconsidered "the realist debates" in 1970s film studies and the neglect of women's documentary filmmaking by feminist scholars. Sophie Mayer's *Lo personal es politico/The personal is political* republished several major essays about 1970s feminist film theory, and included new ones in an innovative bilingual edition.[30] B. Ruby Rich's *Chick Flicks* also includes republished essays about feminist film theory and women's documentaries of the 1970s.[31] More recently Sue Thornham revisits feminist filmmaking of the 1970s and includes close analyses of several documentary films, although her book's major focus is contemporary narrative films by women.[32] *Subject to Reality* joins efforts with these contemporary projects by Juhasz, Mayer, Walker and Waldman, Gaines, and Thornham, which in various ways seek to redress an entrenched inattention to women's documentary practice.

Contemporary Trends

In the Anglophone academy, the term "feminist documentary" circulates with renewed vigor in descriptions of nonfictional films that focus explicitly on gender issues. Most decisively Belinda Smaill made a case for the need to name and describe "feminist documentary" in 2012—a cultural moment in which she observed two contradictory currents: on the one hand a massive popularization of documentary film, and on the other a striking disregard for feminism.[33] In the twenty-first century, Smaill argues, feminist documentary is notable for the way it is always inherently "out of time."[34] That is to say that since gender politics are always out of sync with the present (because they insist on alternative temporalities and ontologies), feminist documentaries are recognizable in part by their untimeliness. Smaill's attention to the temporalities of feminism resonates with the work in this book, which insists that the past was not just there then, but still here now in ways we have not been attuned to.

Domatilla Ovieri, in a recent dissertation on the subject, also offers a valuable definition of "feminist documentary." She writes, "I consider feminist documentary, then, as a film that is *haunted by reality and regarding feminist issues,* namely, issues of gender, power, and processes of inclusion and exclusion."[35] Ovieri's deliberately broad definition is nonetheless remarkably lucid, since it creates room for a range of aesthetic practices as well as diverse political ideals—points of contention in historical debates about what constitutes feminist cinema. Ovieri also shifts the burden of reality in the definition of documentary from notions of transparency or verisimilitude to spectrality. Feminist documentary is not "based on" or "representative of" or "about" reality: it is "*haunted* by reality," in Ovieri's estimation. Reality is thus the fleeting certainty that cannot itself be ascertained in feminist documentary: there, but it is also beyond there; it matters but it is not material. In Ovieri's definition of feminist documentary exists space for films as diverse as Amber Bemak and Nadia Granados's contemporary explorations of lesbian sexuality and global politics in the *Tell Me When You Die Trilogy* (2017), as well as more conventional documentaries such as the celebrated *Miss Representation* (Jennifer Siebel Newsom, 2011).

Furthermore, Ovieri's expansive definition of feminism as characterized by "issues of gender, power, and processes of inclusion," invites us to revisit the archive of women's documentary filmmaking with an eye toward broader relations of power and "processes of inclusion and exclusion" that are not strictly based on female bodies or female experiences. Indeed, Ovieri and I agree that feminist documentary demonstrates a strong ethnographic tradition in which "otherness"—racial, ethnic, religious, national, and otherwise—becomes central to the work that feminist documentaries engage in. Scott has argued that what we might broadly call "feminist methodology" could be summarized in part by the following claims:

> There is neither a self nor a collective identity without an other. There is no inclusiveness without exclusion, no universal without a rejected particular, no neutrality that doesn't privilege an interested point of view, and power is always at issue in the articulation of these relationships. Put in other terms, we might say that all categories do some kind of productive work; the questions are how? and to what effect?"[36]

Following both Scott and Ovieri, who emphasize the dialectical relationships between self and other and privilege and dispossession, I trace the ways that feminist documentary investigates relations of power, especially as these affect the complex production and management of gender in a world to which we wish to belong and share.

Subject to Reality is in part a recuperative project, which aims to insinuate forgotten and neglected films into the canons of feminist documentary filmmaking. However, my aim in this book is not merely additive or corrective. Rather, my claim is that the forgotten ethnographic legacy of women's documentary filmmaking transforms the terms of the debates that have shaped our understanding of both documentary and feminism, especially matters of difference and the aesthetics of realism. Focusing on the shared ethical commitments, contestatory epistemological claims, and politicized realism in these two periods of women's documentary filmmaking excavates and reerects a previously misread heritage—matrilineal, ethnographic, ethnic, and racial—in the entwined history of feminism and documentary.

Subject to Reality also pressures some familiar assumptions about these films and offers alternative analytical tools and methods of reading and interpreting what I hope is a newly relevant archive of women's documentary film production as its concerns became entwined with those of ethnography, feminist politics, and the politicization of film theory. As Juhasz reminds us, the imbrication of academic film study and independent filmmaking means that our work as film scholars has material consequence for archiving and distribution.[37] Films that draw scholarly attention are more likely to be made available to the public.

Feminist artists, activists, and filmmakers today lack access to and knowledge about the diverse history of women's film production because many films are rather difficult to track down and screen. The objects that critics, curators, and scholars deem worth of study, in other words, often determine what gets saved, digitized, and distributed and what gets left on aging and fungible material in the archives.

Rethinking Realism

Our attention to neglected, independent, and feminist films also has conceptual stakes, of course. Because very little scholarship about these films exists, we have few examples of how to analyze films that seem suspiciously transparent in their objectives or appear to be primarily educational or merely historical because of their realism. As Thornham observes, feminist film theory and feminist film practice diverged at a crossroads in the early 1980s and have yet to fully benefit from their shared interests. Similarly, as Waldman and Walker assert, feminism and documentary have suffered from what they call "mutual myopia," existing in isolated spheres of mutual interest.[38] The result of these concurrent modes of erasure is that we lack generative methods to explain how realist feminist films operate at a formal level, what they seek to achieve, and why they should continue to matter. We have yet to conceive of a long history of women's documentary filmmaking, the significance of feminist aspirations to this archive, and modes of reading that can account for the particular ambitions of revolutionary and ethnographic realism.

In feminist film theory in particular, women's documentaries came to light under a single bulb in the midseventies: within the context of the critique of realism throughout film theory. The critique of realism in film studies arose in conversation with structuralism, semiotics, and Althusser; however, many feminist film scholars embraced the ideological critique of realism as they elaborated a distinctly feminist archive of scholarship and practice. As George Kouvaros indicates, the debates on realism in seventies film studies constituted "a defining moment" for the field.[39] Realism was posed as the antithesis of the more highly regarded aesthetics of modernism. Julian Murphet thus explains how what he refers to as the dominant "materialist" mode in seventies film theory in the mold of *Screen* cinema critics Colin MacCabe and Stephen Heath reserved "the noble epithet—'modernist'—only for those properly experimental, avant-gardist film texts that eschewed everything 'realist.'"[40] Throughout the pages of *Screen,* film critics developed a strident critique of realism's "ideological functioning" that also mobilized the work of German playwright Bertolt Brecht.[41]

Brecht's modernist tenets, such as "alienation effects" and "distantiation," which he understood as antidotes to the veiled workings of bourgeois ideology in realist art, were embraced in film studies where the notion of the "classic realist text" was used to denote Hollywood cinema in particular and then documentaries by slippery extension.[42]

The antirealist critical stance in film studies was of course a deeply politicized anticapitalist and sometimes feminist methodology. Yet, as Gaines contends, it went virtually unchallenged for more than two decades; and the hegemony of the antirealist critique would have dire consequences for the material and intellectual legacy of women's documentary practice.[43] Feminist films scholars Claire Johnston, Pam Cook, and Laura Mulvey, in particular, elaborated gender-specific frameworks for cinematic analysis that were indebted to the ideological critique of realism. For these feminist film scholars, the critique of realism facilitated a methodology for thinking through the pernicious meaning-making processes of cinema, which to their minds naturalized a view of the world and thus of women's oppression *as is*. Johnston stated the case against realism most stridently in "Women's Cinema as Counter Cinema," arguing, "the 'truth' of our oppression cannot be 'captured' on celluloid with the 'innocence' of the camera: it has to be constructed/manufactured. New meanings have to be created by disrupting the fabric of the male bourgeois cinema within the text of the film."[44] Flagged by quotation marks, concepts such as "truth," "capture," and "innocence" signal the film theorist's skepticism about the possibilities of representing the oppression of women "realistically" through what she calls "a cinema of non-intervention."[45] While Johnston's critique of realism is widely known throughout feminist film studies, we have failed to stress the significance of the fact that Johnston was explicitly reacting against the rising trend of women's documentary filmmaking, exemplified by films such as Kate Millett's *Three Lives* (1971) and Midge MacKenzie's *Women Talking* (1971). In these documentaries, women speak to each other and to the camera, in the style of feminist consciousness-raising, about their varied experiences as subjects of white patriarchal capitalism. Some feminist critics celebrated these revolutionary films as models of women's emerging consciousness of oppression. However, Johnston pointed out what she saw as a problematic reliance on "cinema verité techniques"[46] and called instead for a mode of women's film practice that would "break" and "disrupt" the illusion of realism with a new "language" of cinema and a newly constructed "interrogation" of reality.[47] Thus, as Juhasz, Waldman and Walker, and others have noted, the feminist idiom of the critique of realism operated in direct collaboration with a rejection of women's documentary praxis. Furthermore, as *Subject to Reality* demonstrates, the legacy of this intellectual antirealist stance is that feminist film scholars have neglected to reexamine prior decades of women's realist documentary practice.

The opposition between modernism and realism, however, as Toril Moi writes within the context of her discussion of Norwegian playwright Henrik Ibsen, "is fundamentally flawed."[48] Drawing from Fredric Jameson's elaboration of "the ideology of modernism" in *A Singular Modernity* as "a set of aesthetic norms" with attendant "aesthetic and theoretical beliefs," Moi explains that (literary) realism is sorely mischaracterized by the ideologues of modernism.[49] "Realism," she maintains, "does not have a built-in commitment to any particular philosophical position. There are many kinds of realism, and realist illusion can coexist with the deepest skepticism in relation to the power of words to make sense."[50] Moi's point is that realism can very well share the philosophical skepticism that undergirds the ideology of modernism. Thus, she sets forth a more elastic definition of the repudiated term in conversation with Erich Auerbach; "realism is neither a specific style nor a specific historical period, but rather an aspect or feature of all kinds of texts," writes Moi.[51] Jameson, too, underscores how realism "by definition" resists becoming "a paradigm of any kind: a form, a tale-type, or even a genre."[52] Recast in this way by both Moi and Jameson, a contemporary return to realism, which animates *Subject to Reality*, demands attention to history, culture, politics, and context: "there are all kinds of realisms," writes Moi, "our task . . . is to account for their specificity, not demonize them all as naïve 'representationalism'."[53]

In the last two decades, a broader reengagement with realism has taken place in the fields of literature, painting, and photography. In film studies, also, the critique of realism has been under serious reconsideration. Ivone Margulies, for example, challenges the hegemony of the critique of realism in her 2002 collection, *Rites of Realism: Essays on Corporeal Cinema*, when she states unequivocally that the anthology "distances itself from the generalized indictment of realist aesthetics as a form of deception."[54] Margulies challenges a conventional narrative in film studies, which remembers the critique of realism as a rebellion against bourgeois values inherent in the ideas of postwar thinkers like André Bazin and Siegfried Kracauer. Margulies repositions Bazin, transforming him from a naïve, passé paternalist into a pioneering thinker whose work was always-already skeptical about the nature *and* artifice of "realism" in cinema. *Subject to Reality* joins forces with this reconsideration of the critique of realism evident also throughout the Visible Evidence series of books on documentary film, including Chris Holmlund and Cynthia Fuchs's edited collection, *Between the Sheets, In the Streets,* Waldman and Walker's *Feminism and Documentary,* and Jane Gaines and Michael Renov's *Collecting Visible Evidence.*[55] Realism has resurged as a site of legitimate critical inquiry, particularly for documentary film studies and in the newly articulated relationship between "feminism and documentary" heralded by Walker and Waldman's collection.

In this vein, *Subject to Reality* offers reading strategies commensurate with a realist style of filmmaking that asks to be read not for what it conceals, but for what it *reveals* about real women's lives and their ethical commitments and political ambitions. I offer new ways to think about realist aesthetics and women's documentary practice by drawing from cultural studies, visual anthropology, postcolonial studies, affect theory, and feminist theory. In its singular commitment to women's practice, close readings, and historical and discursive contexts, *Subject to Reality* offers documentary studies something distinct from other valuable reconsiderations of documentary ethics and politics, such as Elizabeth Cowie's *Recording Reality, Desiring the Real,* Belinda Smaill's *The Documentary: Politics, Emotion, Culture,* and Ilona Hongisto's *Soul of the Documentary.*[56] My readings sometimes emphasize form because women's documentaries are composed of diverse cinematic conventions with long histories in both political and ethnographic filmmaking: interviews, observation, voice-overs, and personal narratives, for example. Yet I focus on the ways these cinematic conventions serve feminist politics, which strive to expose and balance asymmetries of power between women, and ethical commitments evident in projects where racial, sexual, and class differences shape the intimate relationships between the filmmaker, her subjects, and the audience. The overarching narrative that emerges as a result is that early ethnographic and entertainment production, later anthropological cinemas, and the activist films of the seventies were all deeply invested in feminist politics of difference and the ethics of representation.

Juhasz's *Women of Vision: Histories in Feminist Film and Video* from 2001, an interview-based monograph and documentary film that features twenty-one "histories in feminist media," models the thick history of women's film production that inspires *Subject to Reality.*[57] As a feminist film scholar and media maker, Juhasz also engages in a mode of ethnographic feminist practice central to my work, which prioritizes experience, close reading, and attention to the delicate and intimate politics of representation and power. Feminist film scholarship includes numerous and valuable case studies, biographies, and recuperations of women's cinematic and scholarly production; however, as Juhasz points out, these are cyclically remembered and then re-forgotten over the years. Juhasz calls this "a recurring cycle of feminist knowledge and action" whereby "feminists exist and are forgotten, make their work and see it disappear, are remembered and get lost, are rediscovered, erased, and re-represented yet again."[58] My personal copy of *Women of Vision*, a gift from my doctoral advisor Jane Gaines, whose signature graces the title page, bears witness to these material cycles of feminist memory. *Subject to Reality* forms part of this cycle, hoping to interrupt the tendency to forget by drawing out new connections and conclusions from the feminist archives of documentary.

Subject to Reality also participates in a broader effort in feminist studies to reconsider the material history and intellectual, political, and aesthetic legacies of second-wave feminism. Recent reclamation projects include Nancy Fraser's *Fortunes of Feminism,* Clare Hemmings's *Telling Feminist Stories,* Victoria Hesford's *Feeling Women's Liberation,* Kristen Hogan's *The Feminist Bookstore Movement, This Book is an Action* by Jaime Harker and Cecilia Konchar Farr, *Addressing the Other Woman: Textual Correspondences in Feminist Art and Writing* by Kimberly Lamm, *Liberation in Print* by Agatha Beins, as well as numerous others in fields ranging from history to gender studies, to film and media studies, anthropology, art history, and beyond. Academic journals such as *Signs, Camera Obscura,* and *South Atlantic Quarterly* have also published special issues on the 1970s since 2000. In the new journal *Feminist Media Histories,* Amelie Hastie reconsiders *Ms.* magazine's 1970s articles on film and suggests that revised reading practices "might show readers something more subtle than they would expect, let them inspect it, and allow them to draw their own conclusions."[59] As she observes, when it comes to seventies feminism, "This 'something' might be a subtlety in our understanding of both the history and theory of the period."[60] Hastie's attention to "subtlety" suggests that as scholars, we have tended to rely on generalizations and assumptions about what evidence exists in the material and aesthetic archives of the 1970s, especially regarding its subjects (women) and its forms of realism and reality. Revisiting the archive then, equipped with more flexible and less assumptive reading practices, Hastie and others suggest, opens new arenas of research and new nodes of relevance between the archive and the activism and affect of the present.

The Chapters

Subject to Reality comprises four chapters that together provide an account of the anthropological and feminist dimensions, questions, and consequences of women's documentaries during two key historical periods. The first chapter reinvigorates our understanding of the foundations of this anthropological strain in the pseudo-ethnographies of Frances and Robert Flaherty and Osa and Martin Johnson, filmmaking couples working at the intersection of ethnography and nonfiction entertainment in the '20s and '30s. In the second chapter I consider the ethnographic projects of Zora Neale Hurston and Margaret Mead, women who were formally trained in anthropology at Columbia University and were among the early pioneers of filmmaking as ethnographic research. While each of these women has received deserved and sustained attention on her own, *Subject to Reality* connects their biographical, artistic, and politicized lives to one another and highlights their shared ambitions and diverse approaches to documenting the lives of Others.

In chapters 3 and 4, I demonstrate how 1970s realist feminist documentaries resonate with the earlier period of ethnographic and anthropological filmmaking. The driving concerns of many early anthropological filmmakers included the social construction of race, gender, and sexuality and cultural processes of normalization. These same matters would later become the pillars of feminist activism and feminist documentaries of the 1970s. The connections between the early period and the 1970s run even deeper. Both periods of filmmaking also made visible and tangible struggles over the representation of Others and the possibility of solidarity across difference. In chapter 3, "Strangely Familiar," I engage one of the most visible groups of women's documentary films of the 1970s: personal films made by white women about self and family. In *Joyce at 34* (Joyce Chopra and Claudia Weill, 1972), *Nana, Mom and Me* (Amalie Rothschild, 1974), and *Old Fashioned Woman* (Martha Coolidge, 1974) filmmakers turned their cameras on their personal lives and their loved ones. My readings of these films emphasize their autoethnographic qualities: the way that a subject emerges in relation to normalized cultural practices produced by race, class, and gender. I take my cues from other scholars of subjective filmmaking, especially Michael Renov and Alisa Lebow, who insist that films about selves are inherently relational and therefore also about the culture in which that self comes to be. In the case of women's personal documentaries, I argue that reading for "culture" means exploring the ways the formation of whiteness is at once assumed and revealed in these films.

Chapter 4, "Native Ethnographers and Feminist Solidarity," focuses on a group of documentaries that pursue a collective rather than individual form of self-ethnography. In *I Am Somebody* (Madeline Anderson, 1969), *From Spikes to Spindles* (Christine Choy, 1976) and *Inside Women Inside* (Christine Choy and Cynthia Maurizio, 1980), women of color filmmakers expose the struggles their communities face and share with other communities of color. In *I Am Somebody*, Anderson compiles broadcast news footage with original interviews and voice-over to reconstruct a historic strike by black, predominantly female hospital workers in Charleston, South Carolina in 1968. A member of Third World Newsreel, a radical film collective still active today, Christine Choy's *From Spikes to Spindles* also uses interviews, archival footage, and voice-over to tell a new history of New York City's Chinatown. In these films, which have received scant scholarly attention, subjectivity is a collective enterprise and gender is consistently made to matter in terms that resonate with both intersectional and postcolonial feminist theory. Whereas the feminist seventies are often criticized for their lack of attention to matters of race, these films urge a reconsideration of what stories count within our narratives about the racial politics of feminism in the 1970s. Together, chapters 3 and 4 highlight the extent to which women filmmakers in the realist tradition had both convergent and divergent concerns, especially regarding the imbrication of race, class, and sexuality with matters of gender.

This is not to say that all women's documentaries are either realist or anthropological, of course. Rather, I claim that acknowledging the shared commitments of visual anthropology and women's documentary sheds new light on the political and ethical commitments of feminist realist aesthetics, which dominate throughout both periods at stake in this book. Indeed, as *Subject to Reality* demonstrates, women documentary filmmakers have long shared key questions, especially about identity, difference, and solidarity, although they have attempted to answer them distinctly, depending on their political, social, discursive, and economic contexts and personal ambitions. The result of revisiting both periods, and in tandem, is an opportunity to reflect on questions about the ideological processes of canon formation, matters of neglect and scarcity in the archive, and debates about politics (racial and gendered) and aesthetics (especially realism), which are all central questions in film history and theory.

Telling stories about origins, influences, and legacies as I do in this book is a high-stakes endeavor with feminist consequences in and also beyond the academy.[61] As Hemmings has passionately contended, the stories that feminists tell about feminism "intersect with wider institutionalizations of gendered meanings."[62] Hemmings warns that "the amenability" of our stories means we must remain attentive to the habits of grammar, citation, and appropriation that unwittingly repeat and fix narratives about feminism (and its whiteness, middle-class-ness, achievements, failures, pasts, and futures, for example) that could otherwise be rethought and repurposed "to transformative effect."[63] With this in mind, *Subject to Reality* revisits familiar stories about the past, including some of feminism's most beloved and oft-rejected cinematic heroines, in pursuit of what Shelley Stamp calls "a new overarching narrative"—not simply a new arrangement of "individual case studies"—about the history of women's stunning participation in documentary filmmaking.[64] Of course, the history of women and film, as Pam Cook observes, is not a simple tale of progress, improvement, and inclusion; rather, narratives of women's participation in the history of cinema rise and fall according to numerous factors.[65] Likewise, this book revisits key moments in the history of women's work in documentary, but cannot offer a conclusive progressive narrative. Rather, what *Subject to Reality* provides is a new frame of analysis, which brings buried ideas and neglected films to the foreground of feminist film studies. I also take to heart Barbara Martineau's emphatic call to action, which opens this introduction: "Women's films must be seen in the light of revolutionary aesthetics," she writes. "Women must develop revolutionary aesthetics. The context for a revolutionary aesthetic is the struggle by emerging peoples to gain control of the tools which have previously been used to control them."[66] I follow Martineau's shift in emphasis from "aesthetics" to "revolution," which I take as a call to understand the aesthetic commitments of women's documentary films in terms of the politics and ethics they aspire to.

Readers might be surprised that other key figures at the intersection of anthropology and documentary filmmaking do not figure more prominently in this book. For example, connections between Maya Deren's avant-garde aesthetic and her ethnographic explorations in Haiti, most famously in *The Divine Horseman: The Living Gods of Haiti* (1985), are certainly connected to the trends I point out here. Among Deren's influences we should also include African American dancer, anthropologist, and filmmaker Katherine Dunham, a contemporary of Zora Neale Hurston who awaits reclamation. Chick Strand, one of the founders of Canyon Cinema, also stands out for her intellectual training in anthropology and her ecstatic visual ethnographies. In *Fake Fruit Factory* (1986), for example, Strand's emphatic close-ups and discontinuous editing offer partial and yet profound insight into neocolonial labor practices in Central America. However, Deren's and Strand's work is adjacent to rather than embedded in the feminist traditions of realism I focus on in the book.[67] Similarly, although Trinh Minh-ha's scholarship and filmmaking praxis also trouble the interstices of anthropology, feminism, and documentary, her practice consistently challenges rather than reworks the aesthetics of realism that interest me here.[68] Anthropologist and filmmaker Barbara Myerhoff followed in Mead's footsteps, becoming a public intellectual whose work was celebrated in *Number Our Days* (1976), which won an Oscar for best short documentary in 1977. She was also instrumental to the creation of the Center for Visual Anthropology at the University of Southern California, where she worked for decades.[69] These women have all indelibly influenced the development of documentary and its ethnographic strain in particular.

Nonetheless, I hope that the remarkable figures and narratives that do emerge in *Subject to Reality*—and especially evidence about the long-standing concern with matters of racial difference and representation—will contribute to a broader effort to tell and retell neglected, omitted, misread, and misremembered stories about the cinematic and feminist past. There are other films I wish I could have included. *Harlan County, USA* (Barbara Kopple, 1974), raises unique questions about women's participation in labor struggles. *Yudie* (1974) is Mirra Bank's poignant and humorous portrait of her Aunt Yudie, an independent Jewish woman from New York's historic Lower East Side who recommends a daily piece of fruit to ward off negative feelings. Maxi Cohen's *Joe and Maxi* (1978) tracks a tense relationship between a Jewish daughter and her father. Constance Beeson's *Holding* (1971) is a playful early foray into white lesbian sexuality. The intensely personal films of Miriam Weinstein, which have been recently reconsidered by Scott MacDonald, have long fascinated me as well.[70] As I was conducting research for this book, many of these filmmakers, including Mirra Bank, Michelle Citron, Maxi Cohen, and Barbara Hammer, kindly sent me copies of their films when they heard about my project. Extending the scope of my book to the 1980s would have brought in a number of women of color who began making more personal documentaries in the early 1980s, such as Michelle Parkerson, Camille Billops, Lourdes Portillo, Ana Maria Garcia, Allie Light, Lan Brooks, O. Funmilayo Makarah, and others. So many women's documentary films from the past have yet to receive the attention they deserve. This is also true of the 1950s and early 1960s, in which women's documentary film production seems to have gone underground and emerged transformed in the independent and experimental work of Shirley Clarke and Marie Menken, for example. The story of women's work in documentary clearly exceeds the boundaries of this study. My hope is that the work I take on in *Subject to Reality* will inspire others to pursue research on the history of women's documentary filmmaking across the globe.

CHAPTER 1

Filming Among Others

Frances Flaherty and Osa Johnson

In this chapter, I revisit the work of Frances Flaherty and Osa Johnson and write new pages into the story of women's documentary filmmaking, especially during the early years of both cinema and anthropology. Johnson and Flaherty worked collaboratively with their more famous husbands, which has effectively erased their contributions as producers, writers, actors, directors, and promoters of their films. Their lost labor is indicative of the efforts so dear to me in *Subject to Reality*, which asks what it means to recuperate the forgotten matrilineal legacy that has shaped the lives and work of numerous women filmmakers. For Johnson and Flaherty documentary filmmaking was a collaborative endeavor in the interstices of their private and public lives. They built their domestic narratives, global families, and family wealth around "contact films"—ethnographic fictions about their encounters with racial and cultural difference. In turn, these stories, picturized through the veracity machine of documentary, colluded with both patriarchy and white supremacy.

In the late nineteenth and early twentieth centuries, illustrated lectures about exotic lands, often those in the colonial contact zones, and their "savage" or "primitive" peoples drew significant audiences to vaudeville theaters.[1] Burton Holmes, a pioneer adventurer who had started out giving lectures with lantern slides, coined the term "travelogue," which he defined as "the gist of a journey" that should "delight the eye" and "charm the ear."[2] As Ellen Strain and Fatimah Tobing Rony have observed, the late nineteenth century was a heightened moment of "visual frenzy," in which the colonial subject claimed the world as image and thus as object that could be fixed, conquered, and offered back up to the empire as possession.[3] As the decades progressed, performance, photography, and cinema would all be claimed by entrepreneurs and entertainers who largely adopted the "colonial gaze" without question. Optical technologies in particular held sway in the new climate of scientific positivism, such that films and photographs that largely trafficked in racial stereotypes became the logical evidence justifying white supremacy. This history entwined with the coeval development of documentary filmmaking, which would benefit from both currents: its ability to travel the globe and its status as authentic evidence. The "reality" of documentary, its enmeshment with the colonial gaze, and its tendency to suppress the labor of women would all be aspects of the form that women throughout the decades would inherit and continue to grapple with.

In this chapter I begin to excavate the entwined histories of these "regimes of power and knowledge," in Alison Griffith's terms, as together they shaped the cinematic contributions of Flaherty and Johnson. Both women worked in the looming shadows of their more famous husbands, and yet each woman played a significant role in their joint careers. Osa Johnson was vital to all of the films credited to her husband, whether she was cranking the camera or serving pie after a night of filming wildlife from hidden blinds in the Borneo jungle. Similarly, Frances Flaherty's letters reveal that she was instrumental to Robert's career; she generated ideas for projects, networked with potential funders and collaborators, and promoted his work and travel while he was away.[4] Yet both women receive only the occasional production credit. Osa Johnson and Frances Flaherty deserve recognition for their pioneering work in ethnographic-entertainment documentary, a kind of filmmaking intimately structured by ideologies of gender, race, and realism. Their collaborative work with their husbands projected visions of far-flung places to audiences hungry for "authentic" images of the exotic. In subsequent chapters I will tell you more about how these early pioneers—and the complex legacy of gender and race that their stories animate—are vital episodes in the overarching narrative of women's documentary filmmaking.

Frances Flaherty

Historiographies of documentary often begin by referencing the early influence of Robert Flaherty's *Nanook of the North* (1922). "This picture was to have greater consequences than any previous non-fiction film," writes Lewis Jacobs in 1979.[5] *Nanook of the North* "is considered one of the first great documentaries," echoes Patricia Aufderheide in 2007.[6] In the unlikely story of *Nanook*—a film made by a mineral prospector in one of the most remote and coldest places ever captured on film—scholars have rooted out many of the form's best intentions as well as its worst habits. For as much as *Nanook* brings aesthetic reverence to scenes of real life, the film greatly manipulates audiences into believing that the dramatic story of an indigenous man against the brutal forces of nature is a faithful representation of Inuit life near the Hudson Bay in the early 1920s. In contrast to the other "father" of documentary, Dziga Vertov, Flaherty more specifically signals the ethnographic origins of documentary: the romantic desire to capture disappearing worlds and endangered cultural practices. Contemporary ethnographic filmmakers Lucien Taylor and Ilisa Barbash observe, "*Nanook* was remarkable not just for its style but also for its subject matter and approach to its subject. Never before had a non-Westerner been brought alive on the screen with such sympathy and humanity."[7] Robert Flaherty thus leaves us a complex legacy, which bears closer analysis, especially because his body of work has so significantly shaped the ethnographic and gendered history of documentary film studies.

Though he was never trained as an anthropologist, Robert Flaherty shared a fascination with indigenous people and the ethnographic impulse that defined a wide range of visual media from the mid-nineteenth century to the early 1920s when he made *Nanook*. Like so many visual representations of exotic peoples and places, *Nanook of the North* enthralled audiences when it screened in the summer of 1922. Though several distributors initially turned down *Nanook,* assuming erroneously that the public was more interested in "seeing people in dress suits," the film surprised virtually everyone when it had a blockbuster run during its first week of screenings in New York.[8] At a time of increasing modernity and globalization in North America, audiences seem to have craved visions of a (mythical) simpler time when humans enjoyed greater attunement with nature and its rhythms. As Frances Flaherty put it: "When Nanook and Nyla and little Alleggoo smile out at us from the screen, so simple, so genuine and true, we, too, become simple, genuine, true. They are themselves: we, in turn, become ourselves."[9] This wry description of *Nanook* enriches our emotional understanding of the film. Frances Flaherty's labor—the work of promoting the film—is therefore also a unique kind of affective labor; she translates this new visual form and the unfamiliar others it introduces into a familiar humanist narrative of mutual recognition.

By now it is well-known that Robert Flaherty contrived virtually every element of the story in *Nanook,* from the names of his actors to their familial relationships, down to their clothing, modes of travel and hunting, and the domestic scenes he offered to viewers as "life and love in the actual Arctic."[10] In retrospect his blatant disregard for "truth" fomented a crisis in the ontological status of documentary: if *Nanook* marks the origins of the tradition, and *Nanook* is an artful lie, heavily invested in exoticizing indigenous people, then what does that say about documentary—a form of filmmaking supposedly exemplary of the truth principle of photographic realism? Perhaps most pointedly, Rony has deciphered the implications of this Eurocentric ideology at the very heart of the documentary tradition and certainly throughout the Flahertys' body of work. She describes *Nanook* as emblematic of a "taxidermic" impulse, which "seeks to make that which is dead look as if it were living."[11] For Rony, *Nanook* embodies an imperial and romantic ideal preoccupied with its longing for primitive authenticity, and which in turn requires massive artifice to reconstruct its object: "vanishing races."[12] Others have also intensely criticized the film for its stereotypical representation of native Others as noble but uncivilized, backward but charming, wise about nature but naïve about modernity. Perhaps more than any other film, *Nanook of the North* consistently appears and reappears throughout documentary studies—haunting our archives and our scholarship with its stark reminder of the colonial and fictional legacy of documentary. Yet, very little has been said about Frances Flaherty's role in promoting this form of representation in *Nanook*. For example, her use of words like "genuine", "true", and "simple" partially signal her gendered contribution to the ethnocentric worldview that shaped the Flahertys' work. Frances's affective, material, and analytical labor, notable, for example, in her press promotion of the film, receives little recognition throughout documentary studies, which has tended to foreground the more obvious material labor of directors, who were mostly men.

If *Nanook* haunts the history of documentary, constantly reasserting itself as the ur-text of ethnography, what explains the relative absence of *Moana* in these patrilineal narratives? In fact, it was not *Nanook* but the Flahertys' subsequent film, *Moana,* about the idyllic existence of beautiful people in the Samoan islands, that gave rise to the use of the term "documentary" as a way of distinguishing nonfiction films from fictional ones. When the Scottish filmmaker (and another documentary patriarch) John Grierson saw *Moana* in 1926 he raved about the film's poetic imagery, its beauty, and its rapturous representation of nature: "I think *Moana* achieves greatness primarily through its poetic feeling for natural elements," he wrote.[13] However, it was Grierson's observation that *Moana* "being a visual account of events in the daily life of a Polynesian youth and his family, has *documentary value*" that has made the greatest mark on documentary studies.[14]

The origin story of the term "documentary" is often told; however, remarkably little has been said about Grierson's emphasis on Flaherty's gorgeous cinematography and skillful visual narration in *Moana*. Nor have documentary scholars, highly attentive to *Nanook* and Flaherty's other "man against nature films," (*Man of Aran* [1934] and *Louisiana Story* [1948]), paused to reconsider either *Moana* or the gender imbalance at stake in the focus on "man" against nature for themselves.[15] In my story, however, *Moana* opens a new conversation about hidden gendered labor at the conceptual and material birth of documentary film. Recentering *Moana* destabilizes the patriarchal history of documentary filmmaking in a number of ways because *Moana*, far more than *Nanook,* is a film that brings to the surface the collaborative labor and significance of Frances Flaherty, who shares credit on the film as co-writer, co-director, and co-producer.

Indeed, from the beginning of their relationship, Frances saw her marriage to Robert as a strategic partnership and was highly involved in his filmmaking. Flaherty biographer Robert Christopher calls Frances "a significant architect" of his career as a writer and filmmaker.[16] With "Bob," Frances felt she had come up with a "beautiful new scheme of life."[17] In her diary, Frances described her partnership with her husband as a deep commitment to him, but also as a means of fulfilling her own dreams. Bob, she wrote, was "the instrument of my desires, such a nice healthy, interesting, convenient 'tool' . . . surely as my nature and gifts were complementary to his, I could be a real and valuable partner."[18] As Christopher has observed, however, Frances's career as writer, publicist, photographer, and editor alongside her husband has been obscured in most works devoted to Flaherty. Like so many women of the twentieth century who collaborated with their husbands, Frances Flaherty's legacy has only recently begun to receive the attention it deserves.[19]

Throughout their early years of marriage and before *Nanook,* Frances's cooperation with her husband took place largely behind the scenes. Raised in an affluent and cultured household, Frances had benefited from an elite education and experiences abroad. She saw her literary and social skills as the exact and necessary complement to her husband's wild and unschooled talents in photography and exploration. She transcribed his notes, archived his diaries and photographic materials, and took dictation for his writing projects. In the early years, as he slowly began to attract media attention for his expedition photography, Frances wrote and coordinated his publicity materials and coverage. She used her contacts in the world of publishing to secure a book contract for expedition notes that she also edited. In early 1915, during their first year of marriage, Frances worked on the written narrative that would accompany film footage of his expeditions.

Frances Flaherty was both ambitious and optimistic. She was determined to make a life of "profit and pleasure" from her husband's talents, about which she was certain and fiercely protective. "I am willing to slave to the bone for it, i.e. for my ambition for him," she wrote.[20] Indeed, throughout their decades of marriage, art, and travel, Frances Flaherty would make many sacrifices for her ideal of a powerful partnership. She endured years of separation, financial uncertainty, and the more profound injustices of their long-distance intimate lives. Nonetheless, her work has rarely been highlighted in terms of "women's documentary filmmaking." Frances's ethos and vision, especially related to the representation of Others and the translation of their humanity to an audience at home, are key examples of women's suppressed labor in the long history of documentary filmmaking. Despite the fact that Frances was not the technical creator of Robert's films, her gendered labor—affective, reproductive, and as the "emotional translator" of her husband's work—were key to their mutual collaborations.[21]

If her visible work on *Nanook* was largely that of a producer and promoter of the film, and her invisible labor shaped the ethos and reception of the work, her

Frances Flaherty joins Eugene Ormandy (conductor) and C. Robert Fine (sound engineer) at the scoring session for *Louisiana Story* at Reeves Beaux Arts Studios in New York City. (Courtesy of Tom Fine.)

role in *Moana* (and all their later films) was more direct. In a much later interview with acclaimed documentary filmmaker Robert Gardner, Frances describes the journey that took their entire family to Samoa to make *Moana* in the late 1920s. The reception of *Nanook* had been so positive that, as Frances explained, Paramount gave Robert complete license and support as long as he brought back "another Nanook."[22] A friend named Frederick O'Brien had just published the bestseller *White Shadows in the South Seas,* and recommended that they visit a particular Samoan island—"the village was beautiful; the people were beautiful"—and assured them they would find a place of parallel significance to the Arctic.[23] As was the case in northern Canada among the Inuit, traditional ways of life in Polynesia were felt to be quickly and tragically disappearing. O'Brien reportedly told them, "Go. . . . You may still be in time to catch some of that beautiful culture before it passes entirely away."[24] This time Frances, Robert, and their two daughters all went abroad for a long stay in 1923–1924 to work on the film.

As with *Nanook,* the Flahertys had twin concerns in mind. On the one hand, their impulse was ethnographic; on the other, their interests were economic. "Our intention of course was to make an authentic record of this dying culture. That was our mission. On the other hand, we were committed to the box office," explains Frances.[25] Whereas the harsh conditions of Arctic living provided the natural dramas that eventually shaped *Nanook,* life in Samoa was surprisingly blissful and uncomplicated from the perspective of the outsiders. There was no ocean hunter to follow, no tale of survival against the elements to impose. There were instead the everyday lives and rituals of the Samoans, and so the Flahertys had to "let go" of preconceptions, remain "sensitive as unexposed film," and work with the stuff of everyday life: textiles, cooking, ceremonies, and dances.[26] As with *Nanook,* the "drama" of the story was once again fabricated from the contemporary rehearsal of older cultural habits, including dress, courtship, and the ritual tattooing of young men when they came of age. As Grierson pointed out in his 1926 review, *Moana* is gorgeous and quiet, poetic and timeless, and therefore completely noncommercial. The film must have disappointed audiences who were eager to see another version of *Nanook,* for *Moana* did not do well at the box office.

Ever literary, Frances expressed what she hoped the film would achieve: observe, record, safeguard, and pare life down to its basic elements to see one's own humanity reflected. Throughout her writing, Frances often highlighted the humanistic potential of documentaries about foreign peoples and places. For her, both *Moana* and *Nanook* create faithful portraits of unfamiliar ways of life, and in so doing bring us closer to understanding the essential qualities and values that humans share. Her vision manifests clearly in *Moana,* which bears this signature quality of Frances's ethnographic filmmaking ethos. Frances saw documentary film as an opportunity to bridge differences between "us" and "them." Emphasizing shared human qualities: joy, fear, love, and commitment, for example, brought the distant world into a familiar frame. This humanist ethos remains strong throughout women's documentary filmmaking but is thoroughly revised as difference comes to make political and ethical demands on feminist ideals. Just as in Frances's collaborative work with Robert, the complexity of this desire to bridge rather than exacerbate cultural and racial differences would determine what kinds of films were made and how prominently women's bodies, stories, and voices figured within and beyond them.

The repressed labor of women in the Flaherty legacy is not just Frances's, but also that of her daughter, Monica Flaherty. Made from 1923 to 1926, *Moana* was produced at a liminal point in film history, when new sound technologies began to change the industry as well as audience expectations for cinema. According to Kino's featurette, *Moana with Sound: A Short History,* with film historian

Monica Flaherty with Ta'avale Uni, who plays Moana, the older son of Lupenga and Tu'ungaita, in *Moana* (1926). (Courtesy of the Robert and Frances Flaherty Study Center and Kino Lorber, Inc.)

and producer Bruce Posner, *Moana* was shot on orthochromatic film without sound, and originally released with music composed by F. W. Murnau on the soundtrack. Paramount apparently felt strongly that the film needed a musical score to ensure market success. However, the artificial score troubled Monica Flaherty, who had strong memories of the sounds and music of Samoa.

In fact, Monica so loved her time in Samoa and her father's filmed rendition of life there that she decided to restore "authentic" sound to the film and reintroduce it to the public. In the mid-1970s, Monica returned to the South Sea island of Savai'i where the film was made and created a completely new soundtrack. She was accompanied by Richard Leacock. By the 1970s, Leacock was an acclaimed direct cinema filmmaker in his own right, with credits that included *Primary* (1960), *A Stravinsky Portrait* (1966), and *Monterey Pop* (1968). In the 1940s, however, Leacock had been Robert Flaherty's assistant on *Louisiana Story* (1948). He felt he had a keen sense of Flaherty's aesthetic and ethical principles and played an important role in the reconstruction of the sound for *Moana.* To produce a faithful reproduction in the 1970s, more than fifty years after the film was shot, Monica Flaherty and Leacock engineered reenactments in similar places with new people, capturing the voices of contemporary Samoans as they re-created the sound effects, music, and dialogue lost in the silent film. Released in 1980, the new version was called *Moana with Sound.* More recently *Moana with Sound* has been restored again, this time with the substantial advantages of digital technology, intended to more seamlessly marry the Flaherty-Leacock soundtrack with the senior Flaherty's original footage. After more than ninety years and several major restorations, *Moana* is once again on the minds of documentary scholars. As a result, we have a new opportunity to make sense of the hidden labor of both Frances and Monica Flaherty.

Through the artistic, affective, and translation labors and commitments of women like Frances and Monica Flaherty, a new frame for investigating the history of documentary begins to emerge; ethnographic documentary, which we understand as a mode of encounter between cultures and a struggle over power, voice, and the ethics of representation, assumes newly gendered stakes. It is a telling coincidence of colonialism that Samoa is central to the history of documentary in the early twentieth century where gender, anthropology, and documentary filmmaking come together. Samoa of course would soon host Margaret Mead, whose research on adolescent youth in the islands would produce new understandings of gender and sexuality and also launch the young anthropologist into the public eye. And in the South Seas a young woman named Osa Johnson would also become a pioneer of documentary filmmaking with her husband, Martin. With the Johnsons' work, we apprehend another version of documentary film's colonial gaze and the hidden affective, reproductive, and translation labor of women in early ethnographic-entertainment representations of distant cultures. Both Frances and Osa collaborated with their husbands extensively, which makes it difficult to tease out their individual legacies. Further, contemporaneous gender norms surely led these women to diminish their contributions and allow their husbands to take the lion's share of the credit for their work. While it may be difficult to determine what precise material roles they played in the filmmaking, their labor clearly helped shape the early history of documentary.

Osa Johnson

In 1910 Osa Leighty was sixteen, a high school student who spent her Saturday afternoons at the Roof Garden Theater in Chanute, Kansas. She loved watching film melodramas and dreamed of becoming a screen actress. In some ways her dream would come true. She married Martin Johnson, a young showman with big entertainment dreams of his own. According to their biographers, Osa was smitten with the worldly traveler with "country boy manners" and Martin was drawn to Osa's charm and willingness to take risks "while cherishing wholesome home heart values."[27] The two eloped in 1910 after an evening performance and would embark on an uncommon life of travel, filmmaking, and cultural exploration that would make them public celebrities throughout the '20s and '30s. By 1941 Osa Johnson was one of the most famous women in America and yet she has seldom been isolated as a pioneer of documentary filmmaking.[28] The historical record—available in the Johnsons' numerous publications, interviews, biographies, and films—shows that Osa was involved in virtually every aspect of film production, from location scouting to cranking, from instigating action for the camera to promoting the films back at home. Like Frances Flaherty, Osa Johnson's gendered labor shaped the couple's journeys and the ethos of their filmmaking, and yet was discursively domesticated to a "home" realm behind the scenes of active production. It is clear, however, that like Frances, Osa was responsible for the gendered labor of cultural reproduction, as well as the work of translating the emotional significance of their films to wider audiences. To support their careers, Osa took many still photographs, wrote books and magazine articles, apparently organized the safaris the couple would take, and directed the domestic realm of their lives on and off the road. Throughout more than twenty-five years of adventure travel and filmmaking, Osa was a mainstay in the national press, a woman with uncommon technical skill and keen insight into the ways of both the entertainment industry and colonial structures and practices.

Osa and Martin Johnson at the camera during their 1919 expedition to Tomman Island, Malekula. (Courtesy of the Martin and Osa Johnson Safari Museum.)

In the South Pacific, East Africa, and Borneo, she and Martin captured thousands of reels of footage. Although they began their film work documenting the native peoples of Vanuatu, and searching fancifully for alleged cannibals among them, in the twenties and thirties they would devote themselves almost entirely to wildlife, shooting—with cameras and with guns—some of the earliest and most extensive footage of remote regions in Africa. Beginning in 1918 with *Among the Cannibal Isles of the South Pacific,* a lecture film about their first trip documenting the inhabitants of the Solomon Islands, as Vanuatu was then known, and ending just after Osa's 1942 solo lecture tour with *African Paradise,* a silent lecture film, Osa and Martin collaborated on more than fifteen feature-length films and more than thirty silent shorts; Osa also assisted in the production of a television series created from their footage from 1950 until her death in 1953.

Throughout their most successful years, Martin and Osa would promote their partnership as a conventional patriarchal marriage that happened to take place in exceptional locations. Osa was smart and tough, and yet she was also "feminine," a devoted wife and partner who claimed to adopt Martin's dreams as her own. In an article she wrote for *Photoplay,* "A Wife in Africa," Osa assures readers that she is no different from them: "I went along just because I am a wife

. . . just to be with my husband."[29] In the same article, however, Osa advocates for women's rights both at home and abroad. She writes, "every woman should have a right to use her own name and have a personality of her own apart from her husband's."[30] She also informs readers that lions kill three times as many women as men because the women go out unarmed to raise corn.

This attention to gender inequity suggests another side of Osa, somewhat in conflict with the highly touted image of her as a beautiful and dutiful wife. Osa never openly resisted the idea that women had "feminine" responsibilities and talents that should be devoted to the domestic sphere, yet she acknowledged that her life on safari equipped her with unlikely skills for a woman. She wrote, "I did all my own work. I washed and ironed and sewed and cooked. And between times I learned to take a man's share of the work of exploration. I soon could keep up over the difficult jungle trails. I learned to shoot, to manage a boat, and though I had no genius for photography, I learned also to handle a motion-picture camera and to act as my husband's assistant in the darkroom."[31] In his books, Martin also emphasized Osa's unlikely combination of femininity and grit, praising her abilities to bring down a rhinoceros as often as her flair for baking apple pies in rugged safari conditions.

Osa's filmmaking legacy, like that of the Flahertys, poses numerous conceptual challenges, which explains why feminist film scholars in particular have been slow to engage with her work. The Johnsons' early films (from 1918 to 1922) focus primarily on indigenous people and, in retrospect, belie an unquestioned belief in white superiority, which is loathsome by contemporary standards but was not uncommon during an era characterized by ongoing colonial occupation. Martin and Osa, who were always more popular than intellectual, shared these views with Jack and Charmian London and other intellectuals of their time. They had all been influenced by the popularity of travel narratives and a wider fascination with primitivism and the exotic—a trend that begins at the turn of the century with the rise of natural history museums and world's fairs and swaggers into the twentieth century through cinema, music, and visual culture both high and low, from circuses to cubism. As Griffiths observes, "Well before the emergence of cinema, entrepreneurs had been exhibiting native peoples and so-called freaks in their traveling dime show museums and circuses."[32] Martin's story as a filmmaker resonates with Griffith's description. He had started out on the travelogue lecture circuit after his first trip as a bachelor to the South Pacific with the Londons on the *Snark*. He used his photo negatives to make lantern slides and narrated his travels to audiences all over the Midwest near his hometown in Kansas. His show was so popular that in 1910 he opened two theaters, *The Snark* and *The Snark No. 2,* which would together seat more than one thousand people. When audiences started to diminish after a profitable first year, Martin took his show on the road, to nearby towns in Kansas. It was on one of these trips that Martin met Osa. The two immediately began searching for new ways to continue their pursuits in ethnographic-entertainment.

In 1917 Martin found investors willing to fund an expedition to the South Seas with the objective of making a motion picture.[33] He and Osa set off for the Solomon Islands in May 1917 with one Universal motion picture camera, two Graflex still cameras, and 40,000 feet of unexposed film.[34] They would spend nine months traveling by boat around the islands, aided in no small measure by colonial authorities, and constantly on the search for the most remote and least photographed people and places in the archipelago of island nations east of Australia, including the Republic of Vanuatu, the Solomon Islands, and New Caledonia.[35]

The Johnsons' first few films were conceived in the model of the lantern slide lecture, which Martin had mastered after his *Snark* voyage. Later, these were modified with title cards to become stand-alone silent feature films for the entertainment market. The footage from that first expedition provided the material for an hour-and five-minute lecture, *Among the Cannibal Isles of the South Pacific* (1918), which the Johnsons premiered in New York in July 1918.[36] On the tiny island of Tomman in Vanuatu, the Johnsons had captured rare footage of native men, women, and children. Back in the states, an experienced theater manager, Samuel Lionel Rothafel, helped mold the presentation so that it balanced an educational impulse with entertainment value. In New York the program ran for a full week, with three shows a day. Even during this first tour, Osa could be counted on to do the lecture portion alone when Martin fell ill. After the program closed in New York, the Johnsons raised more funds to have the film titled and reprinted, which resulted in a lucrative distribution deal. To produce a film that could circulate without the lecture portion, the footage was cut and titles were added to up the humor and entertainment.

In the opening shots of the silent feature, now titled *Cannibals of the South Seas,* groups of men, some armed with long spears, walk purposefully but peacefully down the beach toward the camera. Several men stare directly into the lens, curious and perhaps confused about the new technology wielded by the white explorers. One young man plays a handheld instrument in close-up. An older man stands practically motionless in what appears to be a portrait made in real time; behind him, other observers are visible, watching the Johnsons watching them. In these shots, Martin's training as a still photographer clearly influences the filmmaking. Islanders are shot individually and framed identically, from the shoulders up. In the majority of these shots, subjects simply stare into the camera, which also remains motionless. Only occasionally does Martin change the camera angle to capture feet in the sand from a low angle, or a group of bodies in motion from a high angle. In the footage that follows, for example, islanders perform a kind of running dance that propels them around a tower made of organic materials. The slow frame rate of the film speeds up their movements, making the dance seem somewhat chaotic and confused, but calm observers on the outskirts of the dance ground the scene for the observer. In all, these alleged cannibals with their natural hair, bone piercings, and bark loincloths remain awesome sights for the uninitiated traveler, but their actions are wildly unfrightening.

Attempts at humor arise at odd intervals and compete with the film's attempt to convey new knowledge and information to the viewer about everyday life and ritual practices on the remote islands. For example, a woman appears with her distressed infant, whose head is wrapped meticulously in layers of material that create a tall cylinder. The title card that follows speculates paternalistically, "The idea may be to make a little brains go a long way." And yet, the narrative constructed by the title cards also makes earnest didactic attempts. After another shot of the mother, who continues to show off her baby for the camera, a title card informs the viewer that the wrapping remains on the heads of children until they reach eight years of age. As evidence for the claim, the film proceeds to present a series of adolescent boys and adult men with elongated skulls. Each subject displays his profile for the camera, turning his head to the right and left. This attention to cranial bone structure would have surely resonated with the discourse of the rising eugenics movement in the United States, a widely accepted pseudoscientific effort to fix race, class, and even moral hierarchies to human genetics that gained popularity in the first decades of the twentieth century. Audiences loved the film and critics wrote favorable reviews that highlighted Osa's charm and presence in front of the camera.[37]

Like most adventure filmmakers of their day, the Johnsons did not concern themselves with the complex problems of making ethical representations of native people. They did not consider themselves amateur anthropologists, but rather saw themselves as entertainers whose responsibility was primarily to their investors. The representations of indigenous people in the Johnson films conform to the demand for thrills and shocks in the entertainment market, and the corollary colonial aspirations of travelogues and adventure films. As the Johnsons' biographers suggest, "Their success very much depended on market forces and a commercial film industry that knew the entertainment value of racial stereotyping."[38] To excite audiences, the Johnsons promoted the South

Production still of a Tomman mother and child from *Cannibals of the South Seas.* (Courtesy of the Martin and Osa Johnson Safari Museum.)

Pacific islanders as savage and irrational, trapped in a distant past when men lived at the mercy of nature in a thoughtless and unpredictable way. Audiences could be both fascinated and appalled by what they saw on screen and use this new "knowledge" about black bodies to bolster their own national racism. Even though nothing frightening actually appears in the film, audiences would have easily cleaved the images of the distant black-skinned islanders to the sensational idea of the black Other as innately violent and irrational.

Upon close study, however, the Johnsons' camera vacillates in these early films between various modes: an attempt at neutral observation, ethnographic representation of native types, and deliberate sensationalizing of native practices, especially as these conflict with Western customs. Without the narration provided by the title cards, the Johnsons' earliest films in the South Pacific are often poetic observations of daily life and everyday rituals and celebrations: marketplaces and bathing scenes, dances and musical performances. Osa appears as often as the native subjects and in their midst, whereas Martin comes on screen stiffly and tends to overwhelm the frame. Osa smiles broadly at the camera, poses arm in arm with the islanders, and hugs the small children. In particular, her appearance on screen undermines the suggestion that these islanders are unpredictably violent or capable of cannibalism.

The earliest films by the Johnsons are curious instantiations of complex desires to capture the veracity of the culturally unthinkable and at the same time make the footage conform to colonial visions of inferior Otherness demanded by the market. It is as if the mere fact of the coeval presence of the native savage with white subject creates its own kind of drama and suspense, which the Johnsons attenuate by placing Osa consistently in the frame. The films seem to continuously pose the question: can these two kinds of people share the frame? the globe? how so? Osa invariably flashes her winning smile at the audience, coos at babies, dances, sips from fancy porcelain cups, and is in general at complete ease in front of the camera. She performs white femininity against and within the backdrop of blackness for an audience no doubt attuned to the racist myths about the desirability and fragility of white women and the savage sexuality of black men. Her soft and comforting presence both produces and also mediates the threat that blackness implies. Thus, Osa's labor on screen as the image of idealized white womanhood shapes the affective dimension of the picture, both confirming and also challenging racist and gendered stereotypes.

The Johnsons would return to the South Pacific Islands in 1919 and make another film, which they distributed in 1922 as *Head Hunters of the South Seas*.[39] However, by the early twenties, investors were less keen on films about primitive others and encouraged the Johnsons to make wildlife films that featured exotic animals in their natural habitats. The shift from ethnographic filmmaking and travelogues to wildlife films was not at all a drastic one in the early twentieth century. Although wildlife filmmaking has a distinct genealogy in the representational practices of naturalists (museums) and hunters (photography and taxidermy), both ethnographic and wildlife filmmaking emerged as "spectacles of colonial power and scientific and pseudoscientific racism," according to Cynthia Chris.[40] Many of the earliest films featuring wildlife were documents of game hunting expeditions in the colonies, including a fictional version of Theodore Roosevelt's 1909 African expedition, *Hunting Big Game in Africa* (William Selig, 1909) and *Paul Rainey's African Hunt* (1912). The wildlife films of the Johnsons were still very much in keeping with the genre of the "safari film," which grew out of the travelogue genre, according to Rony, and were structured around expeditions. The Johnsons' films in Borneo and East Africa, from *Jungle Adventures* (1921) to *Baboona* (1935), their first sound feature, are structured around Martin and Osa's voyages, from the moment they depart the United States by ship to their subsequent docking and repacking, to their camels and mules and porters, to their camping and filmmaking.

In the Johnsons' wildlife films, Osa is featured frequently and always in ways that balance her domestic, feminine talents with her unlikely courage and spirit of adventure. It was during their first trip that Martin had decided, "Osa's true value lay in front of the camera's objective, and not behind the viewfinder."[41] While the films were structured around the couple's photography (not hunting) expeditions into the wild, Osa's experiences—"a fragile beauty in the harsh wilderness"—structure the overall narrative. *I Married Adventure,* for example, which was based off Osa's wildly popular autobiography,[42] grants generous attention to her unique role in the procurement of rare and special footage (thanks to her bravery and skill with firearms). Several times Osa appears in the center of the frame, her back to the camera as she aims a rifle directly at an animal poised to charge. In these scenes, Osa became a veritable Wild West heroine in the spirit of her contemporaries, Annie Oakley and Calamity Jane. Considering the general push to market magazines, motion pictures, and adventure stories to young women, this female-centered approach makes sense for the profit motives that drove the Johnsons. They also demonstrate Osa's complex and central role in the couple's success.

In front of the camera, Osa is strong, courageous, and crucial to the action and the drama. This staged version of Osa was clearly carefully crafted to satisfy audience desires for a beautiful, delicate heroine hoisting her rifle in the middle of the harshest world imaginable. In many of their books Martin and Osa describe Osa as a "crack shot," and recount a number of stories in which Osa magnificently aims to kill in circumstances of extreme danger and pressure. Never mind that the Johnsons always had another marksman on the sidelines whose bullet actually hit the target. Never mind too that these wildlife filmmakers had likely instigated their animal subjects to attempt an attack. The Johnsons' goal was to promote an unlikely feminine heroine, as adept at fishing and hunting as she was at preparing Martin's meals in the tent.

However, there was clearly another side to Osa. On film we cannot see all the times Osa set up the shot, or cranked the camera, or assisted in the darkroom, or sat in the blind for hours waiting to see animals converge at the watering hole. Details about her efforts come readily, however, in the Johnsons' many books, although Martin rarely gave Osa credit for the filmmaking work she did and instead promoted her image as an ideal partner, *feminine* and supportive, gutsy and unusually skilled with a shotgun, but ultimately half of a balanced, traditional couple. Martin also hid the labor of another woman: Lillian Seebach, who worked as his editor for more than twenty years but only received credit beginning with *Simba.* Suppressed within the Johnsons' influential filmmaking is a history in which gendered labor—reproductive, domestic, affective, and visual—mitigates the apprehension of racialized bodies and solidifies the ambitions of the colonial gaze, even as it also challenges contemporaneous norms about gender.

The Johnsons' films about wildlife in Africa presented audiences with unique footage of lions hunting zebras and antelopes, rhinoceroses charging, monkeys grooming, and more. They pioneered the use of aerial photography from planes they had custom fitted for their adventures. Their collective labor resulted in the first sound picture fully shot in Africa. *Congorilla* (1932) pitches a narrative that promises adventure and danger on "the dark continent" with its "primitive savages and primeval monsters." In the first vignette Osa and Martin sit in chairs behind a native musician on the ground. He plays an instrument and sings. Visible to us, but not to the performer, Osa plugs her ears and sticks out her tongue in a way that suggests she does not like the music. The gesture is conspiratorial, with Martin but also with the viewer. It is clear that the spectator of the film is imagined to be a white American in cahoots with the Johnsons as they mock the musician. Structured around the journey, the narrative highlights the difficulty of the travel and includes many scenes of the caravan on the move, always a parade of native people, forever in the service of the white man.

For Chris, both ethnographic films about ways of life in distant corners of the globe and wildlife films in the expansive landscapes of Africa collude ideologically. That is, both forms of travel and adventure cinema share an overriding concern with the preservation of white supremacy. Ethnographic films purport to record disappearing ways of life among humans, and wildlife films aim to capture nonhuman species before they become extinct. Yet in both cases, the cause of the impending disappearance, primarily the consequences catalyzed by colonial expansion, is elided. Chris has persuasively argued that films about indigenous people and indigenous animals both characterize their subjects in decidedly nonhuman terms, as uncivilized, unpredictable, dangerous, and inherently violent. Moreover, wildlife films minimize the presence of humans in the natural landscape, potentially sanctifying colonialism as a project that domesticates wild space and wild animals rather than disclosing the appalling ways it affects human lives.

On the other hand, Pascal and Eleanor Imperato suggest that what we see in the films leaves out the more intimate details of the positive relationships the Johnsons developed with African men and women during their long stays in Kenya, for example, where they lived for several years.[43] One of the connections between ethnographic filmmaking and observational documentary is that intense relationships often build between filmmakers and filmed subjects. Nonetheless, despite the many technological and aesthetic innovations the

Johnsons pioneered, despite the remarkable footage they captured around the globe, and despite their pioneering sense of adventure and performative challenges to the domestic status quo, the Johnsons' films about indigenous cultures, both animal and human, replicate and reproduce the ideological underpinnings of the colonial gaze.

After Martin's death in 1937, Osa continued to build her career. She produced a number of films that recycled footage they had taken during their years together. She was adept at keeping herself in the public eye, even during difficult life circumstances. Her autobiography, which was ghostwritten by scenarist Winifred Dunn, became the number-one bestseller for nonfiction in 1940. The movie *I Married Adventure,* based on the book, did quite well, even though the reviews were not kind.[44] Her follow-up book *Four Years in Paradise* was also a *New York Times* bestseller, and during the lecture tour for the companion film, *African Paradise* (1941), Osa gave one hundred lectures around the United States. By 1942 her second husband and agent, Clark H. Getts, had failed to interest anyone in her next project, *Last Adventure,* which finally came out in 1966. But she continued to find her way into the limelight with a new book, *Bride in the Solomons* (1944), a lecture film, *Tulagi and the Solomons,* which toured in 1943 and 1944, and a television deal in 1950. In 1953, when she was fifty-eight years old, Osa suffered a heart attack and died.

Considering their Eurocentric treatment of both indigenous people and wildlife in their films, it is understandable that the Johnsons' film legacy has received so little attention in the study of documentary film history. Documentary film has often been characterized as a medium best suited for progressive social change, and has tended to vociferously celebrate its leftist progressives, Dziga Vertov, Joris Ivens, Marlon Riggs, and Laura Poitras. And yet, documentary history has been unusually kind to the Johnsons' contemporary, Robert Flaherty, whose *Nanook of the North* remains the ur-text of ethnographic documentary, despite all the ways it shares ideological underpinnings with the Johnsons' work. These observations also suggest that the politics of canon formation in documentary are highly determined by gender and race, which has profoundly impacted the intellectual longevity of women's documentary filmmaking.

What does it mean to reconsider the erasure of the Johnsons in documentary history, and moreover to pull Frances Flaherty and Osa Johnson specifically into the history of women in documentary filmmaking? Well are we aware that the ideological roots of documentary film wind their way back to the heyday of colonialism, when tourism, anthropology, and photography engineered a new world view that granted supreme importance to the mobility and veracity of the photographic image. However, we have not attended to the gendered labor embedded in this story of technological and commercial pioneers; and we have not acknowledged the early suppressed efforts of women like Frances Flaherty and Osa Johnson, who embody so much of documentary's complex history and contradictory desires. The films that Frances Flaherty and Osa Johnson made with their husbands reflect the competing fantasies that sustain documentary filmmaking: on the one hand its didactic impulse and its belief in the humanitarian value of information sharing; on the other its status as entertainment and commodity, which enmesh the form with dominant ideologies about race, gender, and capitalism. Their collaborative, cross-cultural work anticipated the very terms of the debate around realism—its pernicious and liberatory potential, for example—as well as the postcolonial critique of anthropology and the attention to gendered forms of labor in feminism.

Osa Johnson and Frances Flaherty's legacies as pioneers of documentary remind us how deeply the ethics and politics of "real" representations uniquely define this mode of filmmaking. The Johnsons' films are as much representations of a certain vision of womanhood in the early twentieth century—one that pushed norms, but only so far—as they are of visions of colonial expansion and demise. The Flahertys and Johnsons captured the colonial contact zones largely because they knew that this way of life had been changed forever by the penetration of European colonialism. They fancifully sought the most primitive and exotic people they could find largely because no such people existed, except in the colonial imaginary. When the Johnsons turned their attention to animals, they minimized the human impact of their work as well as the legacy of violent colonialism. But the traces remain alive and well in their neglected work.

A history of women in documentary does not necessarily present us with clearly discernible heroines. After all, this is an undue burden to place on the past. Neither does a history of women in documentary present us with lone geniuses in the mode of D. W. Griffith and Cecile B. DeMille, the male auteurs of their day. Rather, as Shelley Stamp's work on Lois Weber has made clear, to reconstruct a historiography of feminist media, we have to "look past the screen."[45] Indeed, the task as Stamp puts it is not so much to recover and re-insert women like Frances Flaherty and Osa Johnson into a tidy timeline of documentary history. Rather, feminist cinematic historiography might instead ask how clear and significant pioneers of the form, like Frances Flaherty and Osa Johnson, have been erased. "What does this 'loss' and 'forgetting' look like? And what are its consequences?" asks Stamp.[46] In both cases, the impulse to forget—likely determined by the complex imbrication of anthropology, cinema, and colonialism at the turn of the twentieth century—means we have yet to ask how this particular legacy of the politics of representation bears out in future decades of women's documentary filmmaking. Women's labor in the realm of documentary consistently builds on that of its antecedents. During the 1970s, more women than ever before took up cameras to tell "true" stories about "ordinary" women in order to challenge dominant myths about gender and femininity in the media. And like Osa and Frances, they would construct cultural documents of selves and others that embed ethical, political, and affective imperatives and complexly negotiate matters of sameness and difference in the realm of the real. Just as Monica Flaherty sought to restore the voices of the Samoan people in *Moana,* so this chapter begins to address the metaphorical silencing of women's voices and their labor in the long history of documentary. In the next chapter, I explore the contributions of Zora Neale Hurston and Margaret Mead, professional anthropologists who pioneered the use of documentary in ethnographic research.

CHAPTER 2

Anthropological Visions Inside and Out

Zora Neale Hurston and Margaret Mead

In the previous chapter, I excavated the suppressed histories of Frances Flaherty and Osa Johnson, whose collaborations with their husbands indelibly shaped the early decades of documentary filmmaking. So much of the popular and academic writing on Flaherty and Johnson contextualizes them as "wives" within their husbands' more studied filmmaking careers. I am more interested in their complex contributions on and off screen to American cinematic illusions of race, gender, and empire in the early twentieth century. Flaherty and Johnson, white, married, middle-class women, prompt a gendered analysis of the regimes of knowledge that shaped early documentary. To detect their contributions, however, we have to study their collaborative films alongside their personal letters, public writings, and promotional work. Thus, the first chapter begins to erect the frame of analysis required, I think, for a new view of women's contributions to the history of documentary. That is, women's labor in the early period clearly exceeds the boundaries of the cinematic frame and includes intellectual, affective, and reproductive labor on behalf of the work and its subjects. As much as Johnson and Flaherty were among a number of women in the early twentieth century who left home (in multiple senses) and expressed proto-feminist aspirations by doing so, they were also completely imbricated in colonial projects. Re-examining their varied modes of filmmaking labor thus opens new ways of thinking about the long and compromised history of women in documentary.

In this chapter, gender, anthropology, and documentary come together again, but distinctly in the careers and legacies of two anthropologists, Zora Neale

Hurston and Margaret Mead, who both made early and innovative use of cinematic technologies. Feminist anthropologists rightly insist that anthropology has played a crucial role in "shaping debates about gender in the United States."[1] Further, the history of academic anthropology reveals a strong tradition of "colorful and strong female practitioners."[2] If Johnson and Flaherty represent a moment when women's gendered labor was distributed across the spectrum of filmmaking labor (as producers, spouses, writers, promoters, actors, for example), then Hurston and Mead draw us closer to debates about women filmmakers behind the camera. Hurston and Mead's intense focus on women's lives and their everyday experiences carries over into the broad archive of women's documentary filmmaking that reached its apogee in the 1970s. So too do their commitments to exploring the differences between women whose lives are variously shaped by race, class, nation, and empire. In both cases, Hurston and Mead turned their gazes and their cameras on women whose lives and voices exist outside the traditional viewfinder of dominant culture. In their films, Hurston and Mead insist that close observation guides the development of knowledge and analysis—a pillar of feminist thought of the 1970s. In the work of Hurston and Mead we glean new meaning about the ways that women are subjects of and to reality—both because of their autonomous positions of leadership behind the camera and their subjective representations of women in front of the camera.

Hurston, in her literary work, and Mead, in her advocacy for women's issues, would also insist that the daily practices of marginalized groups and so-called primitive cultures often reveal strategies that the "civilized" world would do well to emulate. In this sense, they prioritize the ethical commitments inherent to feminism's most ambitious project: producing a political sense of solidarity within an infinitely mosaic category of identity, women. Hurston, who thought of herself as an insider to the rural African American communities she filmed, and Mead, who was always an outsider during her work abroad, challenged traditional hierarchies between male and female, white and black and brown, self and other, us and them, subject and object.

Zora Neale Hurston

> Every fragment, no matter how small, helps reconstruct evolutionary history. And every frame of film, no matter how fragile and incomplete, helps scholars to understand the history of our relationship to culture and ultimately to ourselves.
> —Gloria Gibson[3]

We know that the Johnsons did not consider themselves anthropologists, and neither had formal academic training. They were entertainers and public figures, and when they embarked on expensive projects abroad, they were beholden primarily to the demands of their investors. Zora Neale Hurston, on the other hand, did consider herself an anthropologist, and set out to make motion pictures that would support her research into black rural life in the United States, even as funders with their own agendas also supported this work.[4] Whereas the Johnsons documented cultures in the contact zones of colonialism, Hurston pointed her camera at ordinary folks in places just like the ones she grew up in. She studied their spiritual rituals, their waged labor, and their leisure time, games, and amusements. In her footage, Hurston also captures the essence of everyday life, especially among African American women: gardening, swinging, laughing, singing. In her varied footage, Hurston's position shifts between that of an insider and that of an outsider, illustrating the consistent desire and challenge of generating authentic portraits of Others, even when they are communities to which you sense that you belong. That Hurston would have used a motion picture camera for her research counts as one of the many pioneering acts of a woman most remembered for her unabashed independence and autonomy. Very few anthropologists had experimented with motion pictures by the late 1920s.[5] It remains unclear where and how Hurston learned to use the 16mm camera, but as Elaine Charnov writes, her footage is "remarkable" for how it "anticipates" many of the enduring concerns in visual anthropology about the role of the camera in a field concerned with the scientific validity of objectivity, documentation, and observation.[6]

To highlight Hurston first and foremost as a filmmaker is clearly in tension with the dominant and prolific trend of Hurston discourse, particularly in African American literary studies, where she has become one of the most canonized authors of the twentieth century. Her most cited biographer, Robert Hemenway, does not mention her filmmaking at all. Rather, he tells of her research trips of 1927 and 1929 (when her extant films were made) primarily through her correspondence with Langston Hughes, an archive that comes together, for Hemenway, as "an unintentional documentary of the expedition."[7] In fact, Hurston was one of the earliest women to make documentary films and was certainly the first black woman visual ethnographer. She arrived in the anthropology department at Columbia University at an opportune time. Elsie Clews Parsons, Ruth Benedict, and Franz Boas were together building the discipline by focusing on innovative approaches to race, culture, adolescence, and sexuality—themes very much at the heart of social and political life in the United States in the 1920s (and once again later in the 1970s). Anthropology fascinated Hurston, who was one of the field's first African American scholars. Surely Boas's thinking about the cultural dimensions of racial discrimination, which opposed dominant paradigms about the biological certitude of racial difference, created an environment in which Hurston felt that her interests in the folk practices and beliefs of rural southern blacks would matter. In the following years, Hurston would experiment with fiction, traditional and fictionalized ethnography, theater, music, and filmmaking as she asserted the uniqueness and value of African American cultural practices.

Even before she studied anthropology, Hurston had demonstrated an interest in the traditional ways of African Americans in the South. In 1925 she received two literary prizes that ushered her into the heart of the Harlem Renaissance—both awards were for works that reproduced the everyday speech of rural African Americans.[8] These early works showcase Hurston's persistent commitment to the voices of ordinary people, like the ones she knew and admired growing up in central Florida; they also show that Hurston was willing and eager to experiment with different genres to represent the experiences of African Americans. According to Hazel Carby, "Throughout the 1930s, Hurston is in search of a variety of formal possibilities for the representation of black rural folk culture," including musicals, fiction, graduate school, folk music recordings, and plays.[9] In the 1930s she would travel abroad to Haiti and Jamaica for comparative perspectives on black life. Anthropology, Hurston said, gave her a new "spyglass" to look through, and added to the range of representational practices she would experiment with as an artist, folklorist, and filmmaker.[10]

That Hurston should train her eye on rural blacks in the 1920s indicates her audacity and commitment to a form of black culturalism that valued the daily life and practices of African Americans *as is*. Unlike her educated and outspoken contemporaries, like Booker T. Washington, who espoused faith in the possibility of "racial uplift," Hurston celebrated the traditions and rituals of, in her words, "the negro farthest down."[11] Not only was folklore a relatively new area of research and study in the 1920s, few African American collectors of black folklore predated Hurston.[12] Carla Kaplan notes that it wasn't until the 1960s that sizable numbers of African Americans entered the field of anthropology.[13] In the 1920s, thus, with encouragement from Boas, Hurston was poised to "become *the* authority on Afro-American folklore," inverting the traditional relationship between whites and Others and also pressuring gender norms for black women in the early part of the twentieth century.[14] As an anthropologist, Hurston understood the temporal fragility of cultural expression—the way cultural practices of discrete groups of people change over time, particularly as these groups come into greater contact with more dominant cultures. But more importantly, Hurston recognized the unlikely instances of magic and joy that existed in black communities, despite the poverty, illiteracy, and discrimination they faced in the Jim Crow South.

Hurston's life and her work have been thoroughly explored, and in most contemporary accounts, her studies in anthropology while she was a student at Barnard figure prominently. According to Hemenway, Hurston entered Barnard in 1925 with a full scholarship arranged by Mrs. Annie Nathan Meyer, a novelist and founder of Barnard College, whom Hurston had impressed during her days as novelist Fannie Hurst's assistant.[15] At the time, Hurston was the only black student at Barnard. Hemenway observes, "the Barnard experience was critical to Hurston's development, for she came to New York in 1925 as a writer and left Barnard two years later as a serious social scientist, the result of her study of anthropology under Franz Boas."[16] Boas had recognized Hurston's talent and her passions and influenced her to concentrate on ethnography and folklore.[17]

Boas, too, was unique among his colleagues. Whereas most anthropologists believed that racial difference could be indexed to biology, and used their research to support white supremacy, Boas attempted to prove that ideas about racial superiority were culturally determined and thus products of a certain way of thinking, not being. Perhaps this effort reveals why Boas could see the inherent value of documenting African American culture. He could see that as ideas about race shifted, the cultural practices specific to blacks might change as well. He also had a reputation for training "natives," according to Charnov, because he believed their status as "insiders" could yield more nuanced and accurate data.[18] As Gwendolyn Mikell observes, black anthropologists were extremely rare before World War II, and only two other black female anthropologists pursued graduate work in those decades.[19] Among her many talents, Hurston's presumed ability to gain access to African American communities would have made her a promising candidate for anthropological work. Boas encouraged Hurston to collect folklore, which culminated initially in *Mules and Men* (1935), a collection of myths and stories from African American cultures in Florida, and then *Tell My Horse* (1938), based on research in the Caribbean.

Hurston wrote explicitly about the advantages that anthropological training afforded her, especially considering that her education and social network made her both an insider and an outsider to numerous black and white communities. She described her sense of her own culture as "fitting me like a tight chemise. I couldn't see it for wearing it. It was only when I was off in college, away from my native surroundings, that I could see myself like somebody else and stand off and look at my garment. Then I had to have the spy-glass of Anthropology to look through at that."[20] If her years at Howard University as an undergraduate and in the literary milieu of Washington, D.C. from 1918 to 1924 attuned her ear and pen to the rhythms of black cultural expression, anthropology would eventually provide her with a new understanding of her role both within and outside her community. From Boas, Hurston would inherit the sense that African American experiences deserved recognition within the new discipline's attention to native cultures in North America, that folklore constituted valuable knowledge about cultural practices, and that trained insiders like Hurston had the potential to detect and collect authentic patterns of cultural expression in ethnographic research.

Boas was also among a handful of anthropologists in the silent era to experiment with motion picture technology. Despite what she calls his "flirtations" with silent filmmaking, Alison Griffiths argues that Boas had little influence on the expansion of motion picture methods on anthropology, citing only Mead as a direct successor.[21] However, in addition to Hurston, Boas nurtured and collaborated with several women who would go on to use filmmaking as a way of sharing their research with the public, including Jane Belo, Ruth Landes, and Barbara Myerhoff. Boas had used a motion picture camera in his field research in 1930 among the Kwakwaka'wakw, Northwest coast Native Americans. According to Griffiths and Jay Ruby, Boas's films about the Kwakwaka'wakw "were the equivalent of visual field notes" motivated "entirely by their evidentiary status and practical utility."[22] In his filmmaking, Boas tended to focus on ceremonial and daily life, and never intended his work to be seen by the public. Only in 1973 was the footage restored and edited by George Quimby into *The Kawkuitl of British Columbia*.[23] However, Zora Neale Hurston and Jane Belo were surely influenced by Boas, if not directly instructed in the use of the motion picture camera. Curiously, Griffith understates his influence on future visual ethnographers, perhaps owing to the general neglect of these women's film production within the fields of anthropology, visual ethnography, and documentary.

Here, I join a small number of scholars—Gloria Gibson, Elaine Charnov, Jacqueline Bobo, and Fatimah Tobing Rony—who have all paid serious attention to Hurston's ethnographic films. In Hurston's elusive archive, these scholars have detected foundational themes, techniques, and desires, which resonate with contemporary characteristics of black women's filmmaking, women's documentary, and visual anthropology. Graciela Hernandez observes that Hurston's passions were spirituality, the body, and gender—issues central to her film production as well.[24] Hurston also had a tendency to make her authorial presence known and felt, which draws our attention to asymmetries of power between the producers of knowledge and their subjects.[25] Ethnography, in many forms within Hurston's work, thus becomes a tool to understand the self in relation to Others. Thinking along these lines, Hurston anticipated significant debates in the field of anthropology. Subjectivity, aesthetic innovation, reflexivity, and the commitment to creating just representations of others are all gifts that Hurston's archive bequests to women's documentary history, and especially within the ethnographic current I explore throughout this book.

Before her filmmaking began, Hurston traveled to Alabama and Florida in 1927 to collect folklore while still a student at Barnard College. She set out from New York City bound for central Florida with a $1,400 research fellowship from the Association for the Study of Negro Life and History to support six months of fieldwork in rural African American communities.[26] She had worked out a plan with Boas that involved the collection of songs, tales, jokes, games, and dances particular to African Americans of the South. That first research trip, though influential for her later work, disappointed Hurston, who had yet to establish her footing and her personal style as a folklorist. She complained that people would not open up to her, and she knew it was because she seemed foreign to the locals, overly influenced by her education in the North. When she returned to New York, Hurston and Boas agreed in dismay that what she had gathered was no different from the material collected by white folklorists. Both had assumed that her familiarity with southern black culture would yield something original and were surprised when that did not turn out to be the case.[27] Like so many autoethnographers, Hurston realized that being an "insider" only greased the cranks so much. The traces Hurston bore of her life in the North challenged a tidy commensurability with other African Americans. This crucial lesson about the fragility and the fluidity between inside and outside when it comes to documentary filmmaking was relearned by women in the 1970s, who were eager to consolidate a capacious subject of reality—women—and yet were consistently challenged by the material and psychic differences that mark women's intensely different lives.

Hurston's trip in the winter of 1927 and 1928, which was funded by her white patron Charlotte Osgood Mason, made possible some of the film reels extant today. Mason supported several significant black artists of the Harlem Renaissance, including Hurston and Langston Hughes. Mason had done some field research in the early 1900s among the Plains Indians and considered herself an amateur anthropologist. Scholars speculate that Mason's support of Hurston might have been based on her desire to secure raw materials for Mason's own projects. The white patron's keen interest in the so-called "primitive" motivated her support of black artists in the '30s, but in Hurston, Mason found her anthropological surrogate, someone who shared her belief that ways of life in the rural South should be documented and recorded. According to Hemenway, Mason gave Hurston around $15,000 over a five-year period, and it was her initial contract with Mason, signed on December 8, 1927, that gave Hurston "the wherewithal for her to begin a serious career as a folklorist"—$200 a month for a year, a car, and a moving picture camera to support her collecting.[28] Even so, Mason's mixed intentions are evident in the contract she had Hurston sign. Mason restricted Hurston's use of the material she collected, which would remain the exclusive property of her patron. This partially explains the limited audience for Hurston's footage, which we know very little about. Hurston's extant filmography consists of only eight reels of 16mm film, currently archived at the Library of Congress, and tellingly, in the Margaret Mead collection.[29]

With the support provided by Mason, Hurston set off for the South on December 14, 1927. As Carla Kaplan observes, in a number of ways Hurston was surely an unlikely apparition on the road: a black woman driving alone with a firearm at her side during a period of intense racial violence and legal segregation.[30] Her first stop was a visit to a former slave, Cudjo Lewis, near Mobile, Alabama.[31] She also stopped over in Eatonville, where she grew up, and at the Everglades Cypress Lumber Company near Loughman, Florida before moving on to Mulberry, Fort Pierce, and Lakeland, Florida.[32] Hurston's letters describe both the trials and the joys of her expedition. In a letter to Hughes, Hurston writes, "I am getting inside of Negro art and lore. I am beginning to *see* really. . . . This is going to be *big*. Most gorgeous possibilities are showing themselves constantly."[33] Despite the difficulties involved in traveling alone through the South, Hurston was clearly enthusiastic about her folklore collection and promised Hughes that the material would be valuable for the black folk opera they had in mind.

Hurston's short films include scenes of work, ritual, rest, and play. In several of these, the most striking characteristics are Hurston's willingness to experiment with camera angles, stillness and movement, and positioning and framing. Charnov refers to this expansive formal and thematic range in Hurston's work as unique among contemporaneous amateur filmmakers, who tended to produce more static and less engaging footage.[34] Hurston's film about the Everglades Cypress Lumber Company in Polk County, Florida, for example, begins with a "ghost rider" shot of train tracks, which she must have captured from the front of a moving train. When a man in a heavy work coat enters the frame, Hurston evidently stops cranking and starts up again when he's out of frame. She points her camera decidedly at the hulking sawmill and massive crane that moves the lumber. Workers guide the enormous trunks, but here Hurston seems interested in the scale and fact of the labor rather than individual people. In subsequent shots, Hurston tries to film workers ambling over logs with canteens and kettles, perhaps taking a lunch break from work. The workers seem reluctant to be filmed, however. Several of them keep their backs toward the camera and avert their gazes. A woman hurries over rough terrain to avoid the camera's lens; as Hurston pans the camera slowly to the left, the woman races to the right.[35]

In this footage we get the sense that Hurston's camera is not especially welcome. Rather, we feel the tension between her desire to document the scene and the subjects' unwillingness to be documented. Given the racial stereotyping that proliferated in early cinema, it should come as no surprise that African American workers would be leery of the camera. Mason and Boas's belief that as an African American and thus "insider," Hurston would be granted special access also seems questioned by this film, which attests that the chasm separating the woman with the camera from the workers could not be bridged by racial similarity alone. Hurston's films include several of these surreptitious shots from a distance, as if she had yet to develop a strong relationship with the camera, or a strong sense of what kind of photographer she wanted to be. She is respectful and distant even as she's clearly determined to capture the footage.

In another film, we sense the opposite—that is, that as an African American woman, Hurston was an insider and could seduce other black women to pose for her camera. Hurston's artistic career evidences a consistent interest in the lives and experiences of women. In this footage, a young black woman in a humble cotton dress walks toward the camera in two consecutive shots. Editing in camera, Hurston would have likely asked the woman to approach, stopped cranking, and asked her to approach again. The result is a remarkable series of shots of a young woman descending her front porch steps, walking toward the camera again, and then in a third shot, this time a close-up, smiling broadly for the static camera. In close range, the woman turns her head to the left and to the right, offering her lovely profile in a pose reminiscent of the Johnsons' footage from the South Pacific. In both cases, the filmmakers were likely interested in capturing the physiognomy of racialized subjects, placing their examination of "Others" in conversation with reigning pseudoscience on the biology of race. Hurston had experience with this kind of field research, which she conducted in Harlem in 1926 for Boas. In his antiracist research, Boas also used skull measurements, but he utilized these to disprove dominant theories about the biological inferiority of black-skinned people. The woman in Hurston's footage smiles as she turns her head, seemingly unperturbed by the filmmaker's request, indeed even amused to be the subject of the camera. The woman's body language suggests a comfortable, even playful intimacy between the filmmaker and her subject.

In Hurston's footage, women move within the frame to the unspectacular rhythms of everyday life. In other scenes from this reel, two women lean on a porch railing and laugh; one of them lies down on her side on a simple bench

Zora Neale Hurston's autoethnographic commitments are captured in this intimate close-up filmed in the late 1920s in the rural South. (Courtesy of the Zora Neale Hurston Trust.)

built into the front porch. Hurston intercuts these intimate moments with a long shot of another woman next door who crosses her yard wearing a wide-brimmed garden hat. In this short film, women appear in a range of compositions: near, far, together, alone, active, and in repose. In the hand-sewn dress, the bare feet, the warm smile, the porches, and the lush gardens, Hurston offers a romantic and even emblematic portrait of everyday life in the South. In contrast to the footage of workers in the lumber yard film, this film frames women at their leisure. The film seductively forwards the radical proposition that black women giggle, relax, and expend energies on their own homes and friendships. This is a vision that would have resonated deeply with black feminists of the 1970s, who were determined to assert the uniqueness of their subjective presence in the political landscape. In Hurston's short films, black women emerge in unique ways, without the occluding emphasis on either white women or black men.

All the while, Hurston's attention to form is felt in the broad range of shots, graceful camera movement, and attention to light. This gorgeous film stands out among the extant footage, for it is the only example of Hurston filming women who dare to look right into the camera and smile. According to Rony, "Until the 1930s, it was unseemly in the United States and Europe to face the camera smiling: smiling was considered to make the subject look foolish and childlike."[36] In *Nanook of the North,* when Allakariallak stares directly into the camera during the opening sequence, Rony reads the potential for two modes of interpretation. Perhaps white audiences in North America would see his direct gaze into the lens as childlike. However, it is also possible to imagine that "from the Inuit point of view" Nanook is the one "laughing at the camera."[37] In Hurston's footage a similar tension exists between potential interpretations made from both inside and outside. Whereas the woman's direct gaze might signal her naiveté about motion picture technology, it may also be read as a defiant courage to be looked at, to be photographed, and to be taken seriously as a subject of the camera's reality gaze.

This short film may also serve as a symbolic clue in the Hurston anthropological archive. In the late 1920s and 1930s, when Hurston was engaging in her ethnographic research in Florida and the Caribbean, issues of sex and gender were new areas of anthropological concern. Her Columbia colleagues, Ruth Benedict and Margaret Mead, would emerge as highly influential early feminist anthropologists, and many more would follow. However, Hurston's interest in the experiences of women was unique, following from her own experiences and observations. As Mikell observes, "In her anthropology as in her literature, Zora Neale Hurston offers us a view of Black culture in which women are willing, contributing partners, despite slavery, historical oppression, and the exploitation of colonialism."[38] Black women, in other words, were not solely "subject to reality" in the ways dominant white culture imagined them.

In addition to portrayals of women taking pleasure in themselves and in each other, Hurston was also interested in children. In another film, Hurston begins with an establishing shot captured from far enough away that we see a wide circle of fifteen children holding hands and skipping. One young boy begins to dance alone in the center of the circle and the children stop and clap out a steady rhythm. Behind the camera, Hurston comes closer to the solo performer, capturing him from head to toe as he cartwheels, soft shoes, and lands a few splits for the crowd. The shots become increasingly tight, now framing the children around the circle from the shoulders up, then from the toes up to the knees as feet tap out the beat. In this footage of children at play, Hurston balances the performative aspect of folklore collection with a desire to capture something authentic in the joyful bodies of children. Her precise pacing moves the camera around the circle evenly, capturing the children in medium shots. We observe games as a collective act, we experience children's enjoyment, and we also see Hurston's desire to feature as many individual faces as she can. Thus, Hurston shows an early filmmaking knack for balancing attention to individuals with their place among their community and peers. She also sees the inherent aesthetic qualities of these places and people.

Hurston was not the only African American filmmaker of the 1920s. Scholars have recently paid critical attention to Oscar Micheaux and his contemporaries, among them notable women like Eloyce Gist, who made moral uplift films with her husband. Hurston's contemporaries would have also included Madame C. J. Walker, perhaps the first African American woman millionaire, who made her fortune selling cosmetics to black women. Her filmmaking work aligned with her entrepreneurial spirit; she made educational and training films for her employees. Madame Toussaint Welcome (Booker T. Washington's photographer), Eslanda Goode Robeson (married to Paul Robeson, who had a Ph.D. in anthropology and made ethnographic films in the 1940s), and Alice B. Russell, who worked with Oscar Micheaux, were other black women making films in the 1920s. Among these, however, Hurston's legacy is unique. Whereas Gist and her husband turned to filmmaking to spread their religious ideas and encourage middle-class, bourgeois values among black folk, Hurston sought to mine black communities for an innate, and perhaps romanticized difference that merited serious attention and even celebration. She also sought to highlight the unique lives of women, especially outside the viewfinder of white supremacy.

As an anthropologist, Hurston's legacy is mixed, and largely unacknowledged. In the '20s and '30s, Hurston was sought after for her expertise among African Americans and black Caribbean communities. According to Mikell, she registered for a Ph.D. at Columbia and was courted by Melville Herskovits at Northwestern University. Perhaps funding constraints and the contracts with Mason interfered with Hurston's pursuit of a graduate degree and professional career. Ultimately, she published few traditional academic articles, evidently plagiarized at least one of them, and finally used her folklore collection to publish creative ethnographic works, including *Mules and Men* and *Tell My Horse.* Hurston's literary and filmic output attests to her lifelong interest in representing the ordinary folks of the South; however, she preferred creative means of expression, and she ultimately devoted herself to nonacademic writing, always clearly inspired by her ethnographic eye and ear and her investment in African American culture.

She moved through the illustrious spaces of the Harlem Renaissance, earning both recognition and rebuff from its mostly male stars, including Langston Hughes, Alain Locke, and Richard Wright. Indeed, it was Wright who most vociferously criticized *Their Eyes Were Watching God* (1937), the book that would eventually secure Hurston's place in literary history. Wright attacked Hurston's replication of African American speech in particular, writing, "Miss Hurston *voluntarily* continues in her novel the tradition which was *forced* upon the Negro in the theatre, that is, the minstrel technique that makes the 'white folks' laugh."[39] For thinkers like Wright in the 1930s and Hazel Carby again in the 1990s, Hurston's representation of African American folklore, motivated by a desire for authenticity, suffered from both oversimplification and the romantic (colonial) narrative of discovery that plagued ethnographic writing.[40]

Characteristically, Hurston replied with aplomb; she knew that she and Wright had distinct projects, and though she didn't express her position as inherently feminist or even that of a woman, it cannot be ignored that *Their Eyes Were Watching God* is not only about ordinary folks in a town much like the one she was raised in, but it is also about a woman's experience. This attention to the lives and stories of women, also evident in her filmmaking, would eventually allow Hurston to rise from the ashes of a fallen career and historical neglect. Hurston's cultural ascendancy has been made clear since the mid-1970s, when Alice Walker first recovered Hurston within the context of black feminism. Walker wrote about her rediscovery of Hurston for the then relatively new *Ms.* magazine. She chronicled her journey to Florida, where she found that Hurston had disappeared so completely from collective memory that even her grave was hidden among the weeds. It was Walker who brought renewed attention to Hurston's life and her work, and made her relevant for feminist, literary, and African American studies. Since then, Carla Kaplan notes, "Hurston is now among the most widely read and widely taught American authors."[41] For Walker in the mid-1970s, Hurston represented a singular instance of literary black feminism. Here was a black woman who dared to write about her own people with love for both her rural community and herself. On the tombstone she erected for the then forgotten writer, Walker engraved the phrase, "A genius of the South *Novelist Folklorist Anthropologist*." For film and feminist scholars today, Hurston's legacy anticipates the modes of politicized ethnographic filmmaking that emerged in the 1970s when new generations of people of color once again took up filmmaking as a form of communal self-inscription and resistance.

Gloria Gibson has appointed Zora Neale Hurston the cinematic foremother of black women's filmmaking.[42] In her films, Hurston remarkably turned her camera on her own people, a move Madeline Anderson would echo in the late 1960s for her film about black women hospital workers on strike, *I Am Somebody* (1969), and Fronza Woods would echo a decade later in *Fannie's Film* (1979). Black women's documentary filmmaking is so scant before the late 1970s that only Hurston and Anderson have been identified as precursors to later innovators like Carroll Parrott Blue and Michelle Parkerson. As a pioneer of black women's documentary filmmaking, Gibson writes, Hurston helped establish the dominant trend in which "black women have historically used the camera to document their lives and communities."[43] In biographical films and documentaries especially, Jacqueline Bobo points out, black women filmmakers tend to emphasize the "congruence" between themselves and their subjects.[44] In chapter 4, I examine Anderson's *I Am Somebody*. I focus on the ways Anderson balances a gendered perspective on union activism with a commitment to the universalizing politics of the civil rights movement. In both Hurston's and Anderson's films we see this twin commitment to the specifics of gender and the collective experience of racial and economic oppression.[45]

Margaret Mead

Just as Gibson honors Hurston as a cinematic "foremother," Dolores Janiewski and Lois W. Banner refer to Ruth Benedict and Margaret Mead as the "founding mothers of anthropology."[46] What does it mean to grant a matrilineal heritage to the field of anthropology, and further, to situate Benedict and Mead, women who were also lovers, at the helm? In this complex family history, generations of women anthropologists emphasize a feminist trajectory in the field of anthropology. In the 1920s, most academic anthropologists were men. Pioneering female scholars such as Elsie Clews Parsons at the turn of the century, and then Benedict and Mead in the early '20s and '30s, stood out among them not only because they were women engaged in public and scientific work, but also because they focused on matters of gender and social equity. Parsons, who was the first woman to work with Boas, "touched the lives of most of the women around Boas, whether by providing funds for their jobs or field research or by mentoring their anthropological work."[47] Further, these women anthropologists would shift the field dramatically by focusing on sex and gender as it shaped both men's and women's lives in the United States and abroad. The trends catalyzed under Boas and Benedict's leadership would draw from these currents and also redirect them. Boas is widely credited for catalyzing the birth of modern anthropology, sometimes to the chagrin of later feminist anthropologists, who argue that his male shadow has obscured the equally important contributions of women like Parsons and Benedict.

By 1933 Benedict identified as a lesbian, and beginning in the mid-20s and ending only as a result of her death in the late '40s, she and Mead enjoyed a profound but open relationship of intellectual and sexual intimacy.[48] The two would become anthropology's most famous women; their books appeared on bestseller lists, an unlikely accomplishment for academic writers, and together, albeit in different registers, they developed ideas that challenged dominant perspectives about gender, race, and sexuality.[49] They also helped develop a form of anthropology that was less data driven and empirical and more invested in describing cultural characteristics and practices, and then speculating about the psychological effects of these on the individuals of particular communities.[50] After the more reclusive Benedict died in 1948, Mead would become the most famous anthropologist in the country, and arguably still holds that honor.

Mead's work forwarded radical ideas about the processes of enculturation that shape human social development. Mead also developed strong and original ideas about ethnographic fieldwork, academic publishing, and the use of film in anthropological research and outreach. During her fifty-year career as a public intellectual, Mead published more than 1,300 books, biographies, articles, and reviews. She wrote for *The Nation* as well as *Parents* magazine and *Redbook,* and she appeared frequently on television. Her academic colleagues who criticized her "popularizing approach" to anthropology often scorned these public efforts.[51] Indeed, Mead never held an academic position, but instead worked at the American Museum of Natural History. The result is that although Mead is clearly a cultural icon, Nancy Lutkehaus argues that she holds a "liminal position" within anthropology.[52]

In her lifetime, Mead's status as a "symbol of women's rights and equality of the sexes" rose and fell. In the 1920s, when sexuality was being renegotiated publicly, Mead wrote *Coming of Age in Samoa: A Psychological Study of Primitive Youth for Western Civilization* (1928), which suggested that adolescent sexuality, particularly female sexuality, need not necessarily be considered the "problem" it was perceived to be in the United States. Under the palm trees of the South Pacific, according to Mead's research, young people explored their sexuality without upsetting the social fabric, and potentially enjoyed a more fruitful and less fraught adolescence as a result. This suggestion, and the sexual liberalism that undergirded Mead's positions on youth, sex, and gender roles, struck a nerve in the American public and launched Mead into the spotlight early in her career.

Despite these original interventions, Mead's legacy as a feminist intellectual has been somewhat obscured by controversy over her research methods and her sexuality, as well as the colonial tropes that inform her writing. Mead's descriptions of carefree sex in the tropics resonated with the collective American imagination about Melanesia and a general obsession with "primitivism" in the United States in the early twentieth century. This interest in indigenous cultures spoke of two interlocking cultural trends. On the one hand, the rising dominance of consumer culture, rapid industrialization, and urbanization instigated "the desire for the simpler, more natural world that so-called primitive peoples represented to westerners . . . 'primitivism' as a concept, a mode of thought, and an aesthetic came into being."[53] On the other hand, westerners were clearly "ambivalent," writes Lutkehaus, about the ways of life the indigenous enjoyed in far-flung corners of the globe. Although Mead benefited from the "rage for the dark," as Lutkehaus calls it among countercultural segments of American culture, her work also challenged the imaginary boundaries between so-called civilized and primitive society.[54]

Still, feminist activists and feminist anthropologists kept Mead and her looming shadow at arm's length. Ruth Behar, in her introduction to the influential collection *Women Writing Culture,* for example, writes, "Anthropology in this country bears the shape of a woman—Margaret Mead, the most famous anthropologist of the century." She admits, however, "as anthropologists, we ought to be proud of this robust woman and want to claim her, but in reality many of us are embarrassed by her."[55] Mead gets surprisingly short shrift from her fellow feminist anthropologists.[56] Noting Mead's virtual erasure within feminist anthropology, Kamala Visweswaran remarks that when Gayle Rubin defines the sex/gender system in 1975, essentially reworking Mead's observations of the 1930s, she makes no mention of Mead's work.[57] Even in the 1970s, a key period for feminist studies throughout the disciplines, Mead remained a controversial figure, "difficult to claim," writes Visweswaran. Lutkehaus suggests that this might owe partly to the more general critique of anthropology that emerged in the 1970s after the end of the Vietnam War. Mead became "a symbol of the entire anthropological enterprise and the focus of the critiques that a younger, more politically disillusioned and socially cynical generation of Americans was making of both anthropology and American society."[58] Younger scholars wondered why and how Mead had neglected to consider the political and economic oppression of indigenous people in colonized Samoa in the twentieth century, for example. Bearing these critiques in mind, I ask how a focus on Mead's legacy as a filmmaker and advocate for visual ethnography might help reshape her reception in feminist studies.

In fact, Mead was one of the first anthropologists after the silent era to write extensively about the potential benefits of motion picture technologies for anthropological fieldwork.[59] She held firm and passionate ideas about how film should be used. She was above all interested in the scientific preservation of cultural forms, "so precious and so trembling on the edge of disappearing forever."[60] Her interest in filmmaking had been inspired by her third husband, anthropologist and photographer Gregory Bateson, as well as Jane Belo, an independent researcher and traveler who worked with both Hurston and Mead and would take up formal anthropological studies at Columbia in the 1940s. In the early 1930s, Bateson and Mead met in New Guinea. Mead had apparently seen some of Belo's footage from Bali and decided her own research with Bateson on temperament and gender would benefit from fieldwork there.[61] From 1936 to 1939 she and Bateson pioneered new techniques in ethnographic photography and filmmaking, collecting more than 30,000 feet of 16mm film in Bali and New Guinea, or more than one thousand minutes.[62] Their efforts would result in two books, several films, and a number of published essays.[63]

According to Ira Jacknis, the first scholar to examine their image-based research and production, Mead and Bateson bewildered colleagues with their ideas about film and photography in the late 1930s. It was not until the 1980s, Jacknis observes, that their work "achieved the status of classics" and due credit for originating the field of visual anthropology.[64] Throughout her decades as a public figure, Mead would use her experiences collaborating with Bateson as a touchstone for her published writing about anthropological filmmaking. In the 1950s, she would experiment with ways to turn her footage into finished ethnographic films. And in the 1960s and 1970s, she would also find herself involved in a number of meaningful film projects with the likes of Craig Gilbert (*An American Family*), the father of U.S. reality TV, and Jean Rouch, the patriarch of ethnographic filmmaking in Europe, both of whom made films about her. In the 1970s, Mead supported the creation of the Society for the Anthropology of Visual Communication, under the umbrella of the American Anthropology Association and the Smithsonian Institution. The collaboration also resulted in the journal *Studies in Visual Communication.* Her influence continues to be felt today in the annual ethnographic film festival in her name hosted by the National Museum of Natural History, where she carried out her career.

In her early adoption and thinking about motion pictures, Mead anticipated numerous debates in documentary studies.[65] Though her writing thinks expansively about the potential of the form, her films demonstrate her stark commitments to positivism. Mead herself was subject to reality, but primarily because of her dedication to facts and scientific analysis. She also keenly understood how "reality" was subject to the power of images and was curious about how image making could be used to illuminate debates about gender roles and sexuality. When *An American Family* premiered on television in 1972, Mead was virtually the only commentator who praised the program.[66] Craig Gilbert's *An American Family* was a twelve-part documentary series based on a tumultuous year in the lives of the "members of the real family," the Louds of southern California.[67] Every other outlet, including the *New York Times, Time,* and *Newsweek* decried the series as immoral, unethical, and upsetting. Where they saw problematic voyeurism, Mead detected a revolutionary art form, as important, she proclaimed as "the invention of drama or the novel." The future of televised media, and especially the dominance of reality TV, would bear out her premonitions. Mead astutely understood that watching "the real life of others interpreted by the camera" would fascinate people, and further that it would offer a "new way in which people can learn to look at life."[68] She also had a lingering faith in the indexicality of the recorded image. Even as she acknowledges the mediating role of the camera, she emphasizes the intimacy and suspense, "the actual, what it is really like" guaranteed by the documentary image.

Mead swam against numerous tides in her life, and certainly against the tide in her field when it came to filmmaking. Writing in the late 1970s, she admonished her colleagues for not paying more attention to the possibilities cinema could offer anthropology.[69] She refers to the slow adoption of film by anthropologists as "our gross and dreadful negligence,"[70] arguing that ethnographic filmmaking could create "a reliable, reproducible, reanalyzable corpus," and also assure that the subjects of the films and their descendants would be able to "repossess their cultural heritage."[71] Mead advocated primarily for the filmic collection of objective images that could be reanalyzed by scientists for years to come. Her interest in celluloid as "researchable data," according to Ruby, would never find much support outside the classroom. Nonetheless, Paul Henley argues that the Mead films mark a crucial moment in the history of ethnographic filmmaking. Even though Mead made them as empirical documents, Henley highlights that they also "anticipate, almost despite the intentions of their authors, the event-based forms of documentary representation, structured by a real or constructed chronological narrative, that began to emerge in ethnographic filmmaking" in the 1950s.[72]

Mead and Bateson never set out to make a documentary, "whether in the sense of that term in the 1930s or in the sense that it is used today."[73] The Mead-Bateson collaboration resulted in seven short films, the Character Formation Series, which Mead began editing in the 1950s. Their total runtime is about two hours, which means that these films represent only a small fraction of the Mead-Bateson footage. *Trance and Dance in Bali,* released in 1952, featuring the Tjalonarang theatrical performance of the battle between life and death, has been the most widely watched and written about in their Character Formation series. The twenty-two-minute film coheres around a voice-over written and read by Mead, who identifies and explains each act in the dance.

Although Mead wrote passionately about the need for long, static takes in ethnographic filmmaking, *Trance and Dance* features conventional camera techniques in both narrative and documentary filmmaking. While the film does use several relatively long takes, especially of the witch, the primary character in

A woman performs during the filming of *Trance and Dance in Bali* (1952), with Margaret Mead and Gregory Bateson in the background.

the dance, most of the shots in the film are quite short. Furthermore, the cam-era seeks out the most active figures in the dance, placing them consistently in the center of the frame. The camera, like the dance, transforms the human body into an instrument of art, especially during the scene of trance dancing when performers whip their hair back and forth and pull a ceremonial weapon into their chests repeatedly. In concert with these visual techniques, Mead's voice-over isolates characters, and gives them trajectories in the story of the dance. "Remember this woman," she'll say. As the climax builds, however, the camera changes its tactics and comes closer to the dancers, and films them at eye level and in slow-motion. The aesthetic qualities of *Trance and Dance* may owe to the collaboration by Belo, who operated the camera, and Colin McPhee, who performed the music. Among the Character Formation series, *Trance and Dance,* ironically Mead's most famous film, is the one most at odds with Mead's written treatises on ethnographic filmmaking.

The other five films of the Character Formation series focus intensely on rela-tionships between mothers and their children, vital subjects for Mead through-out her career. Each of the films uses similar techniques, quite different than those at work in *Trance and Dance*. In general, Mead and Bateson's films consist of a relatively static camera, medium shots that isolate one or two characters in the frame, and Mead's conversational and yet didactic voice-over. Bateson and Mead preferred to maintain distance from the scene being shot, engaging in what would come to be known as observational documentary techniques, whereby the cameraperson follows the action rather than instigating action for the purpose of the film. Only occasionally does Mead introduce something like a doll into the scene to catalyze certain behaviors; however, even in this case, the camera remains distant and observant as the scene plays out.

"Childhood Rivalry in Bali and New Guinea" begins with a title card that places the footage in a specific place and time for the viewer, in this case "The Balinese of Indonesia. Village of Bajoeng Gedé, 1936–1938." This is one way the film verifies its authenticity. Another is Mead's omnipresent voice-over. Because the footage was taken without synchronous sound recording, the soundtrack is completely dominated by Mead's voice.[74] Henley describes Mead's voice as occasionally "objectifying" and "heavily burdened with theoretical purpose," especially in the first two films, *A Balinese Family* (1951) and *Karba's First Years* (1952). He means that the films capture and feature only those slices of life that support Mead's theory about the nature of Balinese character. Although Mead's career was dedicated in various ways to understanding "human temperament" or character, and thus some measure of psychology, the subjects in Mead's films emerge as types, "the mother" and "the child," "the neighbor" and "the baby." She does not identify her subjects by name or divulge any differences between them. Yet her attention to the gendered nature of care and reproductive labor emerges strongly in her films, which are keen examples of a feminist ethnographic sensibility. Curious about the way that children were socialized into gender roles and dominant values about sexuality, Mead paid deep attention to mothers and mothering in her films—a prominent feature of women's documentary filmmaking, and certainly in the 1970s, when women made a number of birth films, and as we'll see in *Joyce at 34* and *Nana, Mom and Me* in chapter 3, films about mothers and daughters.

Mead's narration attempts to explain exactly what you see in the frame. The correlation is absolutely synced, often redundantly describing gestures and actions that we plainly discern in the moving images. For example, the film's first vignette is introduced with a title card that reads, "A mother borrows a baby to tease her own child." When Mead's voice enters, she repeats the phrase with only a slight variation: "This mother has borrowed the neighbor's baby just to tease her own child." In the frame, we see a woman seated on the edge of a porch nursing a toddler while holding a baby next to him in her lap. Mead's intention is to describe the Balinese mother's tendency to tease her child, which eventually leads to jealousy and tantrums. Each of the woman's actions is described by Mead, including the obvious, "she nurses the baby," or "she turns her attention again to the borrowed baby." None of these could be misinterpreted by the viewer after the initial title card explains the one key fact, which is that the toddler belongs to the mother while the baby is the neighbor's. Yet Mead allows no variation in the interpretation of the actions on screen. Despite the overdetermined narrative, however, we gain key insight about reproductive labor and about the material strategies by which mothers socialize their children to the values of their communities. These concerns will surface forcefully in the 1970s, and indeed women's documentaries maintain a consistent emphasis on the production of dominant values and behaviors, especially surrounding race, class, gender, and sexuality. Mead's status as outsider to the community she filmed in Bali gave her authority when she returned to the United States and sparked national debates about gender and sexuality in the pages of women's magazines. Balinese mothers socialized their children to conform to dominant norms; American women could harness this observation and rethink the norms they inherited and might reproduce in their future generations. Although Mead didn't voice these concerns exactly, her filmmaking anticipates women's documentary films of the 1970s, which would explicitly confront and rethink dominant values around domestic and reproductive labor.

As the years progressed, Mead's didactic and authoritative voice-over strategies would fall deeply out of favor in ethnographic filmmaking, especially as the "crisis of representation" shook visual anthropology in the 1970s and 1980s. Her tendency to fix meaning and interpretation, whether in her films or in her writing, has made her the object of scrutiny by poststructural and postcolonial

In their "Character Formation" series, Mead and Bateson chose to maintain a static camera on the action. In her voice-over during this scene about mothering, added in the 1950s, Mead narrates even the most obvious actions on screen.

ethnographers. However, less often emphasized is Mead's consistent desire to invert the traditional hierarchy of knowledge between civilized and primitive cultures. For Mead consistently insisted that the practices she observed among the indigenous peoples of Samoa and Bali—for example, birthing, mothering, child-rearing, courtship, marriage, and performance—evidenced logical and meaningful ways of living, often quite superior to the supposedly scientific and rational ways of life in North America and Europe.

In many ways, however, it seems that Mead's legacy is most relevant as a counterexample to feminist documentaries of the 1970s. For example, Mead's voice-overs insist on the expert interpretation of the anthropologist, whereas the voice-over narration in women's films of the 1970s will shift to the expert experiences of ordinary women. Women's documentaries of the 1970s will challenge in particular the assumed and fixed gap Mead constructs between herself and the women she films. Whereas Mead was willing to rethink the value and significance of the cultural practices of others, her voice-overs insist on an immutable hierarchy between the filmmaker who analyzes and the filmed subjects who experience. Observational footage in Mead's films maintains distance, and the didactic voice-over establishes authority. Women's documentaries of the 1970s will resist both of these strategies and increasingly challenge the meaning of differences between filmmakers and filmed subjects.

Mead's films of the 1930s did not in themselves shape the direction of visual ethnography or documentary filmmaking, as Faye Ginsburg has also observed. Despite her desire to advocate for images in a discipline of words, it was Mead's thinking and writing about ethnographic film that would anticipate and perhaps develop an audience for ethnographic documentary. We look back at her work then as we do with Hurston's, with feminist hindsight that attunes us to the gendered ethics and politics at stake and for clues about how these filmmakers decided to tackle some of documentary's most pressing questions about the ethical responsibility of image making, the nature of the aesthetic, and for questions about how images of the real can describe, analyze, and affectively impact our thinking about gender and its imbrication with matters of empire, race, and the visual.[75]

Mead's filmmaking pinpoints crucial historical moments in the development of documentary, ideologies of gender and race, and the influence of anthropology. During these key periods, global political conflicts and national debates would catalyze a reconsideration of social identity, and especially race, gender, and sexuality. The exploration of identity, especially as it is shaped variously by relations over power between us and them, would find key expression and negotiation in documentary filmmaking. Mead and Bateson, for example, recorded their footage in the 1930s in the transitional colonial period that also influenced Martin and Osa Johnson to travel the world and attempt to capture on film exotic and allegedly disappearing cultural practices and natural resources. Mead edited and released the films in the 1950s in a tense and inhospitable postwar climate. However, most of Mead's writing on the use and future of cinema in anthropology happened in the 1970s, an explosive historical moment for documentary film history, feminist and revolutionary politics, and the field of anthropology—all of which struggled to define central terms like truth, justice, and the real.

In the 1970s, anthropologists favored what Mead called a "discipline of words" and struggled to come to terms with the lack of "objectivity" in recordings made on film. Mead, ever the positivist, was sympathetic to these concerns, but also believed that "objective material" could be collected on film if the right techniques were employed. For example, Mead advocated for "long sequences from one point of view," suggesting that the camera be placed on a tripod in a single position and left alone to record. In 1976 Bateson called "cameras on tripods just grinding" and "disastrous."[76] But Mead disagreed with the idea that aesthetic concerns should influence ethnographic filmmakers. She looked forward to technological innovations that would allow anthropologists to make documents without "intervention," for example, with a 360-degree camera that could be "set up and left in the same place" to avoid "self-consciousness" either by the filmmaker or among those being observed.[77] If Claire Johnston, one of 1970s feminist film theory's most influential critics of "nonintervention" could have heard her, she would have balked at Mead's belief in cinematic objectivity. Mead also strongly disagreed with the idea that ethnographic films need be "an art form," saying, "if it's an art form, it has been altered. . . . Why the hell should it be art?"[78] She decried all variations of filmmaking practice, especially camera movement and editing, as "unnecessary variations" that degraded the utility of the recorded footage for scientific analysis.

The effort to downplay the significance of aesthetics as "embellishment" and manipulations of "reality" echoes the manifestos and declarations of radical filmmakers as diverse as Julio García Espinosa's "For An Imperfect Cinema" and Third World Newsreel's anti-bourgeois cinematic imperatives. Although their politics differed, Mead and the radical filmmakers of the '60s and '70s all sought to use cinema as an analytical tool. Documents of everyday life, of struggle, of labor, of mothering and fathering were all necessary to the broader project of reenvisioning life itself, not to mention the structures of neocolonial and neoliberal power that constrained the life choices of so many, at home and abroad. Women documentarians of the 1970s would be emboldened in similar ways by the power of cinematic reality, and equally determined to become sub-jects of a new reality through the gendered lens of autoethnography.

In the chapters that follow, I focus on the ways that autoethnography serves feminist politics. I bring the 1970s to light as a decade of filmmaking deeply in-vested in the politics of difference and the ethics of representation, and thereby initiate a startling counternarrative about women's documentary production and about the feminist seventies. The most familiar story about the feminist seventies is that it was a decade in which "feminism" represented only a narrow slice of white, heterosexual middle-class women and repressed the voices and interests of women of color. As I argue in chapters 3 and 4, autoethnographic documentaries of the 1970s consistently challenge the power dynamics between insiders and outsiders and thereby elucidate the fraught desires for solidarity that characterize feminist action and affect.

CHAPTER 3

Strangely Familiar

Autoethnography and Whiteness in Personal Documentaries

To speak "I" is, after all, firstly a political act of self-awareness and self-affirmation.

—Laura Rascaroli[1]

"The personal," in other words, became a problem for feminism during the emergence of the second wave rather than simply the site of the movement's becoming or future solution.

—Victoria Hesford[2]

This book insists that the history of women's documentary filmmaking demonstrates a consistent tendency to tell stories ethnographically. The ethnographic impulses of documentary—the desire to encounter and know the Other, which simultaneously implicates the exploration of self—have been at the heart of women's documentary filmmaking and significantly shaped the work of many women filmmakers. The previous two chapters established the ethnographic foundations that undergird women's documentary filmmaking. Working out of different contexts and from different impulses, the films of Flaherty and Johnson, Hurston and Mead highlighted the importance of using the camera to see the different but interrelated ways women are subject to reality. In their far-flung anthropological travels, Flaherty and Johnson demonstrated the imbrication of proto-feminist globe-trotting with anthropology's imperialism while also leaving openings to see more into the lives of women. I placed

Hurston and Mead together in the last chapter to reveal how this project moved across racial and ethnic lines in the frame of academic anthropology. Whereas all four pioneers of women's documentary filmmaking reveal the imbrication of anthropology, documentary, and colonialism, Zora Neale Hurston's ethnographic footage in particular highlights the complex forms of autoethnography that exist within this newly configured archive.

In this chapter I focus on personal films white and Jewish women made about themselves and their families in the early 1970s. Invaginated by the political climate of women's liberation, which was itself shaped by civil rights, women filmmakers engaged with cinema to understand themselves better and to share their gendered experiences with other women. Long denied a literal and symbolic voice in patriarchal society, women passionately inscribed and folded themselves into the documentary material of culture and thus demanded and commanded space, permanence, and significance—ontological, epistemological, political, and affective—for their personal lives and unique experiences.

Somewhat like Zora Neale Hurston's autoethnographic films of the 1920s, which I discuss in chapter 2, personal filmmakers of the 1970s cinematically explored the familiar and familial communities to which they belonged. Of course, Hurston's acclaimed contributions to literature, theater, and anthropology attend exclusively to the experiences of rural blacks in places similar to the ones she knew growing up in African American communities in central Florida. Although she almost never appears in her ethnographic footage, Hurston's short films evidence an intimate interest in the people in front of the camera, and she reflexively telegraphs her ethical commitment to them. In her ethnographic films, Hurston picturizes a new sense of African American culture and identity—at a time when new, quasi-scientific racism insisted on the biological inferiority of nonwhite races. Hurston's strategy was to show African Americans, and especially women, at work, at play, in worship, and in leisure—surviving within and living beyond the gaze of white supremacy.

In this chapter, Hurston's radical, intersectional practice provides a sharp lens through which to apprehend later autoethnographic feminist projects, and paradoxically white women's personal filmmaking of the 1970s. Hurston's committed attention to the everyday lives of "the negro farthest down," in her words, directs us to the latent and manifest racial politics of autoethnography.[3] However, the films in this chapter are also related to Osa Johnson's early entertainment films about the exotic lure and white fascination with foreign bodies. That is, although Osa saw herself making films about Others, the Johnsons' films are telling documents of the white self who claims to have access and mastery over the entire globe. Similarly, although the films in this chapter are purportedly about the women filmmakers and their families, they are also telling documents of the formation of white identity, and white femininity in particular. Not unlike Mead's films, too, these films can be read as evidence of specific gendered cultural practices: birthing, mothering, caring, managing affect, and maintaining cultural values within the nuclear family. That is to say, these films do not exactly follow any of the paths blazed by the documentary pioneers in this book, but rather they raise complex questions and suggest new modes of reading evidence of "character formation" in Mead's terms, and thus the identity politics of feminist filmmaking.[4]

In the case of women's personal films of the 1970s, which are exclusively about white and Jewish women, the anthropological legacy of women's documentary encourages us to: (1) read for the autoethnographic valence that resonates within the work, (2) focus on the relations of power that manifest when the female filmmaker enters intimate and reserved spaces of domesticity and familiarity rather than distant or foreign realms, and (3) investigate the dynamics between individual and collective cultural practices and the systemic relations of power—regarding race, class, and gender—that both sustain and contain individuality and collectivity. My goal is to mobilize Flaherty, Johnson, Hurston, and Mead not in the service of whiteness, but rather to reveal the seemingly invisible processes of white identity formation for women in a distinctly politicized historical moment, particularly in films that do not necessarily foreground racial politics as such. Moreover, I draw attention to an anthropological aesthetic evident in these films, which occurs when filmmakers attend deeply to culturally rich and specific details in the lived environments of their subjects.

In what follows, therefore, I gather together a somewhat familiar subgenre of women's documentary filmmaking of the 1970s: personal films made by women about themselves and their families. Like Michael Renov and Alisa Lebow, I am drawn to the personal dimensions of documentary: in particular, the inscription of the gendered self, the politicization of personal experience, and the formal commitments to women's voices and their bodies as sites of knowledge production and as affective harbors.[5] Reading this group of films ethnographically brings new attention to the production of whiteness and its naturalization in these films. For indeed, as Scott MacDonald has pointed out, personal filmmaking and ethnographic filmmaking are essentially "the inverse of each other,"[6] both committed to "the cinematic exploration of the patterns and nuances"[7] of culture, whether distant or familiar. Both forms of documentary filmmaking, MacDonald reminds us, are above all committed to "lived experience," particularly within families.[8] While ethnographic filmmaking implies a detached and imperial gaze at an Other, personal filmmaking acknowledges that the filmmaker/self is implicated subjectively in every kind of documentary filmmaking. Further, and especially in retrospect, the diverse body of personal filmmaking from the 1970s "has increasingly become ethnographic evidence about life in the United States, including the changing role of the filmmaking within family life."[9] I ask, what constitutes the "whiteness" of women's personal documentaries of the 1970s? And why should that matter? How does the representation of white families in these films indicate or even help produce the fraught racial politics within second-wave feminism—even when the documentary thinks it is posing an entirely different set of questions? Further, in what ways might these films by and about women's reproductive, domestic, and affective labor bring whiteness into a form of visibility that is not naturalized but distinctly gendered and politicized?

In white women's personal films of the 1970s, experiences long denied, ignored, or particularized were offered to audiences for several reasons: to give women a platform to speak; to imagine a new and engaged form of listening; and to inspire women to effect change in their lives and join other women in a greater struggle for justice. By inaugurating a cinematic feminist "I," these documentaries constitute "a first political act," which makes the self unfamiliar and therefore a potential site for challenging the demands and expectations yoked to white femininity. In feminist scholar Kimberly Lamm's phrasing, counter-representations of white women have the potential to denaturalize and thus challenge "the dominant visual grammar of white heterosexual femininity."[10] Collectively, these personal documentaries by white women resist naturalized visions of whiteness and femininity and draw meaning and inspiration from the matrilineal stories in their families.

Fundamentally, these documentaries support the idea that the personal was excellent material for documentary filmmaking and for feminist politics—and in particular, that matrilineal exploration was necessary for an understanding of the female self. Lucy Fischer cites Adrienne Rich's observation that the story "between mother and daughter—essential, distorted, misused—is the great unwritten story," and Rita Mae Brown's *Rubyfruit Jungle,* about an artist who makes a documentary about her mother, are clear indications of this second-wave interest in matrilineal stories.[11] White and white ethnic women had to be able to see and reveal the transmission of culture and ideas about gender from mother to daughter and the ways in which that transmission was inevitably sutured to ideas about American whiteness as the unquestioned norm.

Filmmaking was an expensive and technically complex enterprise in the early 1970s, which meant that most women with technical experiences and access to equipment tended to be white, and middle- and upper-class. Many of these, especially the concentration of women documentary filmmakers that I write about here, lived in Boston and New York. Major cities attracted creative laborers because they provided access to grant funding and paid work opportunities in public and commercial media.[12] Writing in *Ms.* magazine about the Second International Women's Film Festival, Amy Stone observes that the filmmakers who emerged in the 1970s were primarily "on the young side of middle age, mostly white and mostly middle class," and that films by "old women, black, Puerto Rican and other women who don't get counted," were hopefully on the horizon.[13] Material constraints thus explain in part why the majority of personal films in the early 1970s were made by white women; however, these material constraints arise from a broader set of racial, economic, and gendered relations of power that are also expressed in these films, albeit in ways that are more often implied rather than explicit. Reading these films for what they reveal about race, rather than what they conceal, opens a long overdue discussion about the formation and characteristics of whiteness in women's personal documentaries. White women had a "foot in" structures of power and resources that allowed them to represent the ways in which they were subject to the realities of the white patriarchal family with renewed and politicized clarity.

One documentary that emerged into visibility against the odds was *Joyce at 34* (1972), by filmmakers Joyce Chopra and Claudia Weill. The short documentary screened widely at women's film festivals and has been written about steadily since its premiere at the Whitney Museum in 1973.[14] *Joyce at 34* seems to squarely address several pressing concerns of women's activism in the 1970s: women's reproductive and waged labor, motherhood, equal treatment, and self-determination. Yet, Chopra hesitates to call it a feminist film. In a review of the first screening, published in the *New York Times, Joyce at 34* is described as "not a feminist film, though clearly aware of feminist positions, but it is a film about people of three generations and many loyalties and ambitions, and many ways of accommodating to life."[15] Chopra describes this review as "one of the most wonderful I ever received."[16] I suspect her enthusiasm for the review has to do with the phrase "not a feminist film." In my communication with Chopra over a decade of exploring this work, I have always wondered about her reluctance to call the film properly "feminist."

Like several other feminist films of the 1970s, and in particular personal films, *Joyce* complicates the mythical harmony of the nuclear family and poses motherhood as a problem for white women's autonomy and freedom, and in generational terms that implicate mother, grandmother, and daughter. Chopra, who worked on several films with renowned documentary auteurs such as Richard Leacock and Robert Gardner, made *Joyce at 34* in 1972 with another woman, something

Chopra describes in the film as the first time she doesn't have to worry "about being taken seriously as a filmmaker." *Joyce at 34* is a highly self-reflexive take on the process of constructing images and narratives about the figure of the white mother. A film about a filmmaker who is also a mother, *Joyce at 34* is about the labor of mothering and the work of filmmaking, and it is the first feminist documentary to explore the range of emotions, duties, and subjective acrobatics between personhood, motherhood, and labor that define motherhood for one individual *from her own perspective*. Formally it makes explicit the technologies of cinematic meaning making, questioning thus its own act of representation; and thematically it grants authority to the mother's own version of her story, insinuating a new politicized maternal figure into public visual discourse.

Joyce's story begins at the end of her pregnancy, meanders through the first year of her daughter's life, and ends with her contemplating a second child. *Joyce* maintains fidelity to lived time and space, to logical flow, and a naturalized trajectory of cause and effect. Yet, *Joyce at 34* also subjectivizes and thematizes "the filmmaker" within the film and strives to expose rather than conceal the means of cinematic production. The dilemmas of motherhood at play in the film revolve around the filmmaker as such, the work of filmmaking, and the labor of motherhood. At the level of narrative, the film participates in a similar mode of exposure: the admission of maternal disquietude, the smoldering ambition in a woman who would also be a good mother, the disruptive arguments that emerge in a white nuclear family in which gender roles are prescribed and also hotly contested. Debates about motherhood were integral to seventies feminisms, and *Joyce at 34* clearly deploys a radical and reflexive cinematic "I" to make political waves in the naturalized placidity of white femininity.

Throughout the film, Joyce's relationship to her filmmaking competes with her relationship with her daughter. Yet, at stake is far more than a simple matter of balancing "life and work." For Joyce, the struggle that takes place is about the definition of self within competing paradigms of white female subjectivity: self as woman, as filmmaker, as wife, and as mother. The trajectory of subjectivity mapped by the film is crooked, winding, and often non-progressive despite *Joyce at 34*'s tight, teleological arc in lived time and space. Near the end of the film, the daughter, Sarah's, progress is clear; she has learned to walk. She masterfully pushes a tall chair past a doorframe and waddles happily at the playground. Yet, "progress" cannot describe the journey taken by the mother. That is, the self-reflexivity of the film attests to a blurring of the discrete categories of filmmaking and gendered labor in Joyce's life. Indeed, for Joyce the possibility of freedom depends on the ability to make gendered labor the raw material and the outcome of filmmaking.

At the end of the film, Joyce remains unclear about how to prioritize and organize maternal and professional desires. The final shot is a close-up of Joyce in a room bright with natural lighting. Voice and sound are initially synchronized as Joyce explains that she both does and does not want to have another baby. When an off-screen voice (presumably that of Claudia Weill, the co-director) asks her why, she begins to laugh as she says, "I think if I have another baby, it would probably be the end." Here, sound and image tracks suddenly split. The visual freezes on the close-up of Joyce smiling, her head thrown back just slightly. Her voice, however, continues to elaborate on thoughts of being able to "just about manage" with "just one" child. She admits that having only one child might be "selfish," but nonetheless, she's fearful that two would be impossible. As she laughs again, sound and image resume synchronicity, and Joyce rejoins her laughing voice once again before the fade-out ends the film. There is a way in which this final splitting at the conclusion of the film hints at the subjective disjuncture that defines motherhood for Joyce. The reason the idea of another baby is laughable to Joyce is clear from her remark that it would be "the end"—the end of her professional career, that is, and in the syntax of the film, the end of a crucial facet of Joyce's life. In the final instance, when the work of creating a film is complete, we continue to wonder about the possibility of Joyce's freedom. The mere mention of "the end" stalls the progress of the visual narrative, just as in the opening scenes where the still images code pregnancy (nonprofessional time) as a time of frustrated waiting. Joyce's nervous laughter in this final shot bridges

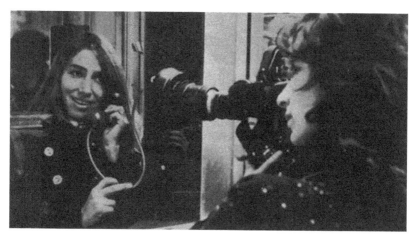

Joyce Chopra and Claudia Weill during the filming of *Joyce at 34* (1972). (Courtesy of Joyce Chopra and Claudia Weill.)

the gap but does not suture over the obvious conflict wrought by the mother's competing desires.

In a sequence when Sarah is six weeks old, Joyce takes the child to her mother's house in New York so that she can work on a new film assignment. As the visual track shows Joyce and Sarah's departure at the airport and flight to New York, it is in voice-over once again that Joyce reflects on how traveling with her daughter has presented seemingly endless complications and has distracted her from thinking about the film she's about to make. The journey to her parents' home also provokes a critical reflection on her changed sense of herself as a daughter. It occurs to her that having a child has filled her with an unexpected but immense sense of "relief" at having done "the right thing." As Joyce admits the regression into an adolescent desire for her parents' approval, the visual track jumps from a shot of the retreating landscape from the plane's window to home movie footage of Joyce at her graduation party at sixteen. The association of regression with motherhood plays into familiar feminist fears about the way investment in reproductive labor saps women of their potential to gain footing in the public sphere. Indeed, throughout the film, and despite scenes in which Joyce acts out and utters obvious maternal satisfaction, motherhood constitutes a sticky web of pleasure, duty, and distraction that Joyce must consistently keep at bay.

The return home in the narrative's present tense, then, is also an internal return to the site of the filmmaker's initial departure from her familial home. The silent home-movie footage of couples dancing at her sweet sixteen party gains new meaning relevant to the present. Significantly, in this segment of the voice-over, Joyce assumes the position also occupied by the spectator who gazes from a location outside the film. Like the spectator, Joyce assumes an almost corporeal presence offscreen through the intimate act of describing the images we both see. The footage freezes individual women mid-dance as Joyce signals them out to the spectator: "There's me . . . That's my old friend Toby . . . There's Gloria." The content of Joyce's voice-over, however, is not about what it felt like to be young or on the verge of independence. Rather, what the home-movie footage plus voice-over construct is a context for Joyce's emergence into motherhood. Each of the friends in the home movie is described in terms of her marriage and maternity. This one has three children already, this one had her first at twenty, this one got married right away, and so forth. It becomes clear that Joyce is an exception in the social scaffolding that contains her white, middle-class nuclear family. In this way, the fact of Joyce's motherhood is rendered both exceptional as well as expected and the visuals emphasize this "late arrival." From the home-movie footage (fixed into the past with the final phrase, "That was eighteen years ago") the film cuts to a shot from Joyce's present-tense perspective in the window seat of the landing plane.

Joyce's mother is a critical figure and presence throughout the film. She lends insight into the ways Joyce's own mothering is both exceptional in the context of her professional life and also in conversation with familial and cultural expectations. In one shot that appears during the sequence when Joyce and Sarah are in New York for the first time, Joyce's mother admits how surprising it is to witness Joyce care for Sarah. Framed tightly in a classic talking-head interview pose, Joyce's mother reveals how unlikely it seemed that Joyce would divert attention from her career to fulfill the duties of motherhood. "I couldn't believe my eyes when I saw her handling the baby, bathing the baby, nursing the baby, which is something I never expected either from Joyce. . . . Just to know that this is number one. This is the number one career at the moment." In the grandmother's discourse, motherhood entails a certain amount of sacrifice as well as the cyclical and repetitive gestures that define labor. As Joyce reveals in the next scene, the primary sacrifice demanded by reproductive labor come in the form of the mother's professional ambitions. Joyce refuses this demand. Instead, the film, which is the product of Joyce's professional work, is also the instantiation of a trace of Joyce's reproductive labor. Thus, the film radically posits the possibility of both/and for women.

Over images of Joyce's mother at the piano, Joyce's voice-off tells us that her mother once hoped to be a concert pianist. Instead, she now occasionally accompanies her son, who did become a musician. A brief history of Joyce's maternal legacy follows in a series of re-photographed still images that tidily match the voice-over: black and white photographs of Joyce's parents' wedding; their first, second, and third children; Joyce's grandmother, who cared for them; Joyce's mother working as a teacher, a profession Joyce admits she never regarded as important because it was performed by women. The emphasis on Joyce's matrilineal heritage provides a framework in which to understand Joyce's present-tense conflict between her maternal and professional desires. The images of the women in her white, Jewish family constitute a collage of professional sacrifices. In her voice-over, Joyce distinguishes herself from this legacy of "women's work," however. If the black and white photographs seem to fix this selfless history in the distant past, though, it becomes clear in the present-tense scene that follows that Joyce, now also a mother, shares more with her mother's generation than she expected.

The film gives the sense that despite the obvious gains made in white women's freedom to self-actualize professionally, systemic gender injustices and white cultural expectations continue to curtail options and opportunities for women in the public sphere. The scene described above ends with a zoom on a black-and-white photograph of Joyce's mother's teaching colleagues. Dozens of teachers, mostly women, are arranged in several tiers; they all smile for the professional photograph. After a jump cut, the same photograph appears in the film's present tense mid-frame in the hands of a middle-aged woman. Brought back to life in moving-color, the photograph stitches together the past and the present, bringing Joyce's life into a continuum of white, maternal subjectivity defined in part by schisms wrought upon working women. In the film's present, a lively group of Joyce's mother's friends—retired schoolteachers—recount their own experiences juggling professional lives with motherhood. In this scene, sound and image are synchronized as women remember how feelings of conflict and guilt dominated their lives. Chopra recounts that she and Weill deliberately incited the conversation by asking the women a question: "Did you ever find it difficult to balance parenting with working?" Yet, the filmmakers were astounded at the flood of dialogue that ensued.[17] In the film, this becomes evident as the women talk over each other, interrupt one another, and generally shout out anecdotes about hiding pregnancies for fear of termination, about children begging them to stay home sick, about feeling lesser than "real mommies" because of their working lives. The cinematic conventions in this scene, particularly the use of synchronous sound, natural lighting, and quick-pace editing emphasize the energetic responses among the women. The collection of stories and the close seating arrangement of the retired teachers around the table emphasize commonality. Though rendered in particular anecdotes, the final sum of the women's experiences is the impression of a collective, systemic problem. Further, their stories are not lore of the distant past, but imminently relevant to Joyce's own present.

The final issue around the lunch table is the topic of women's liberation. "You aren't really liberated if you walk around with feelings of guilt," declares one woman, as others nod in agreement and the sound of dishes clanks in the background. She continues, "You're truly liberated if you can carry on a career and feel that you're doing the right thing for yourself and your children." In sync with the word "liberated" the film cuts to a tracking shot of Joyce. The camera follows her from behind as she walks briskly and balances film equipment in both arms. Here, Joyce is literally "carrying on a career" and the camera races to keep pace with her. At the mention of "feeling that you're doing the right thing," however, Joyce opens a door and begins to pass through. Read in the context of the voice-over, this shot of Joyce poses the matter of her liberation as a possibility: Joyce carries on a career. Once inside the house in the next shot, however, Joyce no longer carries her equipment/career. Instead, she is met with a wailing baby and coos at her sympathetically. It is impossible to know if "feelings of guilt" carry over into the scene with the baby, but certainly the present-tense footage of Joyce leaves the matter of liberation open to interpretation. Is such a thing possible for white women of Joyce's generation in ways not possible for her mother's? Or, rather, does the guilt trip remain exactly as it was?

A few scenes later, Joyce is again traveling and working. This time, however, she leaves the baby at home. Over shots of Joyce as she grabs her luggage and enters the school where they are filming, she admits, "As long as she's with me, all I'll think about is her. And if I don't have her with me, then I can be a person again." For Joyce, in this scene, being a "person" is synonymous with being a focused professional; that is, Joyce must resist that sticky, affective maternal web that threatens her ability to be fully in work.[18] As I see it, the film wavers on the matter of Joyce's liberation, situating her as a maternal subject of feminist politics along a continuum, where the past and the present exist simultaneously and in proximity. *Joyce at 34*, which depends on the structure of calendrical time, asserts the white, maternal feminist subject in a constant struggle with past, present, and future, as well as cultural expectations, personal aspirations, and economic determinations.

Crucially, *Joyce at 34* retains its focus on the singularity of Joyce's experience in contrast to the equally particularized experiences of other white women in the documentary. That is, although *Joyce at 34* projects a feminist reimagining of the transition into motherhood and draws meaning from a reflection on Joyce's matrilineal heritage, the film limits its reflection to *Joyce's* story without attempting to extrapolate meaning about the lives of mothers in general. The use of voice-over in particular secures the film's focus on Joyce's experience as an individual.[19] In the voice-over that bridges the shots of the opening sequence, it is Joyce who reflects on her own state of being and having. In voice-over, Joyce speaks not only to the images on screen, but to an unprojected inner life provoked by her transformation. The highly subjectivized voice-over then collaborates with the image track to constitute Joyce as a unique subject who has authentic access to her own experiences and the ability to narrate the significance of her thoughts and actions. If this mode of storytelling in *Joyce at 34* leaves intact the notion of a subject who is autonomous, sovereign, and self-original, the voice-over nonetheless effects an important feminist endorsement of self-authorship and the authority of experience crucial to second-wave discourses. The reappropriation of the voice-over in women's documentaries such as *Joyce at 34* challenged a previous model of documentary filmmaking in which the male voice connoted authority and held exclusive power to interpret projected images.[20] Here, it is Joyce who reveals *and* interprets her own actions and experiences, and she does so from a subjective location that challenges patriarchal myths about women's relationships to their bodies, their capacities to reproduce, and their proper functions in the domestic and public spheres. The intervention should not be underestimated. In the documentary landscape of the late '60s and early '70s, which was crowded with films about mostly male, public figures, Chopra's film was the first to assert the public significance of one woman's personal journey into motherhood.[21]

And so, if the feminist politics of the film are readily apprehended, why Chopra's reluctance to call the film "feminist"? In Chopra's hesitance I detect concerns about the collective identity politics of feminism and feminist cinema: is feminism about all women? After all, what the film seems *not* to be about is race: no women of color make an appearance in the film and neither does the film explicitly address either the fact that everyone in Joyce's world is white, or that being Jewish somehow contributes to her sense of identity as a white woman. Is a documentary by a woman, for women, necessarily feminist? Who gets to speak on behalf of "women" writ large? Who gets to speak as an individual woman in a nonfeminist way? If one woman describes her personal experiences and connects these to the experiences of other women like her, is she doing feminism? And the perennial question: which women does feminism represent, and whose interests and experiences are excluded or silenced as a result?

Autoethnography

In *Joyce at 34* and *Nana, Mom and Me* (Amalie Rothschild, 1974), the filmmaker finds herself in a moment of transition and turns the camera on herself and her family as a means of self-exploration and subjective renegotiation. In both cases, the filmmakers are college-educated white women brought up in relatively affluent homes, pursue careers in the arts, and are Jewish. Joyce is about to have a baby and Amalie is considering having a child as well. Both young women find themselves drawn to the stories of their mothers and grandmothers; in formal and informal filmed interviews, the filmmakers ask their mothers and grandmothers questions about marriage, motherhood, career ambitions, and unrealized dreams. They invite their female relatives to compare their lives as younger girls and women to the contemporary experiences of women in the 1970s. *Old Fashioned Woman* (Martha Coolidge, 1974), much like *Nana, Mom and Me* and *Joyce at 34*, places the filmmaker reflexively within the frame of inquiry, but also foregrounds the life story of the filmmaker's elderly female relative: her grandmother, Mabel Tilton Coolidge, a stately New England woman who graduated from the prestigious Smith College in the early twentieth century. These related films foreground women's subjectivity across a complex spectrum of white privilege, although they assert themselves primarily as feminist personal documentaries devoid of racial politics.

Although male avant-garde filmmakers such as Jonas Mekas and Stan Brakhage had experimented with autobiographical, personal, and diary films before 1970, women had yet to tell their own stories or stories about other women with the portable 16mm and sync sound technologies newly available to independent filmmakers in the late 1960s. And although women filmmakers like Carolee Schneemann in *Fuses* (1967) and Shirley Jackson in *Portrait of Jason* (1967) had produced gorgeous films that demand attention to subjectivity, sexuality, raciality, and relationality, women had yet to use conventional techniques, such as interviews, voice-over, and observational footage, to document their personal lives and those of their family members.

These films thus belong to a mode of filmmaking Alisa Lebow calls first-person documentaries, which foreground the subjectivity and voice of the filmmaker, whether the film is personal, political, or poetic, and whether or not the documentary is autobiographical.[22] For Lebow, first-person documentaries range in form, subject matter, and address, but they share two key qualities: "subjectivity and relationality," which is transmitted through a filmmaker's direct address to the viewer.[23] These qualities attain to the three films under consideration here. In keeping with their usual designation, I will sometimes continue to call them "personal films," but my understanding of them aligns conceptually with Lebow's notion of first-person documentaries. These are films that speak in the first person and foreground women's subjectivity, especially as their experiences, ideas, and beliefs relate to those of others, and in these examples, other family members.

Laura Rascaroli observes that the act of grouping films together "is a classificatory exercise, one that suggests the existence of a field, of a domain, if not a coherent genre as such."[24] In this case, the field or domain of personal documentaries made by women in the 1970s is a category that has long interested feminist film scholars, because it aligns so clearly with the dominant vision of second-wave feminism and its defining slogan: the personal is political. However, in contrast to other film scholars, I understand these documentaries to exist at a unique nexus where the personal becomes feminist becomes ethnographically relevant. A small number of scholars, including Julia Lesage, Jan Rosenberg, Alexandra Juhasz, and Jim Lane, have examined some of these films closely.[25] However, whereas these authors have tended to fasten the films to the frameworks of autobiography and the politics of women's liberation, I emphasize an alternative relationship between the feminist personal and the sociocultural and read these as autoethnographic films about the gendered, cultural practices of white women and white identity formation.

Among anthropologists who study visual ethnography, the category of autoethnography signals a shift from an interest in otherness to an exploration of selfhood. Writing about *Persepolis,* for instance, Marjane Satrapi's animated personal documentary about growing up during the Islamic revolution in Iran, Mazyar Lotfalian turns to Marilyn Strathern (1987) and Deborah Reed-Danahay (1997) for definitions of autoethnography. "Autoethnography," she writes, "foregrounds multiple plateaus of selfhood, which are revealed as the stories unfold. In addition, autoethnography is about a voice and its 'authenticity'; who speaks and on behalf of whom."[26] In this case, I mine the rhetorical force of autoethnography, which makes manifest the politics of difference and the cultural practices of identity formation to distinguish these personal filmmaking projects from autobiographical films. Traditionally understood, autobiographical films—like autobiographical literature—suggest a film about an entire lifespan, for example Agnes Varda's *Les Plages d'Agnes* (2008). According to Catherine Russell, "Autobiography becomes ethnographic at the point where the film- or videomaker understands his or her personal history to be implicated in larger social formations and historical processes."[27] Thus, the distinction between autobiographical films and autoethnographies lies in the filmmaker's attention to both coverage and culture. Autoethnographies might only cover a brief time period in the filmmaker's life, like Amalie Rothschild's *Nana, Mom and Me,* or indeed foreground the life of another, as in *Old Fashioned Woman.*

Autoethnographies, in other words, constitute a distinct group of first-person films in that they present the filmmaker-self within a matrix of cultural practices, beliefs, and expectations that allow viewers to gain insight about a particular group of people at a particular time and in a particular place. Autoethnographies are therefore distinct from both autobiographies and other forms of ethnographic filmmaking. In contrast to traditional ethnographic portraits of cultural and racialized Others, autoethnography (sometimes also called self-ethnography) implies that "we turn ourselves towards a group of people where we already belong."[28] Following Rascaroli, then, my aim is to regroup a relatively familiar set of "women's personal films" into an alternative category of "autoethnographic films" and thereby illustrate a new way of reading and understanding their contributions to both feminist and documentary studies.

Whereas these landmark documentaries inaugurated key aesthetic and political innovations in the long history of women's documentary filmmaking, they also mark a specific territory of contestation where white women tread uniquely. As Lamm puts it, "hinged between racial privilege and gender oppression," white women both yield power and are subject to the reality of their disempowerment, especially within the stringent norms of the middle-class family, which both venerates and exploits them. My aim is to make the naturalized whiteness in these personal films strange and momentarily unfamiliar. Making whiteness strange through the innovative articulation of a feminist "I" and an innovative anthropological aesthetic with deep roots in the history of women's documentary filmmaking forms part of the films' enduring feminist potential.

Whiteness

Scholars of whiteness do not necessarily agree how or if the notion of whiteness makes a useful contribution to critical race studies or antiracist politics. Nonetheless, "While the definition of whiteness is difficult to pin down," writes Barbara Applebaum, "there is widespread agreement that whiteness is a socially constructed category that is normalized within a system of privilege."[29] In these films, whiteness is made manifest primarily through the normalization of the temporal advantages of knowing the past and imagining the future, as well as through the material certainties of inherited wealth, education, and culture. Undergirding these is the luxurious assumption that one deserves all this and more. Focusing on values, norms, and privileges rather than on racism per se, that is, on the systemic valuation and rewards most often preserved for white people, helps us address how race is produced and maintained in these works, even when their attention to racial politics is largely one of exclusion. In other words, it is not the fact that these films "leave out" the concerns of women of color that makes them problematic for feminist ethics and politics. Rather, the casual acceptance of privilege without attention to classed and racialized structures of power highlights the normalization and naturalization of whiteness within this group of women's personal documentaries.

These personal documentaries of the 1970s tend to insist on the individuality of the filmmaker: Joyce, Amalie, Martha. They are women whose lives, values, wealth, and cultural habits are clearly derived from their families, but the formal structures of the films and the personal voice cultivated in the voice-overs in each of the films also insist on the uniqueness of the individual. This tendency to assert one's individuality and isolate oneself from collective frameworks of class and race identity is ironically itself a marker of both whiteness and middle-classness. Like whiteness, middle-class identity has been elusive as a category of analysis in the academy. According to Chris McDonald, "a number of problems have left the North American middle class under-studied and under-theorized."[30] McDonald draws from the work of sociologist Jennifer Hurstfield, who has noted that middle-class youth rarely use race, gender, ethnicity, or class to describe themselves; instead, they tend to emphasize what she calls "existential references" and are more likely to describe themselves as "I'm an individual," "I'm unique," or "I'm just me."[31] Rather than cultural traditions and community stories, youth from the middle class tend to use "their tastes and consumption patterns" to build identity and distinguish themselves from others, according to Hurstfield.[32] Because whiteness and middle-class values set the dominant standard in the United States, scholars argue that these specific identity practices are normalized and thus made invisible. Middle-classness and whiteness both seem to provide a "blank slate" for members, who ironically sense that they have freely and uniquely defined themselves and are exempt from any larger "group identity."

This gender-neutral assessment of the habits of whiteness and middle-class identity formation, however, cannot account for the feminist politics that conjoin these personal films. That is, although individuals emerge with relative autonomy in *Joyce, Nana,* and *Old Fashioned Woman,* white women assert their individual subjectivity primarily *in relation to* their mothers, grandmothers, and daughters. In other words, these personal documentaries foreground a gendered experience of racial and economic privilege, which is always hampered by dynamics of power that yoke white women to patriarchal demands, especially in the familial and domestic realm. The anthropological aesthetic of these films, evident in the close cinematic attention to detail—the provenance of an heirloom clock, the hairstyle of one's grandmother, the cost of a wedding dress, the food on the table—offers culturally specific descriptions of everyday life. Reading for these details, each film reveals that its vision of white womanhood is far from universal, and instead incredibly specific to the naturalized cultures of wealth and whiteness in which they exist. However, they also signal the particular constraints that limit white women's subjective expansion and point out the sticky combination of racial and economic privilege even as it intersects with gender discrimination. Made visible is the gendered labor that exists within the home and within the genealogies of white and economically privileged families, including reproductive and affective labor necessary to the regeneration of wealth and the integrity of the family tree. In Jewish families, ethnic assimilation into the category of whiteness was also managed by women through the domestic and reproductive labor they were expected to perform invisibly and expertly despite the patriarchal dynamics that shaped gendered relations at home.

Old Fashioned Woman

In *Old Fashioned Woman*, Martha Coolidge begins with interview footage of her grandmother Mabel, who was born in 1886 in Massachusetts. Inserts of archival photographs in the opening sequence reveal a life of stunning turn-of-the-century privilege: women in elaborate dresses, expensive-looking baby prams, and an enormous two-story Victorian home. Several more photographs feature Mabel as a young girl and then as a woman, expensively dressed in lace and exquisitely coiffed in the style befitting an upper-class woman of her era. As she reflects on the significant differences between her life as a young woman among steam trains, house parties, and church events, and the experiences of life in the 1970s, Mabel expresses mild annoyance at the tendency toward "psychological investigation" of "inner selves," evident throughout popular culture in the 1970s. In a classic talking-head shot, Mabel sits in front of a bookcase, gray hair neatly composed in a loose bun, and says, "I can't understand why people are so bound today to know who they are and where they're going and so forth." Despite her mild protest, Mabel is in fact the subject of an introspective project conducted by her granddaughter.

Read as an autoethnographic film, *Old Fashioned Woman* is thus also about the filmmaker, Martha Coolidge. Though she reveals somewhat less about her own past experiences, Coolidge's desire for her grandmother's stories—evident as much in voice-over as through the filmmaker's presence on screen—determines the shape and voice of the documentary. We gather from the voice-over that Coolidge was inspired to make the film as she began to approach the age her father was when he died of cancer during her childhood. "This film started out as a search for the dead lost in the past," she tells us. "My grandmother represents the past to me. While making the film, I discovered she was showing me a new way of looking at my future." Coolidge is not explicit about what clues for the future she gleaned from investigating her grandmother's life, but the film nonetheless reveals the possible connections between the two women's lives, and in doing so suggests a set of cultural expectations for privileged, white women that remained relatively constant even among the political and social upheavals of the late twentieth century.

Throughout the film, Mabel makes consistent use of the phrase "in those days," when she explains how life was for her in the early twentieth century. As she and Martha look through boxes of photographs, Mabel points out the social norms that shaped the lives of upper-class white women and men, but her language is general—as if these realities applied to the general public as opposed to a privileged slice of wealthy Americans. "That's the kind of nightgown little girls used in those days," she says, referencing a long ornate gown. "In those days, men were the head of the family," she explains in response to her grand-daughter's questions about Mabel's relationships with her mother and father. "Father came home at night and that's all you saw of him."

As she narrates these gendered details of her upbringing, Mabel hints at a feminist reconsideration of these stringent norms of white femininity. She also casually describes luxuries like attending prep school and the third-floor dark-room in her home, which was built to support her interest in photography— certainly a hobby reserved for the wealthy in the late nineteenth century, on the other hand, unusual for women at the time. Mabel in other words manifests the unique matrix of white middle-class womanhood: beneficiaries of racial and economic privilege, white women were nonetheless constrained within the fa-milial order in notable ways in Mabel's generation. The power to create images, for example, which Mabel enjoys because of her race and class, cannot grant her freedom from the gendered expectations of women's constrained visibility. It is up to Martha, the filmmaker, to revive the power of the image contained in the photographs to do work in the service of feminist politics and feminist cinema.

In another memorable sequence, Mabel describes her life in college. She entered Smith, a woman's college, in 1908, wearing a red winter dress with chinchilla furs. She studied botany, psychology, history, Latin, French—whatever interested her, because her future did not require that she train for paid labor. As a college junior, she went on a specially chartered Mediterranean tour with friends and family. The trip's guests included an art professor who gave lectures on the sites they visited, including the Pyramids at Giza. Personal photographs portray young women wearing elegant silk dresses and carrying parasols as they ride horses in the desert. "We were dignified young gentlemen and ladies in our day," Mabel recalls. The dedication to covering and protecting their white skin with expensive materials illustrates the privilege that undergirds this image. However, these educational riches would have been rare for women at the turn of the century, and so these photographs also illustrate the way that Mabel was always ahead of her time, consistently conforming to and also challenging the norms of white femininity.

Rich details about an imaginary "we" narrated nonchalantly by Mabel, and included with obvious curiosity and admiration by her granddaughter, generate a nuanced though naturalized portrait of gender constraint as well as race and class privilege in the early twentieth century. They also reveal the parameters of the filmmaker's own possible trajectory and future—here, the range of gendered norms that she will decide to adhere to or resist. Broadly, these details include decisions related to family, marriage, and wage or nonwage labor. Martha has a wider range of options in the 1970s than her grandmother did in the '20s and '30s as a young woman. Despite the affordances of wealth and whiteness, Mabel admits that her career options were limited by social norms for women of her class and race. "We could only be teachers or nurses" in those days, and "I wasn't going to be a teacher or a nurse," she says. Growing up, Mabel explains that the social expectations were clear to her. She was to get through high school and college and then "brighten the corner," as a popular saying went at the time. She thinks she would have chosen music if she had had the freedom to choose a career, but instead: "I was a volunteer. We all volunteered in those days." Coolidge asks her, "What should people get out of life?" Her grandmother's answer is: "Respect. You should all want the respect of your friends, and the love of your family and your relatives and so on." She has a few other key suggestions as well: "Strive for success in life" and "What's the use of living if you can't live happily?" What she does not say, however, is that respect, success, and happiness are all deeply bound by social expectations determined largely by one's gender, class, and race.

Thus, *Old Fashioned Woman,* as is hinted at in the film's title, is an interesting template for dominant gender norms of the early twentieth century, especially among white women with economic, social, political, and cultural clout. Mabel became the wife of a governor, and in her own account, influenced her husband's presence in the public sphere. She explains her life as one devoted to her marriage and her family ("family is the most important thing"). In her advanced age, she is the keeper of heirlooms, traditions, and customs. In the final scene Martha and her extended family sit at a lushly set table enjoying the annual Thanksgiving feast. As the credits roll, the camera singles out key members of the party: great-grandchildren, grandchildren, and sons and daughters. In medium shots that briefly isolate each family member, each of them enjoys the traditional spoils of the holiday: turkey, sweet potatoes, green beans. Moving busily among the seated family members are several working women in uniforms; they serve laden plates and pour the wine, but unlike the family members, they are not identified by name. Like so many of the privileges captured by the film's anthropological aesthetic, they are merely there in the background, supporting the dominant narrative about the importance of family and ritual.

Highlighting the affordances of generational wealth and whiteness, the film also zeroes in on the consistent domestic demands on women throughout the decades. What form of "I" is able to emerge within these possibilities and pressures? The relationships between the past and the present—between Martha and Mabel—are all bound by social norms and cultural expectations, which we can retrospectively analyze as determined by race, class, sexuality, and gender privilege. Will Coolidge also become a heterosexual wife and mother, wear an expensive wedding dress, host catered family gatherings at her stately home, become the support system for a more public partner? Or not? If not, will her future be resonant with her grandmother's generation? What future possibilities exist for women buoyed by the privileges of race and class, but also seemingly hampered by the constraints of gender?

Coolidge presents her grandmother within past privileged norms, but also as resonant with contemporary feminist politics. Despite her pastness, for instance, Mabel holds contemporary, liberal views commensurate with those of her granddaughter's generation, especially around gender and the environment. Toward the end of the film, Coolidge includes observational shots of Mabel outside her home as she collects twigs and sticks for the fireplace in a brown paper bag. In voice-over, Mabel expresses concerns about the environment and wishes people were thriftier. The sounds and images coalesce here, presenting Mabel's "old-fashioned" ideas about recycling and reuse as surprisingly contemporary. She also voices concerns about population explosion and the earth's limited resources, which were progressive political concerns at the time. Seeming to test the limits of Mabel's liberalism, Martha asks her grandmother about abortion, and she says, "I believe in it." She also believes in equal rights and equal pay. That is, despite that her views represent those of a particular class, race, and sexuality in the twentieth century, they are also in line with many contemporary concerns that could be read as "feminist"—also seemingly uncoded by race and class.

Old Fashioned Woman demonstrates that relatively privileged women of the feminist seventies saw their futures in relation to a particular set of familial and societal norms. For them the options seem expansive: they can choose to marry or not; choose to have children or not; choose careers that provide intellectual fulfillment and offer opportunities for introspection and self-realization. And yet, the frame of yes or no is also the sign of a constrained set of possibilities, especially within the domestic realm. They are women for whom feminism held possibility and promise for a revised future, which was, crucially, also consistent with models of white femininity they excavated from the past.

The Production of Whiteness

Old Fashioned Woman makes it clear that women sustain that temporality often at the expense of their own autonomy. Individuality, choice, and struggles that are primarily domestic and related to dominant albeit gendered values and norms characterize the feminist impulse of these films. However, women's personal films of the seventies have more often been criticized for problematically navel gazing at bourgeois concerns, and concomitantly assuming that these represent the experiences and interests of *all* women. In contrast, my claim is that these films warrant a different critique. That is, although the films are exclusively about white women, I disagree that they are not also key feminist interrogations of racial politics. As the work of Richard Dyer and Ruth Frankenberg makes clear, whiteness is too often left out of discussions about difference and representation.[33] The result is that we continue to take whiteness for granted without exposing the purposeful ways that it is constructed socially and cinematically. Thus, this chapter takes its title from Richard Dyer's landmark book, *White,* in which the author argues that a key move in understanding how whiteness works in cinema is by "making whiteness strange."[34] "The point is to see the specificity of whiteness," writes Dyer, "even when the text itself is not trying to show it to you, doesn't even know that it is there to be shown."[35] The anthropological aesthetic invites a closer investigation of how whiteness is produced within the films, just as the critical discourse surrounding the films over the past forty years has reproduced the "whiteness" of women's liberation by criticizing these films as absent of race.

Following Dyer, I am interested in the ways that whiteness is "produced" in these films about domestic reproductive labor and affect—as a result of certain ways of seeing family, work, and time. As Victoria Hesford writes, although women's liberation sometimes stands for "a hopeful and exciting feminist moment," it also suggests "a white middle-class rather than women of color feminism . . . and a depressingly racist and essentializing feminist moment."[36] In *Feeling Women's Liberation,* Hesford claims that narratives about women's liberation have tended to misunderstand and overgeneralize its political claims, as if feminism meant something singular and inevitable in the 1970s, which either succeeded or failed depending on the account. In contrast, Hesford urges us to explore the complex and contradictory archive of women's liberation "as an array of rhetorical materials that sought to persuade and enact a new political constituency and world into being."[37] In particular, Hesford observes that the dominant retellings of women's liberation have naturalized its "whiteness" and "its so-called bourgeois preoccupations—its revolt against marriage, the vaginal orgasm, and housework, along with its fight for the legalization of abortion and for sexual harassment laws."[38]

Hesford's intervention is significant. It is not that she asks us to refute the naturalized account with more correct details from the archive, nor "reconstruct some hidden, originary truth of the movement."[39] Rather, what Hesford encourages is an engagement with the archive that historicizes "the production of women's liberation as a *white* women's movement."[40] I take Hesford to mean that we need more reflection on the social, cultural, and intellectual means by which women's liberation came to seem so obviously white and middle-class. In hindsight, this body of films and the film criticism they inspired were clearly part of that process. They provide, therefore, an opportunity to explore what Daniel Bernardi in another context calls "the voice of whiteness" in women's personal documentaries of the 1970s.[41] In these films, I argue, whiteness is produced primarily through the uncontested norms and privileges that define women's personal experience and self-exploration. That is, while whiteness is not "ontologically empty," in Linda Martín Alcoff's terms, it also is not fixed, stable, or homogenous.[42] Indeed, Alcoff describes whiteness as "an organically emergent phenomenon" with "economic and political power," historical and subjective contours, and lived-in personal experience.[43] Similarly, these documentaries suggest a tense relationship between living whiteness and testing it, especially in the realm of the domestic.

It is especially curious to think about whiteness through these films, the majority of which were made by Jewish women about Jewish families. (*Old Fashioned Woman* is the exception.) Thus, *Nana, Mom and Me* and *Joyce at 34* are similarly self-reflexive autoethnographic projects, and they also indicate the ways that in the late twentieth century, whiteness expands to comfortably encompass Jewish women. Both *Nana* and *Joyce* exemplify the characteristics and affective contours of Jewish first-person filmmaking, as defined by Lebow. In her landmark study, *First Person Jewish,* Lebow retraces the discursive shifts in the early twentieth century by which Jews came to be perceived as white first and (maybe) Jewish next. A push toward assimilation in the 1950s resulted in a generation of secular Jews, like Amalie Rothschild, Joyce Chopra, and Claudia Weill, who were all young women in their twenties and thirties in the 1970s, when they made these personal films. If their parents had to struggle with becoming white in earlier decades, few traces of this emerge in the narratives of their daughters. As in many of the films examined by Lebow, personal films by white, Jewish women in the 1970s make sometimes subtle, brief, or no reference to Jewish religious or cultural practices. In some cases, like a scene of a family Seder in *Joyce,* the Jewishness of the films is readily apparent. That is to say, though these films are all by women whose lives were in some ways shaped by Judaism, that fact is lived and expressed in different ways. What the films share, however, is a comfortable acceptance of the idea that to be Jewish is to be white in the America of the 1970s.

Whiteness, however, much like Jewishness, is expressed in these films in ways that require some measure of decoding. As Lebow observes, discussion of *Joyce at 34* in the 1970s and 1980s tended to focus on her class and race with no mention of how being Jewish shaped Joyce's self-construction in the film.[44] Historically, these films point to the epidermalization of whiteness, where skin color serves as an alibi for the ethnic specificity possibly contained under the skin. That is, just as none of these films are about Jewishness per se, they are also not explicitly about having light skin, of being Caucasian or of western European descent. In fact, the Judaism and the whiteness of the filmmakers and filmed subjects seems to be naturalized or, in fact, muted in these films. And yet the anthropological aesthetic and autoethnographic presentation make them important objects of inquiry here. Indeed, the richness of the details seen and heard throughout these films invites an investigation into the way that ideologies about race, gender, ethnicity, and religion come together to seem so seamless and acceptable. As Lebow and her interlocutor Faye Ginsburg attest, secular Jewish filmmakers who came of age in the '60s and '70s tackled the subject of identity from a distinct position from the generation that preceded them. Whereas their parents' generation would have been much closer to the brutal, racializing history of the Second World War, the generation of filmmakers I consider here share "a lack of clarity and assurance as to the precise elements constituting a contemporary, secular, Jewish identity," writes Lebow.[45]

And yet, these are stories about women and thus focus on the gendered demands of reproducing culture within the domestic realm. Following Lebow then, it becomes clear how and why the family, and female relatives in particular, figure so prominently in *Joyce at 34* and *Nana, Mom and Me,* and how a focus on genealogy in these films exhumes the latent autoethnographic ("a study of one's own culture") and ethnoautobiographic ("a culturally grounded study of oneself") dynamics that structure racial and ethnic identity.[46] Although Lebow's focus is on another set of first-person films, including *Thank You and Goodnight* (Jan Oxenberg, 1991), *Nobody's Business* (Alan Berliner, 1996), and *Complaints of a Dutiful Daughter* (Deborah Hoffman, 1994), she offers key insights about how the family structures self-inquiry in first-person films.[47] The nuclear family represents "the psychological ground zero of modern identity construction," she writes.[48] That is, the family is a key site for self-construction, since our familial lives produce the primary cultural templates that we tend to conform to or resist. Moreover, the family has become a distinctly cinematic construction since the introduction of amateur filmmaking technologies to the domestic market in the 1960s. Archival images thus figure prominently in personal films about the family. And while family films tend to express a commitment to history, "the only history that seems to matter is that which can be traced through ancestral lineage or gleaned from the faulty and erratic memory of living relatives."[49]

Jewish women's personal documentaries, moreover, highlight the gendered nature of cultural reproduction within families, which makes particular demands on white women even within the constraints of religion and the privileges of class and visible belonging.

Nana, Mom and Me

Nana, Mom and Me begins reflexively as a complicated endeavor. Amalie Rothschild, the filmmaker, explains that her plan was to make a film about her aging Nana. However, the film becomes—as its title indicates—an exploration of the way that all three generations of women—Amalie, her mother, and Nana—interrelate. Like *Joyce at 34, Nana, Mom and Me* is also inspired by reflections on motherhood. Twenty-eight years old when she made the film, Rothschild explains in the opening voiceover that she is contemplating having a child. "In anticipation of a 4th generation," she observes, she is suddenly interested in the "continuity" between generations. "I see a lot of Nana in me," says Rothschild. Similar to Martha in *Old Fashioned Woman,* Rothschild sees herself as a link in the lineage of women in her family: women who become wives and mothers and expect happiness in their futures. The benefit of having, holding, and seeing one's forbearers stable, healthy, and near goes without mention in *Nana, Mom and Me.* However, generational integrity and a positive relationship to the past and future are arguably material evidence for the social formation of whiteness. As Alcoff observes, "To say that identities are material is not only to mark the perceptible physical correlates of identity, but to draw attention to our lived environments."[50] Just as the environment inhabited by the women filmmakers in these films evidences material traces of privilege, so too does an attachment to generational knowledge and its expression throughout the film. After all, Alcoff reminds us, "social identities are the residues of history that make up part of the context within which we must fashion ways of being in the world."[51] This is true of both public and private histories, including "the traumatic or inspiring memories of our ancestors' struggles."[52]

In the case of Rothschild's family, "struggle" is primarily a psychological response to the very real constraints of gender experienced by women in her family. In one touching scene, mother and daughter are driving in suburban Baltimore. The film cuts between shots of tidy, affluent row houses out the window to shots inside the car where Rothschild and her mother talk about Nana's marriage. Were her expectations for marriage met? How did her husband's long illness affect her grandparents' married life? Rothschild's mother is generous and thoughtful in her responses, but she admits that she doesn't know, has never asked, has never wondered about her mother's emotional life as a wife. Rothschild's autoethnographic practices, on the other hand, draw out these details. *Nana, Mom and Me* is thus a project of memory making; the film reconstructs the matrilineal history of the filmmaker—a history that is supposed to link to a generational story as a natural succession of lives and experiences. And so the film is also an exercise in social identity formation, because the "raw material" of our "histories and lineages," explains Alcoff, produces the modes of interpretation by which we fashion our social selves.[53] The ways we connect, interpret, analyze, and respond emotionally and intellectually to the world has everything to do with the structures of meaning and feeling that are taught to us in our families. In the case of relatively privileged, white families like Rothschild's, the driving concern of generations of women has been the desire to self-actualize (determine what one does with one's time, body, and space), and although this takes place within the normative constraints of womanhood for individuals of this particular race and class, the choices and decisions are most often interpreted as individual and unique.

As she describes her upbringing and youth, Nana consistently mentions the controlling power that social norms and expectations had over her choices and behaviors. Like the grandmothers and mothers in each of these films, Nana

Three generations of women in *Nana, Mom and Me.* (Courtesy of Amalie Rothschild.)

had musical talent as a girl, but never realized her potential, according to the filmmaker. "In keeping with the times, her gifts were only developed for mar- riageability," explains Rothschild in voice-over. Nana confirms this perspective in the following shot of the family at the dinner table, while they are eating, appropriately, steamed crabs. "My mother wanted me to be a real lady," says Nana, as she details how her formal education was complemented by lessons in embroidery, millinery, and dressmaking. These classically feminine skills were of course valuable to white women of the middle and upper classes, who had the benefit of a formal education in addition to training in acceptable modes of femininity. This was also true for Nana despite the fact that she did not grow up wealthy, but rather with what Rothschild describes as "pretensions to wealth."[54] Rothschild's creative choices in *Nana, Mom and Me* both connect this matrilineal history of desire and constraint and also demonstrate how the demands on white femininity change over time, such that filmmaking becomes an accept- able albeit still rare vocation for women of the 1970s. *Nana, Mom and Me,* thus, as well as *Joyce at 34* and *Old Fashioned Woman,* consistently mark the filmmaker's place in time as they expose the pliable and intractable ways that white women are made subjects of reality.

In another scene, Rothschild and her sister sit in front of a reel-to-reel tape player and listen to their grandmother complain about the new habits of young people. Nana doesn't agree with Rothschild's decision to live with her partner before marriage. "You've become very bold and very brazen, and that part I don't like," says Nana. "You don't care what you say or how you express yourself. Publicly you don't give a damn." Her grandmother complains that Rothschild made her abortion public, that she lived with her husband before marriage, and that she asks too many questions. She tires quickly of her granddaughter's persistent interrogation, especially when Amalie asks if her grandmother also had an abortion. Nana's response is sharp: "Now, listen. I've asked you not to question me. Don't question me because I don't want to think so much about what went on in my lifetime." Nana's voice becomes a diegetic voice-over for the scene. The tapes spool in the background as the two sisters sit and listen. They snicker at moments they disagree with. These three women and two genera- tions exist in the same sonic space, but they are meant to seem worlds apart. Separated physically from the scene, the grandmother becomes a distant voice from another time and space—different and distant in an essential way.

Charmingly cantankerous throughout the film, Nana often seems like a relic of time gone by. She makes grumpy comments about the social conduct of young people in the 1970s, and especially her granddaughter's. "There's too much envy going on in the world today. Children don't respect their older people. Want to live their own life and do it their way." Nana clearly thinks that remaining true to dominant norms and expectations befits the women of her family, including her daughter and granddaughter. And although Rothschild often highlights the differences between her life and that of her mother and her grandmother, the striking similarities in their social identity formation—and the role that domesticity and creativity play within that dynamic—hold the generations of the Rothschild women tightly together. Rothschild seems to want to highlight Nana's conservatism—her attachment to the ways of the past, especially those modeled by her more affluent husband's family. Despite these micro-differences, however, the generational stability and the similarity of their concerns are tied intimately to the racial and economic privileges granted by whiteness, financial security, and the gender norms that constrain white, middle-class women.

The anthropological attention to the lived environments pictured in the film also conveys the material realities of social and cultural identity. Numerous and treasured family portraits feature women in elaborate dresses, with fur and lace. We do not merely infer wealth from the inclusion of the photographs; in fact, Nana mentions the quality of fabrics and the cost of the garments, likely because she was also a skilled seamstress and made her own clothes. Ever attentive to highlighting the success of her marriage and the way it preserved and accumulated modest wealth and status for later generations, Nana expresses her pride in so much finery. She also explains that her marriage elevated her class status, a feat Nana's own mother did not think her capable of. In addition to taking care of an ailing husband for decades, Nana's major source of pride in the film is the fact that she married "up" and leveraged, though not without difficulty and setbacks, a more prosperous future for her children and grandchildren. Her successes, in other words, were intimately tied to her reproductive labor and her ability to both sustain and advance the next generation and its social and material status. Any dreams she may have had about her personal creative success were subsumed by the social demands affixed to her gender.

Nana's daughter, also Amalie, speaks eloquently about the pressures she faced from Nana growing up, especially because of her looks. Rothschild's mother is a handsome woman in the film. Her thick red hair, pale skin, and prominent nose do not immediately identify her as ethnic, and yet one gathers from her description that Nana's goal was to make her fit the norms of Protestant whiteness, especially by taming her hair. "I was raised to be a conventional person and to do what everyone else did and what was accepted," recalls Rothschild's mother. "When we grew up everything was a pattern, and I didn't know people who were unusual and who were original and who were thinkers and creators. I just didn't even know that people like that really existed. . . . I just didn't have any idea that there was any way to live except the way I was raised." The strength and security that these women found in social and cultural norms makes sense because the norms to which they aspired to were in fact tailored for women like them.

In contrast to her representation of Nana, Rothschild eagerly represents her own mother as a dynamic, independent, creative feminist. Whereas she asks Nana to narrate her experiences as a wife, Rothschild focuses extensively on her own mother's work as an artist. Much of the film takes place within her mother's studio, or in conversation with her mother who describes how her marriage to a man she loved allowed her to see herself anew, not simply as an obedient daughter, but as a woman, a wife, and eventually, an artist. Rothschild's mother is clear that the privileges of wealth opened her to a creative life and to an independent sense of self. "After being married I did not have to earn a living," she acknowledges, and so she turned to painting. Rothschild films her mother in front of her vibrant, abstract canvases. She asks her mother to describe the work, but the older Amalie is reluctant to explain her ideas and inspiration. The refusal frustrates the filmmaker, who suddenly asks her, "Why are we here together in the first place? Why am I trying to get something out of you; I'm not even sure what it is!" Amalie's mother does not hesitate to give a poignant and astute reading of the film: "You are using your own life to create a film which is autobiographical in content yet its ostensible title and subject matter deals with another person." She explains that the project is clearly Rothschild's attempt to explore herself by understanding her mother and her grandmother. And then she says, "Why are you asking me these questions? I should be asking you!"

The spontaneous exchange between mother and daughter draws out the significance of the family as a source of raw material for the interpretation of social identity, and in this case gender, whiteness, and financial security. Although stated neutrally as an effort to "understand" oneself, the knowledge one gains about oneself from the history of one's family has much to do with the way that class, race, ethnicity, and religion has shaped the family's experience in the world. In the case of Rothschild's family, *Nana, Mom and Me* evidences a long history of struggle in relation to social norms for middle- and upper-class white women. The progressively autonomous lives of women in the family suggest that the future holds promise for women of this place, race, and class. Rothschild's earnest desire for a child is in line with the histories of women in her family, as is her creative dedication to film. However, her ability to question, choose, announce, dissent, and divulge are privileges that are new to her matrilineal line. She projects these new '70s modes of thinking back to her mother and grandmother, and the results suggest that each generation brings a wider range of independent choices to a nonetheless stable set of values.

As they recount how they were raised, and interview the women that raised them, and as they struggle both with and against certain norms, the filmmakers who made these films lay bare the architecture of white middle-class values and expectations in the early 1970s and the ways these consolidated a particular rather than a universal feminist subject. As Saba Mahmood observes, the critique of the nuclear family by white middle-class feminists in the 1970s expressed a culturally specific desire for autonomy and freedom—liberal notions Mahmood understands as particular rather than universal.[55] In contrast, women of color argued that "freedom, for them, consisted in being able to form families, since the long history of slavery, genocide, and racism had operated precisely by breaking up their communities and social networks."[56] Whiteness is therefore produced not in a discourse of race and skin color in films about white women, but rather through the performance and struggle over class values and gendered familial structures.

Throughout the '80s and '90s, women's personal documentaries of the '70s—like the women's movement itself—were often accused of perniciously claiming to offer universal perspectives on women's experiences.[57] My claim is precisely the opposite. That is, it is the fact that these films claimed to offer *merely* personal, individual, and unique experiences that demonstrates the racial politics at stake. In these films, it is the claim on particularity—not a claim to universality—that indicates how whiteness operates. Further, the critical discourse surrounding these films—often written by feminist film scholars who emphasized the exclusion of race inherent in the universal claim—paradoxically contributed to the production of the women's liberation movement and its cultural production as innately white and middle-class. In fact, the films I gather in this chapter have gone relatively unexamined and have become mere citations in the recurrent feminist critique of both documentary realism and the racism of the women's movement. Read for latent clues about white identity formation, such as faith in genealogy, self-actualization, career, and temporal integrity, women's personal documentaries take on new significance to a field of study intent on dismantling cinematic white supremacy, and dominant visual ideologies of class and gender.

CHAPTER 4

Native Ethnographers and Feminist Solidarity

> What I am doing is creating a historical record. I feel that it's important for black artists to interpret their feelings and experiences. Who else is going to interpret or document these feelings? Who else is going to create that painting and who else is going to deal with our triumphs and our sufferings if it is not us?
>
> —*Varnette's World: A Study of a Young Artist* (Carroll Parrott Blue, 1979)

Carroll Parrott Blue's *Varnette's World* showcases the painter Varnette Honeywood, an African American artist who describes her work as representing "black lifestyles on canvas." Blue's documentary foregrounds Varnette's personal story and artistic ethos in a manner similar to other feminist portrait documentaries, like Mirra Bank's *Yudie* (1974) and Amalie Rothschild's *Woo Who? May Wilson* (1970). The documentary weaves together observational footage of Varnette, for example at work, where she designs art programs for children in public schools, and in her church, where she sings in concert with other African Americans. Varnette also tells us her story eloquently and voices her commitment to Afro-centric aesthetics and practices in filmed interview footage. Interspersed with these sequences are striking montages of Varnette's paintings, colorful and abstracted visions of everyday life in African American communities, which she hopes convey positive images of black culture. *Varnette's World* is at once an exploration of an individual artist and a portrait of a community that coalesces around a shared archive of images and a shared sense of the unique valence of blackness in the United States. Varnette sees her role as an interpreter and translator of the affect and image archive of her community—artistic and emotional labor that she indicates must come from within: "Who else is going to interpret or document these feelings?" Varnette and Blue both commit to this call to black artists to represent the "feelings and experiences" of their community.

In this chapter I explore matters of difference and solidarity in films by white women and women of color about communities of color. We might be tempted to think of this chapter as a corrective gesture of inclusion, or in other words, as the inverse of chapter 3, which focused on films by and about white women. In fact, both groups of films are about the confluence of gendered and racial identity formation, either implicitly as in *Joyce at 34, Nana, Mom and Me,* and *Old Fashioned Woman,* which I analyze in chapter 3, or explicitly as in *From Spikes to Spindles* (Christine Choy, 1976), *Inside Women Inside* (Christine Choy and Cynthia Maurizio, 1978), and *I Am Somebody* (Madeline Anderson, 1969), which I discuss in this chapter. That is, rather than read one group of films as excluding women of color and the other as correcting that exclusion, which echoes a standard but by now tired narrative and periodization of racial politics in feminist studies, I argue that both groups of films are most productively read as coeval autoethnographies: studies of the mutual imbrication of selves and Others, some individual and others collective, all of which are subject to the realities of gender, class, and race, albeit distinctly. Some of these films tell stories that focus on the role of the individual within the community and others foreground the collective solidarity of the community and the place of the individual within it. Each of these films explores the reality that haunts feminist documentary, especially when the subjects of reality belong to communities of color in which gender is both central to and exceeded by the demands of collective struggles against racial and economic oppression.

Chapter 3 focused on first-person documentaries, to use Alisa Lebow's term, to show that rather than excluding racial politics, white women's personal documentaries reveal the naturalized structures of white and gendered identity formation, which makes it possible to see the ways in which the construction of white femininity is premised on racial exclusions.[1] The feminist potential arises in personal documentaries from the radical instantiation of the "I" that makes white women's particular struggles within white patriarchal capitalism newly visible. Working deftly against dominant social tendencies to either a) universalize the experiences of white women, or b) depoliticize the raciality of whiteness, white women's personal documentaries enact complex feminist politics. The anthropological aesthetic evident within the films in fact denaturalizes whiteness by drawing attention to all the ways it is carefully manufactured both socially and cinematically.

White women and women of color all made a wide range of documentary films in the early 1970s, including personal, experimental, biographical, animated, and movement manifestos. As much as white women like Joyce Chopra and Amalie Rothschild were interested in the newly radical act of making personal stories about themselves valuable to political struggle, others committed to featuring a racially and economically diverse range of women's voices in their films. Women of color filmmakers also made first-person and personal films about individuals, like Carroll Parrott Blue's *Varnette's World,* and they made expansive films about newly coherent communities of color as well. The radical realist aesthetics of feminist documentaries about intersectionally oppressed women forcefully picturizes the coming together of communities of color by highlighting personal experiences in voice-over and interviews, by foregrounding images of women working and producing culture, and by highlighting the interimbrication of the personal with the collective.

Disenfranchised communities are at the center of these films: exploited laborers, incarcerated women, black women, and the poor. I begin with a reading of *The Woman's Film* (SF Newsreel, 1971), one of the earliest feminist documentaries to evidence the emergent concerns of seventies feminisms: revolution, collectivity, and critique. Featuring filmed interviews and observational and staged footage of women laboring inside the home and eventually demonstrating out in public, the film highlights a feedback loop between individual experiences and collective reparative action. Made by a group of white women, *The Woman's Film* also highlights the anthropological tensions and ethical dilemmas inherent to making films about Others. Third World Newsreel filmmaker Christine Choy and her partners, Susan Robeson and Cynthia Maurizio, self-identified women of color, produced three key films about the collective experiences of communities of color: *Teach Our Children* about the Attica Prison uprising, *From Spikes to Spindles* about New York's Chinatown, and *Inside Women Inside* featuring interviews with diverse incarcerated women. These films take up Varnette's call for insiders to interpret and translate the affect and experiences of their disenfranchised communities for the "historical record." Madeline Anderson's *I Am Somebody,* which foregrounds the role of the individual within the activist struggles of a collective, forcefully underscores the power of identification between filmmakers, filmed subjects, and viewers to enact justice in the service of black women workers. Placed together in this chapter, these films paint a complex picture of how community, solidarity, and racial and economic differences among women shape feminist politics in documentaries that balance the ethnographic tension between selves and Others, insiders and outsiders, privilege and oppression.

Ethnographic readings of these documentaries center our attention on the relations of power between filmmakers, subjects, and audiences, and foreground the ethical and political imperatives that drive the revolutionary aesthetics and economies of representation in these films. Autoethnographies are explorations of a designated "self" that also reveal a broader matrix of cultural practices, beliefs, and expectations. As viewers of autoethnographies, we pay attention to the aesthetic practices and thematic choices filmmakers experiment with as they construct documents of justice with attention to the ethical demands of representing formerly repressed and newly visible political subjects. Indeed, considering that autoethnographers turn inward, toward communities with which they share a sense of belonging, their films evidence both the "auto" (or subjectivity) of the filmmaker as well as the "ethno" or the racial and ethnic communities to which that self claims to belong. This investigation is crucial to studying the oft-neglected cultural production of women of color. Zakiya Luna's research on women of color organizations argues, "with few exceptions, researchers have paid insufficient attention to strategies of collective identity creation in spaces created by and for women of color, or how patterns of marginalization are avoided or reproduced in these spaces."[2] As a space of feminist practice, women's documentary filmmaking of the 1970s engaged powerfully in the act of collective identity formation for women of color to work against patterns of marginalization. The radical assertion of the "I" in these films works toward the coherence of a collective identity in films by women of color, connecting diversely oppressed groups on and off screen to the liberation struggles of feminism.

Radical movements of the early 1970s were contingent on notions of solidarity. And yet, collectivity and solidarity require that diverse groups of individuals imagine themselves as belonging together, to and with each other. Luna calls this the "gender and race logics of collective identity construction."[3] In the United States, where gender, race, class, and sexuality have always already etched the fault lines of difference, oppression, and privilege, collective politics require constant negotiation over which subjects belong at the center of which movements, and how to work through and with difference to achieve collective goals. In the context of political documentaries, just as in the conceptual battles over ethnography, matters of representation refract these tensions between inside and outside, self and Other, us and them. Autoethnography is key to detecting the way women's documentaries of the 1970s play a role in these ethical and political negotiations and the visions of justice they seek. Beating within the heart of the archive of women's documentary filmmaking of the 1970s, and especially in the autoethnographic films that concern me here, are a vital set of questions about the distinct and powerful ways that feminism manifests in these matters of representation, about who gets to speak for feminism and whom feminism speaks for, with, and in feminist scholar and filmmaker Trinh Minh-ha's formulation: nearby.[4]

Difference on Screen

The Woman's Film emerged out of debates within Newsreel about the role of women within the organization. A New-Left filmmaking and distribution collective, Newsreel was at the center of the political cinema scene in the United States in the 1960s and 1970s. Caroline Gil-Rodríguez's institutional history of the enduring radical film collective recounts the experiences of women in Newsreel, who were generally assigned to clerical duties and felt shut out of filmmaking opportunities.[5] As the women's movement and movements for racial justice gained momentum in the United States, women and people of color within Newsreel demanded more opportunities to make films by, for, and about their communities. *The Woman's Film* was one of those projects. It was made collectively by a California-based crew of white women, and focused primarily on poor and working-class women across a spectrum of race, including white, black, and Chicana activists. The majority of these women were filmed in their consciousness-raising groups. The film screens a vision of women's liberation as a coalition movement where the most oppressed members of society inhabit the center of the frame, both figuratively and literally. Writing about the women in the film, one reviewer remarks, "They do not, in the wildest stretch of the imagination, fit anyone's image of militant supporters of Women's Liberation."[6]

The trajectory, membership, and even name of the Newsreel collective would shift decisively in the early 1970s, from a mostly white and male leftist group to an organization devoted to the struggles of third world people in and outside the United States, and thus from Newsreel to Third World Newsreel. In its original formation as Newsreel, the filmmakers in the collective generally claimed an inexpensive and anti-bourgeois notion of cinema, keen on shocking what they understood as bourgeois aesthetic sensibilities. According to Christine Choy, an early member of the New York collective, "Originally we wanted to raise people's political consciousness in looking at films, and we considered politics more important than actual filmmaking."[7] Early films produced by the collective, such as *Columbia Revolt* (1968), about the student takeover at Columbia University, infamously share "anti-conventions" such as shaky camera work, blurred focus, erratic editing, and a lack of narrative cohesion. This style emerged partly because members of the collective worked with limited funds and were also new to filmmaking, and partly this can be explained by the urgency with which films were made. As demonstrations erupted in cities with Newsreel chapters, such as Boston, Detroit, Chicago, Ann Arbor, and San Francisco, filmmakers rushed off to record the scenes of protest. Their short 16mm films covered the civil rights movement, anti-war demonstrations, feminist activism, and political groups such as the Black Panther Party and the Young Lords. Moreover, Newsreel filmmakers traveled with their films and facilitated Q&A sessions with audiences. According to the organization's self-authored historiography, "The goal, though, was not just to educate, but to inspire action for change."[8]

The Woman's Film marks an early attempt to draw out the potential of these revolutionary and aesthetic ambitions in the service of radical feminism or, in Kristen Hogan's terms, "feminist accountability" around race and class.[9] For the "bookwomen" at the heart of Hogan's chronicle of the rise and fall of feminist bookstores, accountability meant ensuring "a feminist dialogue to define, grapple with, and evolve a shared set of ethics and ideas about how to live by those ethics."[10] Although filmmakers may not have documented their commitments to accountability in the same way that bookwomen did, their films manifest similar politics of accountability to anti-racism and anti-capitalism. In an interview published in the inaugural issue of *Women & Film* in 1972, Judy Smith describes the process of making *The Woman's Film,* which she produced, directed, and edited with Louise Alaimo and Ellen Sorin. Asked about whether the filmmakers prioritized the aesthetics or the information at stake in *The Woman's Film,* Smith replies, "this film came from the people. We when started out to make this film we decided that we weren't going to write the script, that the ideas would come from those women, that—like what Mao says, from the people to the people."[11] *The Woman's Film* brings the tension between art and propaganda to the fore in the mind of the interviewer from *Women & Film.* However, Smith's reply to the question of whether content or form guided the film's production aims at a slightly different target, one perhaps just left of the art versus propaganda mark. Smith, instead, explains how the philosophy guiding the production of *The Woman's Film* came from global radical movements for liberation. Quoting Mao, she points at once to the inspiration for the film, the reason for its form, and the purpose of its content: from the people, to the people. Smith's vision of feminist filmmaking draws its inspiration from the radical left, and refracts the aesthetic potential in the service of feminist liberation politics, which centered the concerns of poor and working-class women.

Smith thus links the film to Marxism and decolonization movements throughout Latin America and Asia; she also conjures the feminist practice of consciousness-raising—the hallmark political program of the women's liberation movement. A broad range of seventies feminists, including radical feminists such as the New York Radical Women and Redstockings, held fast to the idea that women needed to completely rethink *thinking* as a way of getting closer to the truth of women's oppression. Likewise, the Combahee River Collective, for example, references the significance of consciousness-raising in their "Statement," explaining how the process of "talking/testifying" generated new understandings among the women about "the implications of race and class as well as sex."[12] Rather than understand women's oppression through theoretical models created by the class of oppressors, feminists sought to access an untainted mode of understanding their roles in society, their relationships to each other, and the multilayered oppressions that many women faced.

Although the women interviewed in *The Woman's Film* are racially, ethnically, and economically diverse, they tell remarkably similar stories about disillusionment and domestic entrapment. They struggle to find existential and material fulfillment within severe social and economic constraints, and are limited variably by controlling husbands, demanding children, exploitative bosses, or state bureaucrats. Each woman is often isolated from other influences and centered in the frame, commanding the full attention of the spectator. There are no psychologists, social workers, or feminist spokeswomen interpreting the narratives of these poor and working-class women. Granted full command of the time and space of the frame, each woman is validated as the expert of her own experience, witness to her own transformation, and evidence for women beyond the frame of a newly possible subject of feminist politics. In one telling sequence, a close-up still image of a woman's head thrown back, mouth howling, explodes into a grid that repeats the image column after column, row after row.

Formally the film's accumulated interviews enact equality and justice at the same time as a repetitive rhetoric of shared experiences surfaces in the soundscape. Across scenes in which women of different classes, races, and activist allegiances collectively analyze their material and political conditions, the cinematic mode of production insists on audiovisual equality to make a case about women's collective oppression. In scenes where women speak both to each other and to the camera, they arrive in aggregation at the realization that their/your oppression is systemic rather than individual. "The only way things are going to be livable is for a complete changeover to be made," explains one young mother. "Change has to come through changing minds," concurs another. In the aggregation of these similar scenes, women's voices echo and reverberate with passion and commitment to collective action.

Through the sheer force of repetition, the voices create a chorus, a consensus, and a collective body that does not diminish differences among the women. In the final sequence of the film, the diverse women featured throughout appear as leaders at rallies and demonstrations, galvanizing other women to resist and revolt. No longer framed in formal interviews in domestic spaces, the women have emerged as public speakers. They yell, scream, and chant. As the accompanying musical track makes clear with the refrain, "I woke up this morning," by sharing their experiences and uniting their energies, women have finally woken up to the truth of their collective oppression by patriarchy, capitalism, and racism.

A wide range of screenings and extensive media coverage suggest that News-reel hit home with their first film by, for, and about women. In a review entitled "'Woman's Film': A Look at Poverty," the *San Francisco Chronicle* announced "Women's liberation now has its own full-length film, with more good humor than anger."[13] *The Woman's Film* enjoyed successful runs in New York and California theaters. Newsreel filmmakers also screened the film to diverse audiences, ranging from movement meetings and university screenings to a room of male telephone company employees.[14] In April 1971, the film reached the museum circuit with a screening at the Museum of Modern Art in New York City as part of a series programmed by John Hanhardt entitled, "What's Happening."[15] Positive reviews of the film erupted in print media from Berkeley to New York.[16]

The Woman's Film mobilizes the two key concepts at work in consciousness-raising: personal experience and identification, or the ability to see one's experiences reflected in the Other. Sharing personal experiences granted women in consciousness-raising groups a newfound authority over subjectivity and reality: their individual and collective realities. The "Redstockings Manifesto" expresses the vision in these terms: "We regard our personal experience, and our feelings about that experience, as the basis for an analysis of our common situation. We cannot rely on existing ideologies as they are all products of male supremacy culture. We question every generalization and accept none that are not confirmed by our experience."[17] In the film, each woman is the expert of her own being in the world, the author of her story about living in it, and the executor of her narrative describing the experience of being subject to a reality shaped by gender, class, and racial ideologies. By granting women the authority to generate alternative epistemologies through personal experience, the Redstockings' notion of consciousness-raising aspires to a radical reconfiguration of both collective identification and collective knowledge: women as a class allegedly shared a unique perspective on the world, which had been hitherto unrevealed and hence presented a potential site of tremendous political power in the service of all women.

However, not all women identified equally with the notion that gender was the primary form of oppression they faced. The rhetoric of the "Redstockings Manifesto" imagines a mode of identification that would bridge women *in spite of* their differences; gender, in other words, above all, defined women's being in the world in the political vision of the radical feminists. "We identify with all women," declares the 1969 "Redstockings Manifesto." "We define our best interest as that of the poorest, most brutally exploited woman. We repudiate all economic, racial, educational or status privileges that divide us from other women. We are determined to recognize and eliminate any prejudices we may hold against other women."[18] In this call for solidarity, identification hinges not on identity between women (the recognition of difference is boldly stated in the manifesto), but on the identical recognition that gender is *the* defining feature of all women's lives. This claim would structure tense debates about race, representation, and solidarity within the discourse and filmmaking of the women's movement.

Difference in Theory

A tense but vigorous dialogue about race has always been a defining feature of seventies feminism, although popular and academic discourse often neglects the debates about race politics that took place there. In feminist theory, a time-line of race politics suggests that diversity belongs to the 1980s, while essentialism (aka white feminism) characterizes the seventies. The "story" feminist theory tells itself about itself, according to political theorist Clare Hemmings, is "a developmental narrative" that moves from "unity and sameness, through identity and diversity, and on to difference and fragmentation"—stages that correspond to the decades of the seventies, eighties, and nineties respectively.[19] Throughout feminist theory, one reads these debates as taking place within neatly defined decades, characterized by an ostensible unity and homogeneity. As a result, conversations are "fixed," as Hemmings asserts, into tidy decades, where conversations both begin and end. The "women of color critique" is widely understood to have emerged only in the 1980s, heralded by landmark interventions such as Gloria Anzaldúa and Cherríe Moraga's *This Bridge Called My Back*.[20]

However, this periodization problematically occludes material evidence from the archive of feminist discourse of the 1970s, including the documentaries in this chapter. *The Woman's Film,* for example, evidences the fact that feminist activists and scholars robustly struggled with the fantasy of race-blind gender solidarity virtually since the moment it emerged. Many (and mostly white) radical feminists, like the filmmakers of *The Woman's Film,* often argued that by

destabilizing gender oppression in the capitalist economy, the women's liberation movement would force the unraveling of all systems of domination, including racism.[21] On the other hand, black women often responded with fury, daring
white women to see how their perspective ("be patient; it'll come") was a direct
result of their race privilege and an indirect attempt to grasp onto rather than
dismantle white supremacy. There might not have been much agreement across
racial divisions, but there certainly was a great deal of blunt and significant
dialogue. The constellation of films in this chapter shed light on various positions in this dialogue: the radical feminist proposition that women constituted
a cohesive class, and the emergent consciousness of women of color, which
resisted the dominance of white women's perspectives on both oppression and
liberation.

The production of the women's movement as white throughout and beyond the seventies has consistently occluded the diverse coalitions that enacted
feminist politics on and off the screen. Victoria Hesford demonstrates the ways
that, in the seventies, media representation and engagement with the women's
movement often produced a vision of women's lib as an entirely white endeavor.
In her analysis of the *New York Times* coverage of the major women's liberation
marches and protests of 1970, Hesford reads a consistent "ambivalent affect,"
especially on matters of race. Again and again, Hesford notes how "class, race,
and ethnic differences" are "subverted by the need to reassure the reader that
members of the women's movement are the familiar women of middle-class
suburbia."[22] She elaborates, "For the *New York Times,* as for the national media as
a whole, black feminism was left off stage, its presence occasionally glimpsed
. . . but mostly ignored—its invisibility a threatening spectrality that provided
the necessary shadow for the media's organizing of the meanings of women's
liberation in relation to white, middle-class femininity."[23] Perceived as a threat
to the acceptance of the progressive agenda of women's lib, the participation of
women of color was left off the page, and increasingly, throughout the decades,
out of the stories that feminism tells itself about itself.

The neglected archive of women's liberation documentaries, which is
haunted by the realities of multiple oppressions, however, evidences an alternative story about the racial makeup and ethos of feminist activism and discourse of the 1970s. As in *The Woman's Film,* women's lib publications, essays,
and manifestos continually draw attention to difference, but also insist on the
commonality of all women based on a shared oppression located primarily in
the fact of gender, rather than class, race, or ethnicity. Radical feminists envi-
sioned a women's movement that would account for and encompass all women
despite their differences. Ginny Berson for the Furies, an early lesbian-feminist
collective, for example, imagined that together, women could "figure out how to

put an end to the sexist, classist and racist system which oppresses them."[24] In a 1968 pamphlet, Beverly Jones and Judith Brown proclaimed about women: "We are a class, we are oppressed as a class, and we each respond within the limits allowed to us as members of that oppressed class. . . . There is no personal escape, no personal salvation, no personal solution."[25] From the beginning, radical feminists sought to emphasize women's collective oppression, what Jones and Brown also refer to as "our common identity" and "our common plight."[26] The dramatic shift from the personal to the collective meant that only a collective solution, a revolutionary movement, would address the concerns that women allegedly shared. Marlene Dixon optimistically submitted a version of women's liberation as an all-encompassing movement:

> whose base encompasses poor black and poor white women on relief, working women exploited in the labor force, middle class women incarcerated in the split level dream house, college girls awakening to the fact that sexiness is not the crowning achievement in life, and movement women who have discovered that in a freedom movement they themselves are not free.[27]

In pamphlet after manifesto after position paper, emerging women's groups consistently referred to the movement as addressing a collective of "women" writ large. Although particularizing gestures are peppered throughout the documents accessible today, more often, white women resort to analogizing their oppression to the oppression of African Americans (occasionally even ranking these such that "women's" oppression appears *worse* than that of black men's).[28]

Women's liberation literature also demonstrates that early women's groups were aware that among their ranks, noticeably fewer women of color were actively participating. In *Notes from the First Year,* Carol Hanisch and Elizabeth Sutherland staged a mock "conversation" in which they responded to typical questions posed to movement activists by both men and women. In answer to the comment, "But other people are *more* oppressed than you," for example, part of their response addresses the notion the Combahee River Collective would term "simultaneous factors in oppression": "There may be several things holding you down at once. If you're a woman, it's men and the capitalist system. If you're a black woman, it's also racism."[29] A subsequent question directly targets the relationship between white and black women in the movement.[30] The response, though stated in simple and direct terms, evidences complex logic and confused affect behind New York Radical Women's inability to recognize the particular needs and demands of black women. The full question reads: *"You make a lot of analogies to the black movement. How do you see your relationship to black women?"* The response begins, "At the moment our group is largely white. Occasionally a black woman will come to meetings and that's great. Our meetings are open to all women. However, there is a reluctance on the part of white women to assume that black women want to be part of an 'integrated' group. We figure black women may want to get together themselves first. Furthermore, we're all sisters but some of our problems are different."[31] Cellestine Ware, writing in 1970, continued to notice how "remarkable" it was that despite the frequency with which women's liberationists made analogies to the black movement and professed allegiance in oppression, "they are seemingly unable to attract black women to the female liberation cause."[32]

Hanisch and Sutherland's response suggests they did not assume to know what black women wanted and whether black women desired a political subjectivity outside black liberation struggles: "We figure black women may want to get together themselves first. . . . Many militant black women see their struggle as a fight alongside their men for survival; some say that only middle-class white women can afford to worry about their freedom as women."[33] Hanisch and Sutherland seem to be tacking back and forth between several concerns: a desire to acknowledge the hegemony of white women in the movement; the white-skin privilege that separates white women from black women; and black women's likely critique of white women's abstract desire for freedom while black people continue to struggle for the immediate goal of survival. White women admit a failure to recognize themselves in the struggles of black women, yet they go on to utter an aspiration for a future movement in which "all women will eventually be able to get together and fight for certain programs. This should result in a lessening of white supremacist attitudes, too, as white women get together with non-white women around similar needs."[34] These perspectives shed new light on the radical feminist politics of *The Woman's Film,* which manifests the white feminist desire to bridge racial and economic differences between women and work together on "similar needs" of gendered oppression.

Throughout movement literature and filmmaking, white women demonstrate that they were not ignorant of the absence of black women among them, nor did they blindly pursue an agenda that spoke for women in universal terms; however, as the films in chapter 3 show, neither did white women often prioritize an explicitly anti-racist agenda. White women had difficulty seeing their struggle as coterminous with black women's struggles. That is, Hanisch and Sutherland leave organizing around "the woman issue" among "nonwhite women" out of the program and politics they develop for a more generalized "women's liberation"—even if only "for the moment." The trajectory imagined here presupposes separate spheres of organization where nonwhite women determine their needs as women and then "get together" with white women to work collectively *as women.* Although the title of the staged conversation suggests a universal, gender-as-class mobilization, "Women of the World Unite," Hanisch and Sutherland's answers demonstrate that white women clearly had trouble imagining what it would mean to open the notion of "gender oppression" to the intrinsic differences they acknowledge exist between women; more significantly, they did not conceive of the women's movement as innately anti-racist, or responsible for troubling the waters of white supremacy.

The Woman's Film both exemplifies and challenges these radical feminist desires for solidarity, and also manages to encompass both an anti-racist and an anti-capitalist agenda; it envisions a women's movement as a coalition that prioritizes the struggles of women of color and poor and working-class women *as women*. Moreover, by framing diverse individual women and groups of activist women with consistently applied time and space constraints, notions such as authority, experience, and expertise are dispersed, decentered, and defamiliarized. Experience belongs to each and every woman diversely and uniquely, while at the same time identification with the accumulated recorded narratives and images allows viewers to locate themselves within the new world of racial and economic justice constructed by the film about women. In the film's closing sequences, all of the women emerge in the public sphere as advocates for their diverse priorities. They show up bodily and vocally on stage, in the streets, surrounded by diverse women and calling other women to the cause. The vision of feminist politics in the film is one that prioritizes not only gender but also race and class. The filmmakers hoped that women viewers would "identify with the experiences and feelings of the women in the film" and embrace the idea that "women are strong when united, and when they work together and support each other, they have the power to bring about meaningful and necessary changes in this country."[35] Feminist documentaries thus played a crucial role in contesting the white-washed vision of women's liberation in popular media.

Similarly, in *Janie's Janie* (1970), another Newsreel release, directed by Geri Ashur with a New York–based crew including Peter Barton, Marilyn Mulford, and Stephanie Pawleski, identification operates precisely within a framework of difference signaled by the "Redstockings Manifesto." *Janie's Janie* features the story of a white, single mother of five in Newark, New Jersey. The film's narrative is motivated by Janie's journey to independence, her transformation from her father's Janie to her husband's Janie to the final realization: Janie's Janie. In the opening shot of *Janie's Janie*, a woman's figure in the center of the frame walks away from the camera, toward the front door of a modest row house. Children rush out to meet her and assist her with the grocery bags she carries home. *Janie's Janie* thus begins on the outside of Janie's intimate life, following her toward the heart of her story: her domestic life inside the home. Inside her house, Janie continues with the motions of her life even as she answers delicate questions

about her abusive father and controlling husband. She dresses the children, pre-
pares a chicken for the oven, and folds laundry, all the while smoking cigarettes
and constructing the narrative of her raised consciousness. The film stitches
together excerpts from several different interviews to create a narrative trajectory that follows Janie through her young life under her father's strict rule to
her dashed hopes of salvation through marriage, to her final realization that
solidarity among women is the only answer that will lead to structural change
for the working poor. In the film's final shot, Janie walks toward the camera with
a colleague, her body in motion in public. Janie heads past the camera into the
distance, a new, public and collective horizon before her. Like *The Woman's Film,
Janie's Janie* tracks a "classic" arc in feminist documentary, from personal lament
to collective, public activism. Feminist documentaries consistently demonstrate
that collective thinking, feeling, and seeing transform women into revolutionary subjects of reality, poised to topple white patriarchal capitalism.

Both *Janie's Janie* and *The Woman's Film* project the impulse to cast a multiply
oppressed figure at the center of women's liberation. At a time when the mainstream press sought the least-threatening spokeswoman for the movement
in Kate Millett, featured on the cover of *Time* magazine in 1970, the women of
Newsreel shared the opinion that "women's lib" was about identifying with
the most disenfranchised among them. Structured around the trajectory from
the personal to the political implied by consciousness-raising, *The Woman's
Film* and *Janie's Janie* encourage women to see their own oppression mirrored
in the narratives of all women, despite the obvious differences in their material lives—to identify, as the "Redstockings Manifesto" suggests, with "the
poorest, most brutally exploited woman." As a result, the films retrospectively
construct an ethnographic mosaic of diverse women at a moment of collective
transformation. If traditional ethnography hoped to capture the disappearing
ways of life of distant communities, the feminist ethnographic desires of seventies feminist documentaries catalyzed cultural transformation, showcasing
American women who eagerly cast off the patriarchal ways of the past in favor
of a revolutionary drive toward an alternative future.

Solidarity Troubles

The potential for solidarity evident in *The Woman's Film* and *Janie's Janie* did not
always resonate with women of color, who like Varnette in Carroll Parrott Blue's
film see a need for women of color artists to rise up and tell the stories of their
communities. After all, embedded in the radical visions of Newsreel's films
about women exists the material fact that white women continued to helm

projects about others. The power differential that separates those that have access to the means of production and those that are subject to the reality visions of dominant culture remains a potent indicator of the limitations of radical feminist discourse. Despite an espoused insistence on concentrating on the most oppressed, that is, the feminist desire for solidarity that consciousness-raising was meant to catalyze, often lent itself to repressing difference. A powerful fantasy throughout seventies movement rhetoric, literature, and film, consciousness-raising became equally problematic for the movement and for theory. Based on similarity, consciousness-raising suppressed the significance of difference. Based on sisterhood, it made claims about womanhood that were soon critiqued as essentialist and exclusionary. Although the slogan for radical feminism insisted that "we are one, we are woman," the fact was that this rhetoric of sisterhood, as soon as it was uttered, came under assault in the movement from working-class women, lesbians, and women of color.[36]

Black women, as individuals and as collectives, published scores of articles, essays, and position papers throughout the years of the women's liberation movement. Evident throughout is a sense of immediate discontent with the logic, goals, and sense of exclusion emerging from a coalescing movement of white women. The Combahee River Collective statement, for example, makes plain that black women's experience of feminism and consciousness-raising requires them to go "beyond white women's revelations" about oppression. They write,

> The major source of difficulty in our political work is that we are not just trying to fight oppression on one front or even two, but instead to address a whole range of oppressions. We do not have racial, sexual, heterosexual, or class privilege to rely upon, nor do we have even the minimal access to resources and power that groups who possess anyone of these types of privilege have.[37]

In the early 1970s, black women consistently challenged white women to hear their resistance to a singular, unified movement based solely in an aspiration for freedom from gender oppression.

Toni Morrison's 1971 article, published in the *New York Times Magazine,* minces few words about the racism at work in women's liberation. Titled, "What the Black Woman Thinks About Women's Lib," the article offers a pat answer to the issue posed in its title: "Distrust. It is white, therefore, suspect."[38] Morrison claims to speak for "the black woman," explaining in broad terms that her skepticism toward the women's liberation movement stems from the fact that black women see white women as "the enemy." According to Morrison, black women see white women as grasping for power—white power that would be lorded over black women, not shared with them. She buttresses her analysis by relating a similar reflection shared by Ida Lewis, a former editor in chief of *Essence*. In her interview with Nikki Giovanni, Lewis dismisses the women's liberation movement as "a family quarrel" between white women and white men.[39] Despite the fact that Lewis admits she supports the goals of women's liberation, she understands that the role of black women "is to continue the struggle in concert with black men for the liberation and self-determination of blacks."[40] Morrison (and Lewis) explain the absence of black women in the women's liberation movement as a matter of racial politics: liberation for black women was impossible in a framework that refused to engage with racism explicitly.

For Morrison, women's liberation was a movement of elite, white women demanding access to the highest ranges of society. She writes, "The early image of Women's Lib was of an elitist organization made up of upper-middle-class women with the concerns of that class and not paying much attention to the problems of most black women."[41] If white women's demands come out of their own historical relations with white men, counters Morrison, so are black women's relationships to black men demarcated by a shared history—a history defined above all by white supremacy. Even as white women fight for liberation, Morrison quips, "someone's nice black grandmother" shoulders the responsibilities of the liberated woman's home; "If Women's Lib needs those grandmothers to thrive, it has a serious flaw."[42] According to Morrison, white women are regarded as children, "never as adults capable of handling the real problems of the world"—and it is this feeling of "superiority" to white women paired with black men's formidable opposition to women's lib that makes black women reluctant to sign on.

Although Morrison makes no reference to the possibility of a black feminist subject, other authors did articulate the possibility of gender-based organizing for black women. When Maine Williams presents the friction between black women and the women's liberation movement, she gives specific examples why black women see their oppression as primarily race-based; black women, she explains, "have not yet developed a feminist consciousness."[43] According to Williams, the "middle-class" mentality of the women's liberation movement seemed at odds with black women's needs—most black women saw little attempt within women's liberation to incorporate the problems that affect poor and working women, including domestic workers, factory employees, striking telephone workers, and women in prison. As a solution, Williams argues, white women must refrain from speaking *for* black women, but allow black women to speak for themselves. She cites the emergence of a black feminist consciousness in the creation of the Black Women's Alliance, formed in New York to address the specific oppressions of black women and to avoid the bitter anti-male sentiments of the white women's movement.

For black women writers it was important to stress the ways in which black women were not only differently struggling in the world of white power, but how for them the struggle was also *more* urgent, *more* violent, and *more* complex because of the multiple oppressions that yoked them. How could they be sure white women would not continue to benefit from their race privilege? In other words, what in the world did they have to gain from joining their struggle, appearing in their films, allowing them into their communities?

By, For, and About in Newsreel

These early writings by black women on the politics, methods, and discourse of the women's liberation movement illustrate the inability of black women to sign on to a movement dominated by what they perceived to be white women of privilege. Black women refused to be spoken *for* by the discourse of the white women's movement, but they also refused not to be spoken *with*. This struggle over solidarity, difference, and the racial politics of leftist activism also shaped the direction New York Newsreel would take in the early 1970s.

Filmmaker Christine Choy joined Newsreel in 1971 and was immediately struck by the gendered and racial dynamics at work in the organization, and especially tensions between white leftists and what Cynthia Young calls "U.S. Third World Leftists."[44] "Films were being made about blacks and women and (rarely) working-class whites," Choy remembers, "but none of these subjects had access to power within the collective. As in the larger culture, the women (almost all white) were subordinates and sex objects."[45] Moreover, Choy recollects dissatisfaction with the way people of color were represented in films made primarily by whites. She explains,

> I saw white people making films about Blacks and Hispanics, for instance. And I felt there was a lack of depth in the representation of how minorities really feel in this country. A few of us began to recognize that to deal with issues affecting our community (Third World communities), it would be better to take our demands further and to take control of the whole process.[46]

Though she does not name them, *The Woman's Film* and *Janie's Janie* might be examples of the kinds of films Choy became weary of during her early days at Newsreel. For Choy, the commitment to solidarity through difference espoused by these films was yet another manifestation of white privilege. Writings by black women about solidarity also demonstrate that leftist activism that lacked an anti-imperial, anti-racist, and anti-capitalist agenda did not attract people of color. Increasingly, as Choy's recollections illustrate, people of color saw their political struggles as more analogous to those of third-world movements in the throes of anti-colonial revolution than to white leftist movements in the United States.

Young observes that U.S. minorities identified with third-world minorities, especially as the radical cinemas of Latin America reached U.S. leftists in the '60s and '70s. Young theorizes that the two groups "articulated," in Stuart Hall's terms, around a shared experience of state sponsored oppression and violence.[47] Newsreel increasingly distributed and screened films about revolutionary politics in Cuba and Vietnam, for example. As members of the collective, Choy and Sue Robeson traveled to international conferences on cinema in the mid-1970s.[48] They also came to the conclusion that white people should stop making films about people of color. Eventually, the white leadership of Newsreel split along class lines, and later left the collective altogether. The filmmakers of color who remained committed to producing films "by and about Third World peoples in the United States."[49] Debates about the representation of people of color in leftist filmmaking and in women's liberation discourse parallel contemporaneous debates in ethnographic filmmaking. In the 1960s David James writes, "As a result of the civil rights movements, minority social groups who previously had been both politically and cinematically marginalized and who had been represented only by the external agencies of the entertainment industries began to make their own films, representing themselves, their own communities, their own histories."[50] Throughout political filmmaking, activism, and academic discourses, U.S. people of color took possession of the right and responsibility to represent their own interests and their own communities, and this proposition—as radical as it was reasonable—indelibly shaped the future of leftist organizations like Newsreel.

Teach Our Children, a documentary about the Attica prison rebellion, was Third World Newsreel's first film "made by filmmakers of color about communities of color."[51] *Teach Our Children* was also the first of several prison films made by Third World Newsreel, who understood the military-industrial complex as a key manifestation of state-sponsored violence against people of color. In several interviews about her decades-long career in documentary filmmaking, Choy explains that when they made *Teach Our Children,* the filmmakers wanted to focus exclusively on the experiences of people of color; they deliberately "eliminated everything that had to do with whites. This film, made by two women all about men, contains only images of Blacks and Latinos."[52]

Although not necessarily "native ethnographers," because the filmmakers in question did not feel bound by the disciplinary demands of anthropology, Choy and Robeson's film participates in the intellectual and political upset catalyzed when "insiders" document their own communities. According to John Jackson, native ethnographers instigate distinct changes in ethnographic practice: "Here, ethnography is not just a research method; it is also a new work ethic, a new scientific policy, a new kind of salvage ethnography that saves natives from the abuses of feigned neutrality."[53] Jackson also acknowledges that in comparison to the "outsider anthropologist," the native anthropologist carries a distinct charge: "Once scientistic and objectivist claims for privileging the outsider anthropologist over the insider began to fall away, however, another political project became even more important to the native anthropological cause: the use of ethnographic research for the explicit political benefit of one's people, the co-natives under study."[54] Native ethnographers are expected to provide representations of their co-natives that are not only more accurate and commensurate with the experiences of their communities, but also that concretely advance their political causes.

In this sense Choy and Robeson clearly act as native ethnographers, determined to rewrite the history of representation as well as create material evidence for a political cause: the end of the carceral society. In *Teach Our Children,* solidarity is bridged across racial difference and in distinction to militarized white supremacy, exemplifying a third-world political consciousness. Choy and Robeson include men, both black and Latino, in their film, and they explicitly refuse whiteness. In fact, what creates the web of solidarity in the film is the way these identities cohere in their opposition to that one major force: white imperialist supremacy. As Luna points out, few scholars have attempted to define what they mean when they use the term, "women of color," which is generally used to signal non-whiteness, despite the many differences that fracture the term empirically. Similarly, their embrace of third-world politics meant that Choy and Robeson saw themselves (an Asian American woman and a black woman) closely aligned with incarcerated people of color. Their documentary thus enacts the ethics and politics of a native ethnography, which is often based on sense of identification between the filmmaker and the filmed subjects and the uniquely "native" charge of responsibility for the social situation represented.

This notion of solidarity makes sense, according to Natalie Havlin, who observes that in the later reflections of women of color feminists of the 1980s, such as Cherríe Moraga, 1970s third-world feminism and its vision of collectivity provided key inspiration.[55] Moraga recalls that the Third World Feminist Alliance of the 1970s published essays that connected "Racism, Imperialism, and Sexism," in *Triple Jeopardy*, and advocated for "domestic worker and welfare rights, the political prisoner movement, the sterilization of Black and Puerto Rican women, reproductive rights, and the liberation of Palestine."[56] She describes women of color feminism of the 1980s and particularly the writing contained in *This Bridge Called Our Back* as "one liberation tool at our disposal"—a tool of the heart, the psyche, and a "theory of the flesh"—an "intercultural conversation and confrontation in order to build an unyielding platform of equity among us."[57] The third-world feminist films of the 1970s, and especially the work of TWN, thus share characteristics with women of color feminisms as well as native ethnographers, including an indictment of "a feminism prescribed by white women of privilege" and a commitment to "the process of discerning the multilayered and intersecting sites of identity and struggle distinct and shared—among women of color around the globe."[58]

From Spikes to Spindles

Choy's next film, *From Spikes to Spindles*, draws her closer to her own ethnic community and positions her more squarely as a native ethnographer, but the resulting film still produces a complex understanding of ethnicity, community, and what it means to be Chinese or Chinese American in the United States. The documentary, which was the first by, for, and about Asian Americans, opens with a provocation that illustrates the coherence of as well as the tensions within the Chinese community in New York. The opening sequence centers on Peter Yu, a "young engineer" and bystander at an altercation that broke out after an automobile accident in Chinatown. "Without provocation," according to the voice-over, bystanders were pushed and harassed by NYPD. Yu was beaten, taken into custody, and charged with assault and resisting arrest. In hand-held observational footage, we see a firetruck and some police pushing their way through a buzzing crowd in Chinatown during what appears to be a large protest march. The voice-over tells us that in response to Yu's arrest, various groups and organizations "rallied" both in support of Peter Yu and "also the dignity of the Chinese community."

The film also immediately acknowledges that "community" is a contested term, and that behind the scenes of solidarity on screen reside fierce differences of opinion, which necessitate the "conversation and confrontation" highlighted by Moraga. An on-the-street interview with a demonstrator who speaks in Cantonese hints at disagreements between various organizations who proposed different dates for the protest. A spontaneous interview with a white police officer standing in front of the offices of the Chinese Benevolent Association

(CBA) suggests collusion between that organization and the police. Footage from a crowded community meeting following Yu's arrest features snippets of speeches that highlight internal disagreements between speakers regarding the most appropriate response to police intervention and violence. One passionate, elderly man calls for unity in Cantonese. "Don't separate," he urges. "I've been here for 50 years, and had many hardships. That's because of racial discrimination. If everyone starts to divide along family names, races, territories and nationalities, it is not unity. WE MUST UNITE!"[59] The more staid leader of the CBA suggests in contrast that the meetings are an unnecessary distraction. *From Spikes to Spindles,* which was the first documentary about New York's Chinatown, boldly constructs an unsentimental portrait of a complex community, united by a common sense of racial discrimination and divided by diverse ideas about how to acknowledge and combat what the filmmakers clearly see as their collective disenfranchisement.

Subsequent interviews aggregate a mosaic of personalities, experiences, and nationalities among the residents of Chinatown. A seventy-eight-year-old man who was born in San Francisco shuffles through old photographs of his parents, who wear traditional clothing unlike his own Western apparel. Next, a woman filmed in close-up, and identified only as "Garment Worker," explains that she came to the United States from Hong Kong with her five children, while her husband stayed behind. The subtitles translate her experience into English: "It was very hard at first because the children needed me. I worked even when I was sick. No work, no food, that's all." Fifteen-year-old Judy narrates her immigration to the United States with her dad. She is filmed in a stairwell, wearing a T-shirt and bell-bottom jeans, as she sits and talks to a producer. She explains that she was obligated to work instead of study because of the debt she and her father owed to the "boss" who "brought us over." "We have to work," she sighs, her chin resting in her hand, her voice resigned: "and if we don't like it, we have to move back." Though she speaks initially in Cantonese, she finishes her thoughts in English; Judy is clearly bilingual and bicultural and represents the unique experiences of a new generation of children who were born in China and raised in the United States. These meditative autobiographical dimensions of the film arise consistently, marking the way the experiences of the "I" designate a vital entry into the collective.

Despite strong differences, these three interview subjects share resonant experiences of displacement, adaptation, and loss. As if to highlight these shared affective characteristics of their diverse backgrounds, the film intercuts contemporary observational footage of Chinatown's hustle and bustle with archival footage and photographs of earlier waves of immigration. The voice-over

The hustle and bustle of New York's Chinatown in *From Spikes to Spindles*. (Courtesy of Third World Newsreel.)

bridges these two temporalities, explaining that those who are "called politely Chinese Americans" are "immigrants still trying to adjust to a new world." Once again, the voice-over stresses community and shared experience, even in the face of differences: generational, temporal, national, and ethnic. The woman who delivers the voice-over speaks English without the trace of an accent, and yet also speaks of a "we," as when she says, "faces and images from *our* history" over the archival footage. The voice of the woman narrator, an index to the woman filmmaker, brings the collective together, bridging past and present, diverse constituencies, the I with the we.

The second major segment of the documentary didactically recounts the history of Chinese immigration to the United States, stressing the contributions of immigrants to the nation's economy and infrastructure, and lamenting the violence and discrimination that they continually faced despite their contributions. Photographs, drawings, prints, and paintings illustrate the voice-over narrative as the historiographic account moves through the westward expansion, the Civil War, and the migration of Chinese communities east toward New York City. As if to verify the account, interview footage with the director of Naturalization Services in New York adds detail, nuance, and a progressive view of the value of immigrants to the U.S. economy and cultural landscape.

At the heart of this historiography are matters of labor, and the story of a people whose primary draw to the United States has been the opportunity to work, save, and prosper. And yet, because wage labor often depends on and produces gender norms, the film makes it clear that the history of the Chinese community in New York has produced different experiences for men and women. In the 1970s, according to the documentary, the largest single source of employment in Chinatown was in garment factories, and the largest single industry in New York remains the garment industry. As detailed by an ILGWU (International Ladies' Garment Workers' Union) male union representative, garment workers thus constitute the largest "economic and financial base in the Chinese community." Since the vast majority of garment workers were women (80 percent, according to the documentary, and the majority of these from Hong Kong), their "position" was "raised," according to the translation of the union representative's comments.

Throughout, *From Spikes to Spindles* subtly highlights the experiences of women within the community, asserting the collectivizing potential of gendered experiences. At the end of the film, it is unity that the work stresses: unity of the Chinese community, and of the Chinese community with other minority communities. The film is thus a document of the history of the Chinese community in New York, as much as it forms part of the unifying discourse that would produce such a thing as a Chinese community against such powerful differences of region, language, gender, class, and religion. Sharing the space and time of documentary reality, the subjects of the film occupy a collective aesthetic and temporal world of experience and possibility.

Michael M. J. Fischer argues that ethnic autobiographical literature of the 1970s and 1980s, including for example Maxine Hong Kingston's *The Woman Warrior,* raises new questions about "how culture operates" and about how ethnography might as a result be repurposed from a mode of knowledge about primitive others to a form of "cultural criticism."[60] Writing in the midst of reflexive reconsiderations of ethnographic writing in anthropology, Fischer suggests that "listening" to new "ethnic autobiographies" provides clues about how to describe the "actuality" of the late twentieth century. He writes, "the ethnic search is a mirror of the bifocality that has always been part of the anthropological rationale: seeing others against a background of ourselves, and ourselves against a background of others."[61] In linking autobiography, ethnography, and ethnicity, Fischer highlights the process of "cultural emergence" of ethnic identities in the United States in this politicized period, which he contrasts with a legacy of more traditional "naive efforts of direct representation" by others.[62]

Fischer's account of ethnic autobiography provides several important observations for the present study. For Fischer, ethnic identity is continually emerging in each new generation; and rather than something handed down by the past, it is future-oriented and constructed through aesthetic practices, including literature and film, in the present. Thus, to read autobiographical novels (fiction and nonfiction) is not to seek the stable contours of a particular ethnic group, but rather to ask what formal strategies different ethnic subjects employ in their constructions of community and solidarity.

Following Fischer, I read *From Spikes to Spindles* not as a document of Chinese Americanicity, but rather as cultural criticism about the making of a radical, collective Chinese American identity in the 1970s. For the filmmakers, Chinese Americanness is explored through the history of immigration, labor, language, and discrimination by white supremacy and capitalism. The film's major strategy is the use of first-person interviews to share personal experiences related to these topics. *From Spikes to Spindles* situates itself strongly in the present, opening with an event that took place in the same year. However, the film clearly finds the past relevant to the present and takes a substantial didactic turn to the first presence of Chinese in the United States in the nineteenth century. It is also future-oriented, echoing the call for unity expressed by several speakers in the film. Staying away from more obvious cultural markers such as food, dress, and music, *From Spikes to Spindles* creates a sense of ethnic solidity through the shared experiences of struggle. Ethnicity emerges in the conversation and confrontation between feeling and being in the contested and racially managed space of the everyday. How does the history of Chinese immigration to the United States inform how people live today? How does the history of white, patriarchal capitalism constrain forms of being for others? In the film's final sequence, other young people of color express solidarity with the struggles of Asians and Asian Americans. As a Chinese American young man explains toward the end of the film, "Other minorities, too, must unite. America is made up of many nationalities. We all have to unite."

Inside Women Inside

Solidarity is also the major emphasis of Choy and Robeson's later film, *Inside Women Inside,* which is more specifically about women's experiences in three different prisons. *Inside Women Inside* highlights a diverse range of women: the majority of them black, some of them white, some mothers, some grandmothers; all of them are criminalized by the state. The film is comprised primarily of interviews in which women describe their deplorable living and working conditions in prison. Unlike *From Spikes to Spindles, Inside Women Inside* contains no voice-over, but rather in the style of *The Woman's Film* allows each woman to be the expert of her own personal experiences. By 1978 the imperative to exclude white people was also diminished, and solidarity with the incarcerated women clearly extends to incarcerated white women as well. Overall, the film stresses the intense oppression and lack of freedom that all the women share; it is their state of incarceration, their truncated liberty, and their dehumanization that makes them a community. Numerous shots of cells and long pans across iron bars create the visual impression that the women are treated more like animals in a zoo than humans. An eerie soundtrack produces a sense of discomfort and fear throughout. Yet, the film also works to particularize the faces of the women, framing them in close-ups that constantly emphasize their individuality and the unique landscape of each face despite the dehumanizing conditions of prison.

Choy and Robeson focus on the way that labor and capitalism collude with patriarchy to shape the unique form of discrimination endured by all women in prison. Women are shot working at sewing machines, not unlike the shots of garment workers in *From Spikes to Spindles* and resonant images of women at work in the opening sequence of *The Woman's Film* as well. Highlighting the collective labor of women in factories, laundries, domestic, and commercial spheres consistently demonstrates the ways that patriarchy and capitalism structure the uniquely gendered experiences of women of all races. The incarcerated women in *Inside Women Inside* also speak eloquently and sharply about their unpaid labor. "This is like reverting back to slavery days," remarks one woman. "Instead of bringing us over on a boat, they bring us from the jailhouse. Instead of bringing us from Africa, they're bringing us from Harlem and the Bronx. But it's all the same game. They've copped us for 400 years, they'll cop us again. But it's going to blow eventually." We occasionally hear questions from the camera crew, such as: "How do you feel about not getting paid?" And answers from the women: "I don't feel too good about that." The filmmakers are also clear that incarceration presents unique challenges for women. Women in jail face uniquely gendered problems because many of them are the primary caregivers of children. Whereas men usually leave behind women to care for their children, women struggle to find others to replace them and raise their children.

Choy and Robeson's TWN films are important examples of the types of selves and communities produced in 1970s women's documentaries about communities of color. They also manifest a form of documentary filmmaking in which solidarity is not a fantasy of similarity as much as a native responsibility toward other oppressed groups. The filmmakers illustrate the native ethnographer's political responsibility toward her community; and they also demonstrate the fluid networks of identification and collectivity among third-world communities in the seventies. Despite significant historical, geographical, and ethnic differences, third-world communities stand together, willing to examine the ways dominant ideologies of race, gender, class, and sexuality imperil them similarly. The "auto" or self at stake in these feminist autoethnographic TWN films is constructed by the material and psychic conditions of existence among the oppressed. The filmmakers would likely agree with women's liberation rhetoric that the personal is political (or "the political is profoundly personal," in Moraga's terms)[63] and that one's own experience constitutes the starting ground for political action and revolutionary thinking; the filmmakers would also say that the gender (and particularly, gendered forms of labor) are key to understanding the broader kinds of discrimination that most concern them: bodily and psychic exploitation by capital, violence by the state, and cultural annihilation.

Madeline Anderson's *I Am Somebody*

As is clear from the title, *I Am Somebody* foregrounds the attenuated relationships between the individual and the collective in racialized communities and the ways that highlighting the experiences of the individual generates new insight about the coherence and politicization of the community. The film documents what labor historians Leon Fink and Brian Greenberg describe as "one of the South's most disruptive and bitter labor confrontations since the 1930s."[64] From March 20 to June 27, 1969, hospital workers at the Medical College Hospital of the University of South Carolina in Charleston carried out a strike call from Local 1199B after twelve black union activists were dismissed from their jobs. More than four hundred workers went on strike that summer in Charleston, demanding union recognition. Significantly, all but twelve of the strikers were women, all of them black. Anderson's documentary film, which was commissioned by the Hospital Workers Union Local 1199, is a sharp example of autoethnography in the vein of Zora Neale Hurston's ethnographic work. Anderson is both of the community she films (black women workers) and separate from it, since she was a professional woman from the North. In Anderson's film, dynamics of identification shift between race, gender, and class, constructing solidarity variously and fluidly among African Americans, women, and workers.

Anderson explains that with *I Am Somebody* she hoped to create a film that would reach the Charleston women workers in particular: "But I didn't want it to be just a compilation, that is, just an episodic record. I wanted some kind of personal touch that the women strikers could identify with."[65] Anderson describes a desire to create a documentary that would exceed its function as document and serve rather as a catalyst for identification between the women in the film and the representation of their moment in history. The "personal touch" was key to the goal, which Anderson realizes by foregrounding the experiences of Claire Brown, one of the strikers. The strikers in this case were black women workers: new faces on the scene of labor marches and a new collective subject of both political action and filmic reception. With *I Am Somebody* Anderson thus assembles a radical political act of representation and recognition: she puts black women workers at the center of the civil rights movement in 1969, at the heart of a labor campaign, and through the film product itself, in the center of the feminist film culture of the seventies.

Because Moe Foner, who served as the head of New York Local 1199's educational and publicity campaigns beginning in the early 1950s, recruited Anderson to make a film about the strike after the events he wished to publicize had already occurred, Anderson assembled *I Am Somebody* almost entirely from newsreel footage garnered from major broadcasters. Much of this footage bears the stamp of the journalistic conventions of the time: interviews with workers, hospital leaders, and state officials are framed similarly in frontal medium shots; scenes of marches are often unsteady, where the camera constantly seeks a better angle on the action; and celebrity marchers and speakers, such as Ralph Abernathy and Coretta Scott King, receive a disproportionate share of the camera's attention. Only after the filmmaker had compiled an initial rough cut from footage selected from the archive libraries of ABC, CBS, and NBC did she shoot additional footage of the striker Claire Brown, a mother of five and an obstetrics technician at Medical College Hospital.[66]

Characteristic of the communal autoethnographies and native ethnographies of women of color in the seventies, *I Am Somebody* forwards a political vision intent on balancing the individual with the collective, and in this case black women workers within both labor politics and what the film calls "soul power." That is, Anderson's documentary wants to account for black people's collective will to be recognized as properly human, as well as black women workers' specific aspiration to be distinguished as uniquely subjugated by a function not only of race, nor of race and class, but of race, class, and gender.

Addressing the collective politics of race, *I Am Somebody* consistently references the visual and verbal lexicon of the civil rights movement, and certainly with its title—a phrase that emerged from the movement and was later made famous by Jesse Jackson. By using the political rhetoric of the civil rights movement, *I Am Somebody* lays claim to a politics driven by a collective will to assert the most basic humanity of black people. At several points in the film, a chorus of voices chanting the refrain "I am somebody" accompanies footage of the marchers as they demonstrate peacefully and are arrested in droves. To "be somebody" in the discourse of the documentary is to be recognized as a group by (white) power as belonging among the human. In the opening sequence, a shot of a carriage horse's galloping hooves cross-fades into a shot that features hundreds of marching human feet. The cinematic transition literalizes the transformation from nonhuman to human that the film and the strike work to produce in the political recognition of black people. A voice distinct from narrator Brown's announces, as if reading from the march manifesto, "We as black people in South Carolina have awakened to the fact that we are no longer afraid of the white man and that we want to be recognized, not because of our race, but because we are human beings."

The realist aesthetics of representation in *I Am Somebody* do not simply index political work in the realm of the real, but in fact constitute the political act of demanding justice. Nancy Fraser distinguishes between two categories of injustice: socioeconomic and cultural.[67] According to Fraser, socioeconomic injustice stems from the political-economic structure of society and includes exploitation, economic marginalization, and deprivation.[68] Cultural injustice speaks to what she calls "social patterns of representation, interpretation and communication," such as cultural domination, disrespect, and nonrecognition.[69] The solution to socioeconomic injustice lies in the redistribution of economic resources; cultural injustice, on the other hand, demands recognition as a remedy. The distinction between these two understandings of injustice, Fraser admits, is analytical rather than realistic. In life, the two are entwined, often creating what Fraser describes as a "vicious circle of cultural and economic subordination."[70] *I Am Somebody* manifests this "interimbrication," as Fraser calls it, between socioeconomic and cultural injustice. The hospital workers in the film constitute a class; the literal demands made by the strikers address their economic exploitation by calling for the right to unionize, as well as for their right to receive better wages and better hours. Yet with support from civil rights leaders, the hospital workers' strike becomes a collective struggle of the black community. The specific politics of redistribution embed a logic of generalized recognition that encompasses the entire population of black people in Charleston.

This matter of recognition—the demand to be recognized as human—is fundamental and established a priori to the particular struggle by black female hospital workers at stake in the film. In the opening march scene, for example, there is no mention in the voice-over that the march was part of the hospital workers' strike. In shots of the march, the frame repeatedly fills with the upper bodies of men and women, black and white, as they march arm in arm, dozens deep in the streets. The images attest to a peaceful demonstration, interracial solidarity, and massive collective will. However, only posters and paper hats, which display UAW, AFL-CIO, and 1199, the hospital workers' union name and number, reference the labor politics at stake. Reverend Ralph Abernathy speaks in voice-over of the success of the Mother's Day march. As he relates his feelings of excitement when he saw more than fourteen thousand people marching in solidarity that day in Charleston, the image track features a shot of the reverend arm in arm with black women. His presence at the march and the authority granted to his reflection in voice-over code the event as significant within the context of the civil rights movement. He makes no mention of the hospital workers' union when he says, "I just knew that this would be the beginning of a new day in Charleston." This opening sequence thus creates the framework within which the hospital workers' strike gains general relevance to the struggle of all black people in their demand for recognition.

However, it is primarily through the original footage of Claire Brown and her first-person voice-over narration that *I Am Somebody* answers the need for a "personal touch" that Anderson mentions in her interview with the editors of *Film Library Quarterly:* to make a film that the hospital workers would identify with. The film's attention to Brown's personal political becoming utters an unambiguously gendered take on the events that took place that spring in Charleston. It is through Brown that we apprehend what Abernathy calls "a new day in Charleston" in the opening sequence of the Mother's Day march. Following the march, the film cuts to the first sequence of Anderson's original footage of Brown. Brown is framed in close-up, cropped at the shoulders, as she stands in front of a bathroom mirror. In the foreground, her hand moves a cloth in circles over her reflection. "It *was* a new day," Brown emphasizes with authority in the voice-over while she repetitively wipes the mirror clean. As the voice-over continues to describe the success of the Mother's Day march and the coalitions between civil rights groups and the labor unions that made the event a tremendous success, the framing zooms out to capture both Brown and her reflection. She circles the mirror a few more times with her cloth and then checks her reflection and starts to exit the bathroom.

Situated in a decidedly intimate space in her home, Brown is at first introduced to the spectator indirectly, through the mediation of the looking glass. The film here emphasizes the act of looking and the process of creating a clear image, a true reflection. As we gaze at Brown, she gazes at herself. She does not return the camera's gaze but rather ignores it, performing for the camera the act of seeing herself. Two simultaneous moments of mutual recognition are thematized. Not only does the film invite the spectator to know Brown, it suggests that first of all, Brown must work to know herself. As she wipes the surface of the looking glass, Brown metaphorically apprehends her own image more clearly. In the act of looking at herself, Brown instantiates the process of becoming a political subject made possible through participation in the hospital workers' strike.

This exquisite representation of subjective formation also appears in *Fannie's Film* (1979), Fronza Wood's unique portrait film about Fannie Drayton, an African American woman in her sixties who is the cleaning woman in an exercise studio for professional dancers. *Fannie's Film* juxtaposes an intimate personal voice-over by Fannie with two tracks of footage. In one set of images, the lithe and muscular bodies of white dancers bend and lift with rhythmic precision. Interspersed with these are shots of Fannie cleaning the studio, spraying here, collecting towels there. All the while her rich voice-over proclaims her unflappable happiness: she was raised well and comfortably in the South, married a kind man, pays all her bills on time, and generally feels successful and blessed by her life. The filmmaker's sense of irony is more clearly on display in her fictional short, *Killing Time* (1979), about a woman fitfully preparing her outfit and postmortem pose after her suicide. However, *Fannie's Film* features a striking collision of shots of young, beautiful white dancers who embody one vision of fulfillment and success compared with the spry African American woman who voices her own vision of happiness.

Whereas the gaze constructed by the shots of white bodies is beautiful but also voyeuristic, the way we are invited to watch Fannie as she goes about her business implies a certain kind of familiar and yet unexpected beauty. This is especially true in the shot of Fannie wiping down the mirror in which her own image is reflected. Only this shot is slowed down in the film, stretching across several seconds, emphasizing the point that it is not how the filmmaker or the viewers see Fannie that determines her sense of self; it is how Fannie sees herself that matters to the filmmaker. Woods grants us access to Fannie only through the disconnection between her voice and body. Our knowledge about her life is partial and only discernible in the context in which she allows herself to be known. We are not granted access to Fannie on her way home, in her living room, or with her family, only her image in public and her personal narrative about her own life.

In the last sequence of *I Am Somebody,* two juxtaposed scenes seal the seam between the politics of recognition at stake in the strike and the self-recognition achieved by Claire Brown. The first scene takes place at a press conference in which a black female spokesperson for the strikers announces their victory. She is seated at a square table with a cast of officials, reporters, and spokespeople.

Claire Brown and Fannie Drayton discover themselves through a demand for cultural recognition in *I Am Somebody* and *Fannie's Film*. (Courtesy of Third World Newsreel and Women Make Movies.)

Her torso is framed dramatically against a background of male suits and ties. She reads from a statement, which details the terms of the agreement between the strikers and hospital officials. Beyond the facts and figures of the redistribution agreement achieved by the strikers, the final words she reads declare the accomplishment most sought by the strikers: "We are returning in a new relationship of mutual respect and dignity between the workers, the county council, the hospital administration, and the entire community." When asked by a reporter what exactly the workers accomplished by striking, the woman, Ms. Simmons, declares boldly and without hesitation: "We gained recognition as human beings for one. We gained that recognition . . . as human beings." She nods emphatically and looks at her interlocutor directly. As she continues to stare down the male voice that interpellated her, her face dissolves into the cut. In the shot that follows, a white bird framed by a blue seaside dips gracefully in the wind. The transition here, from boardroom to blue sky, clearly alludes to a new space of freedom made possible by the success of the strike and the revolutionary realist aesthetics of the film.

During the feminist film movement of the 1970s, *I Am Somebody* was taken up and claimed as a distinctly, even classic feminist documentary. At the Flaherty Seminar in 1970, *I Am Somebody* screened alongside other feminist documentaries such as Amalie Rothschild's *Woo Who? May Wilson*. In 1972 Anderson's documentary was included in the First International Festival of Women's Films, the signature event that marked the emergence of a second-wave feminist consciousness in the realm of cinema. Alexandra Grilikhes brought *I Am Somebody* to audiences at Philadelphia's First International Festival: Films by Women. As women's film festivals proliferated throughout the United States and Europe,

I Am Somebody found receptive audiences. In many of the earliest published materials on feminist documentaries, *I Am Somebody* is routinely mentioned as a documentary relevant to feminism generally and to black and working-class women specifically; it is placed unselfconsciously alongside dozens of documentaries featuring new perspectives on women, by women, and about women.[71]

However, *I Am Somebody* was also one of the first films by and about *black* women, about black women workers more specifically and about black workers more generally. The meaning of community throughout the film is fluid, but also circumscribed by race. For the black women workers featured in the film, as was the case with Christine Choy's TWN films, community is created primarily in contrast to white capitalist patriarchy. It is largely in response to their disenfranchisement and to their dehumanization that black women workers in the film come together, and where Anderson in the role of native ethnographer aligns her goals with theirs. Though race, gender, and class clearly shape the experiences of women in the film, *I Am Somebody* is about a form of political solidarity constructed through shared experiences of oppression, arguably the most consistent form of reality that haunts feminist documentary.

In a number of significant ways, *I Am Somebody* directly corresponds to the legacy of autoethnographic or native ethnographer films made by Zora Neale Hurston in the early twentieth century. Both black women used the technologies of cinema to humanize the cultural practices and political ambitions of other women in their communities. Although neither woman directly filmed herself, both responded to what Jackson calls the "native politics" that shape native ethnographies: a sense of shared responsibility for justice, in this case for other African Americans, and especially other black women. Resonant with the characteristics of the native ethnographer, these women filmmakers elaborate the claims made in writing by black feminists: that gender exists in a complex matrix with class, sexuality, and race, and only a struggle that addresses all of these will yield the radical humanist politics of both recognition and redistribution that black women urgently needed.

One of the most entrenched stories about the 1970s that gets reworked in recent feminist scholarship centers on the politics of race and sexuality in the women's liberation movement and '70s feminism. Here, too, women's documentaries stand to make valuable contributions because of their constant commitment to exploring the activist and affective webs of solidarity and difference that shaped feminist politics. Kristen Hogan explains that the origin stories narrated by women who started feminist bookstores around the United States "contradict remembrances of 1970s feminism as straight and white. Instead the work of these dykes with a vision adds to the valuable narratives of a more vibrant movement history and establishes feminist bookstores as sites that, at their beginnings, drew together lesbians and their allies from across racialized difference to attempt to enact feminist futures."[72] Similarly, Victoria Hesford asks not why women's liberation was an exclusionary movement, but investigates what she calls "the production of women's liberation as a *white* women's movement."[73] As I argue in chapter 3, feminist documentary films of the 1970s and the responses they elicited from feminist film scholars clearly contributed to the production of whiteness Hesford identifies. Revisiting the films, I argue, offers a new framework for thinking through the subjects of reality—the category of women, the racialization of some bodies and not others, the activist and affective needs for solidarity and difference—that determine the complex racial politics of feminism.

Subject to Reality aims to tease out the less-often publicized activist and affective ambitions of cinematic feminisms, especially as these intersect with contemporary feminist commitments to both solidarity and difference. Feminist scholars have argued convincingly over the past decade that putting race at the center of a discussion of the second-wave women's liberation movement deeply upsets the singularity of feminist activism in the seventies and its corollary assumptions of racial homogeneity. That is, once we acknowledge the multiple fronts on which women waged their struggles, the coherence of a singular movement of white women becomes untenable. Rather, what we find in the late sixties and early seventies is a landscape of feminist activism by racially and economically diverse groups and organizations of women, which are impossible to generalize as existing and cooperating within a singular "women's liberation" movement.

Arguably since the 2016 presidential election in the United States, in which an overtly sexist and xenophobic white man with no political experience triumphed over a highly educated white woman with far more credentials, feminist activism has resurged with new vitality and a vociferous commitment to intersectional politics. Once an academic term in feminist scholarship, intersectionality reigns as a contemporary form of popular feminism, often alongside a strident critique of mainstream or "white" feminism.[74] For example, despite the feminist tone of Hillary Clinton's 2016 presidential campaign, women of color were quick to point out that 53 percent of white women voted against Senator Clinton, and helped propel her opponent to the White House.[75] What kind of affective or activist solidarity can exist between women who voted for Senator Clinton or Green Party candidate Jill Stein and those who voted for their opponent? When more than a million women took to the street in the Women's

Marches of 2017, debates about the racial politics of feminism dominated the U.S. media coverage of the emergent movement.[76] Throughout the public sphere, mischaracterizations of seventies feminism were abundant, especially in the shorthand notion that the women's liberation movement of the 1970s stands in eternally and simplistically for "white feminism." As *Subject to Reality* illustrates, women's documentary films of the 1970s belie other stories about the feminist seventies, especially about the racial politics of those subject to the realities of patriarchy, capitalism, and white supremacy.

Conclusion
When the Walls Come Down

Women's documentary filmmaking has long been a powerful site of political and ethical negotiation for those subject to different forms of reality depending on their social and political identity, including race, class, sexuality, ethnicity, religion, and nationality. Throughout this book I have elucidated how this negotiation has been rendered cinematically by women filmmakers committed to the aesthetics of documentary realism, including interviews, voice-over, narrative coherence, observational footage, identification, and aural intimacy. I have also argued that we can apprehend this trend productively by engaging with the intellectual and material history of ethnographic documentary filmmaking, what I call an anthropological aesthetic, and the dilemmas of outsiders and native informants.

In the first and second decades of the twentieth century, Osa Johnson and her husband Martin pioneered entertainment ethnographies about far-flung islands and their mysterious villagers in ways that supported white supremacy at home and buttressed the colonial project abroad. In the twenties, Frances Flaherty and her husband Robert continued the trend with more serious films about "noble savages" and man's plight against the forces of nature. By the late twenties and early thirties, when Zora Neale Hurston and Margaret Mead began making proper ethnographic films, anthropology and film had a deeply intertwined history. Although the relationship between cinematic image-making and the new scientism of anthropology was at first (and perhaps still is) somewhat ambivalent, as Alison Griffiths notes, ultimately—starting with figures like Margaret Mead—the two would become deeply interwoven, motivated by similar impulses of documentation and a desire to record the inexorable passage of time and culture for an uncertain but inevitable future. In the late 1960s and early 1970s that future would become powerfully tangled with the affective and activist goals of feminism. Women's documentary film-making formed a key site of feminist praxis throughout the feminist seventies. In the language of cinematic realism, women documentary filmmakers spoke passionately about personal experiences, political ambitions, fantasies of soli-darity and revolution, and commitments to difference and racial and economic justice. They continue to do so today. Attention to the long history of women's documentary filmmaking reminds us of the complex and ambitious desires of feminist aesthetics and of the political and ethical dilemmas that attend to projects devoted to the redistribution of power on and beyond the screen.

While important predecessors in feminist filmmaking include experimental artists like Gunvor Nelson, Deborah Wiley, Ana Mendieta, and Carolee Schnee-mann in the late 1960s, feminist documentary in the way that I think of it in this book was inaugurated with films that captured women's demonstrations and protests, such as *The Jeanette Rankin Brigade* (1968), *Up Against the Wall Ms. America* (1968), and *She's Beautiful When She's Angry* (1969)—all made by mem-bers of Newsreel, who prioritized the political potential and utility of cinema. In the early 1970s documentary film held gorgeous promise for feminist film-makers and activists who imagined that authentic images and stories about the experiences of other ordinary women would encourage more participation in what seemed to be an imminent social and political revolution. Across the heterogeneous archive of women's filmmaking of the 1970s, the gritty realism and immediacy of documentary film projected the many fantasies of feminism: embodied knowledge, empathy, recognition, solidarity, and action. It should come as no surprise that today, women continue to make documentary films with similar strategies and resonant ambitions. Feminist documentary film-making remains a vital aspect of feminism, consistently revising the visual grammar and ideological forces of gender, race, ethnicity, and class.

Throughout *Subject to Reality,* I have insisted that women's documentary film-making deserves renewed attention—not just because of what can be gleaned about the past lives of feminism and documentary—but also because women's anthropologically inflected documentaries resonate powerfully with the pres-ent. When I first saw films like *Joyce at 34* (Joyce Chopra and Claudia Weill, 1972) and *Janie's Janie* (Geri Ashur et al., 1971), I was struck by how relevant they seemed to me. These films about white mothers balancing marriage, work, and self-actualization spoke directly to my life, which was unfurling four decades later. Surely this was because the issues they explored echoed my own life at that time in the early 2000s. Like Joyce Chopra, I was in my early thirties, struggling with the new normative domesticity seemingly required by heterosexual, white, middle-class motherhood. Women's documentary films from the 1970s looked and sounded uncannily familiar—as if I had somehow seen them before or knew them already. At the time, I was also working in programming at a local documentary film festival, watching dozens of films each week, many of which were also made by women about gendered concerns like motherhood, sexuality, women's health, and body image. I found the contemporary films remarkably similar to those from the seventies. Newer films included familiar feminist documentary conventions: personal voice-overs, interviews with ordinary women that centered on personal experiences, and observational footage throughout. They also vibrated with similar commitments to intimacy, personal revelation, and a desire for self-inscription.

What I found strange was that no one in the United States that I worked with at the time—not the programmers, filmmakers, or critics—used the term "feminist documentary" to describe contemporary work by and about women. I remember the moment that Julia Lesage, who learned about my work at a Visible Evidence conference, generously invited me to review a group of contemporary "feminist documentaries"—anything I felt was necessary and important. At the time, I did not have a clear sense of what the category "feminist documentary" would contain or exclude; I never did take her up on her offer. There are libraries full of what we could call "feminist documentaries"—films about rape and sexual abuse, human trafficking and adoption, lesbian marriage and labor activism. But I could not conceive of a coherent archive, nor did I understand its boundaries—the term seemed both overly expansive (any feminist issue?) and overly limited (only films that self-announced as feminist?).

In the past few years, however, renewed interest in documentary films about feminist issues has become evident, even in popular media. In 2014 *Ms.* magazine published a list of "Top Ten Feminist Documentaries Streaming on Netflix," which included *Miss Representation* (Jennifer Siebel Newsom, 2011), *The Invisible War* (directed by Kirby Dick and produced by Amy Ziering and Tanner King Barklow, 2012), and *After Tiller* (Lana Wilson and Martha Shane, 2013)—about gender issues in the media, sexual assault in the military, and reproductive rights, respectively.[1] In the years following, popular media articles on sites ranging from *HuffPost* to *Bustle* continued recommending "feminist documentaries," such as *!Women, Art, Revolution* (Lynn Hershman Leeson, 2010), *Dark Girls* (Bill Duke and D. Channsin Berry, 2011), *Girl Rising* (Richard E. Robbins, 2013), *The*

Hunting Ground (directed by Kirby Dick and produced by Amy Ziering, 2015), *Hot Girls Wanted* (Jill Bauer and Ronna Gradus, 2015), and more—films about art, race, empowerment, sexual assault on college campuses, sex work, and beauty.[2] In 2015 Laura Poitras became the twelfth woman to win an Academy Award for best documentary for *Citizenfour,* a sharp portrait of whistleblower Edward Snowden—not necessarily a film about gender issues, but a stunning closing chapter to her post-9/11 trilogy about surveillance, military intervention, and American geopolitics. At Sundance in 2016, women documentarians won top awards in several categories, including Kirsten Johnson for *Cameraperson* (2016) for best documentary and Rokhsareh Ghaem Maghami for *Sonita* (2016), which garnered an audience award. Powerhouse producer, distributor, and director Ava DuVernay has also claimed feminist space for her range of fictional, activist, and documentary projects with deeply intersectional commitments. Feminist curation projects, film clubs, and collectives have sprung up all over the globe. In her eloquent take on "new feminist cinema," British scholar and critic Sophie Mayer observes, "Any narrative of twenty-first century cinema could be, and perhaps should be written through feminist films."[3]

In 2015 the "discovery" of *The Year of the Woman* (Sandra Hochman, 1973)—a documentary about women's political participation in the 1972 Democratic National Convention—made mainstream news when it was suddenly made available on Vimeo by journalists interested in Shirley Chisholm's presidential bid. In her multimedia feature story on the film's discovery, Rebecca Traister explains that as a journalist who covers women in politics, she had read about the 1972 convention where women like Bella Abzug, Gloria Steinem, and Germaine Greer urged Democrats to advocate for women's issues. She imagined "the convergence of powerful women, the late nights, the arguing, the swearing, the marching, the drum circles," however, "It never occurred to me that I would ever see it, that I *could* ever see it, since one of the enraging challenges feminists encountered in Miami was that the men holding the news cameras refused to accord them the respect of recording their project."[4] At the end of her rapturous account of the film, which was made by a collective of women that included Barbara Kopple and Claudia Weill, Traister writes, "Good god is it liberating to watch a bunch of loud-mouthed broads who do not give a rat's ass about violating safe spaces without trigger warnings."[5] Traister finds the film refreshing, relevant, and an important reminder of how fiercely women fought, how deeply they felt, and how urgent their demands for gender equity in politics remain. Traister and I agree that "lost" feminist documentary films of the past contain valuable lessons about activism and affect for contemporary audiences.

In some ways, we have also become more comfortable with the idea of the woman filmmaker than ever before. In so many other ways, of course, the industry, and especially Hollywood, continues to limit the influence and success of female creators.[6] In the realm of documentary, one of our most prominent female documentarians, Laura Poitras, has made her remarkable career by creating films about men, war, and global politics. Her attention to global inequality, masculinity, and state-sanctioned violence against Others certainly instantiates transnational feminism. However, the lack of women in her films makes Poitras a more viable subject for discussions about female auteurs than for a definition of feminist documentary. Poitras's success and her subject matters are no doubt related to the complex history of women's documentary filmmaking that I explore in this book. However, the example of Poitras also raises a question about the viability of feminist stories within the public sphere. The year a woman filmmaker receives the academy's highest award for a film expressly about gender politics, we will know that feminist documentary has finally begun its long-awaited journey from margin to center.

How will feminist film studies respond to that moment, which is no doubt on the horizon? Throughout *Subject to Reality* I have drawn expansively from a wide range of critical methodologies developed throughout the past five decades of academic film and feminist study. The early chapters depend on historiographies, biographies, personal archives, and popular reviews as well as postcolonial, film, and feminist theory to develop arguments about the complex roles women like Osa Johnson, Frances Flaherty, Zora Neale Hurston, and Margaret Mead have played in the overarching narrative about feminism and documentary. Later chapters depend less on biographical and contextual material, and instead prioritize the discursive and activist impact of feminist documentary filmmaking during the revolutionary period of the 1970s. Subtending the book, however, I maintain a commitment to close readings, in which I consistently return to the ethics and politics of form—in *mise-en-scène,* patterns of editing, and other cinematographic strategies.

Lucas Hilderbrand recently dubbed this an "amphibious" approach, "moving between cinema and media, history and theory, formalism and cultural context."[7] This multivalent reading practice is surely the result of my academic training, which has been shaped by numerous debates in film and literary studies about the politics and ethics of interpretation and a destabilized boundary between the object of inquiry and the subject who inquires. More concretely, however, this book is indebted to the ongoing challenges posed and navigated by feminist film and media scholars. As Sangita Gopal observes, "Feminism reminds us always to think about frames and stakes with regard to media content and form, as well as its proliferation and diffusion." "It is salutary to recall," she continues, "that feminism guided early film and media work not only in generating theoretical and analytical models but also in researching and promoting women's media and reexamining and assembling archives."[8] In film theory, we often recast the seventies as the age of Grand Theories, where clear theoretical camps existed in distinct intellectual territories. Because that was the moment that let down feminist documentary, I have tended to resist strict theoretical regimes. Instead, my thinking has been deeply inspired by thinkers that prioritize questions about subjectivity, whether they focus on representation, subject formation, form, or authorship. For me that feminist genealogy includes the landmark work of Vivian Sobchack in *Carnal Thoughts,* Trinh Minh-ha in *When the Moon Waxes Red,* Alisa Lebow in *First Person Jewish,* and Alexandra Juhasz in *Women of Vision.*

Firmly committed to the feminist goals of theory, praxis, promotion, and reexamination, *Subject to Reality* concludes with two personal stories that reveal contemporary encounters with the transhistorical power of feminist documentaries. This will, I hope, demonstrate how writing this book has attuned me like never before to the explosive scenes of solidarity and difference that have shaped the work of women in documentary. If on the one hand the "subject of feminism" poses a question for feminist theory, and on the other, matters of both reality and difference have shaped the politics of contemporary feminist activism, then women's documentary practice continues to hold promise as a key site of negotiation between filmmakers, filmed subjects, audiences, and critics. In particular, I am convinced that in the affective and activist feedback loop that continues to define documentary and its audiences—no matter its ever-changing technological forms of expression—exists the potential, both effervescent and ephemeral, for scenes of connection, analysis, and solidarity.

Scene One

As I was finishing *Subject to Reality* in Dallas, Texas, I received an email from filmmaker Signe Taylor with an invitation to attend the Texas premiere of her latest documentary, *It's Criminal* (2017). Signe mentioned that the film was based on an undergraduate seminar taught at Dartmouth College by Ivy Schweitzer and Pati Hernandez. I graduated from Dartmouth in 1996 with a bachelor's degree in women's studies. During my time there, Ivy was a beloved professor, mentor, and friend. We have reconnected several times over the years, and each time I tell her how instrumental she and other women faculty were in my decision to become a feminist academic. I immediately wrote a reply to Signe and accepted her invitation. My primary motivator was my commitment to Ivy, but I could tell by the description of the film that *It's Criminal* was also intimately related to the book I was writing.

It's Criminal follows two parallel groups—Dartmouth students and incarcerated women—as they participate in Ivy and Pati's service-learning course at Dartmouth titled "Women, Prison, and Performance," in which they will collectively write and perform a play. My persistent claim throughout this book has been that women's documentary filmmaking has a deep and complex history of attempting to rethink asymmetries of power and create solidarity between women in the service of feminist politics. Indeed, that because of its constant attention to the viability of the category of woman, feminism manifests an enduring commitment to the affective, ethical, and aesthetic dimensions of solidarity and difference. *It's Criminal* extends this essential feminist legacy into the present. Taylor's documentary resonates strongly with the early consciousness-raising documentaries of the seventies archive, like *The Woman's Film* (1971), which is also structured around transformation and feminist awakening. *It's Criminal* also embeds the anthropological aesthetic of close detail and the ethnographic ethos of examining cultural practices among distinct groups, which I highlight in chapters 3 and 4.

The documentary starts on the first day of a new semester as Professor Schweitzer introduces the class to the project and explains that the course involves weekly sessions at the women's unit in a local prison. The camera zooms in on the nervous facial expressions of undergraduates as they pay close attention to Professor Schweitzer's candid description of the intense experience they are about to undergo: "This class in not like the typical Dartmouth class," she says. "It asks more of you and it will change you." By stitching together archival footage, interviews, and observational techniques—the documentary charts the transformations that take place within both groups of participants separately as well as collectively—the students and the incarcerated women experience independent paradigm shifts within their cohorts, and they change their behavior toward one another as the weeks progress. The students gain new insight about their Ivy League privilege and also about the ways that race, class, and gender discrimination create the conditions by which some lawbreakers land in prison and others go free. The incarcerated women learn this, too, and this knowledge changes their perception of themselves, their choices, and the students who come to work with them.

In the early weeks of the course, the distance between the students and the incarcerated women manifests primarily through body language and silence. The women in orange suits watch the students with occasional suspicion; some

Four women featured in *It's Criminal*: Georgia, Malika, Thandar, and Charlotte (2017). (Photos by Charlene Music. Courtesy of Signe Taylor.)

sit apart from their small groups, some assert themselves bodily, daring the students to judge them for their way of speaking, sitting, laughing. Students in casually expensive shorts and T-shirts mostly attempt to focus on their assigned tasks, notebooks and pencils in hand, staying close to the other students and bonding over the awkward task of working within the integrated groups. As the weeks pass, however, the dynamics between the women shift perceptibly. The uncomfortable silences and separations fade away as the groups brave more personal conversations, find shared interests, learn to appreciate each other's humor and struggles.

In the interstices of these scenes, interviews with individual participants illuminate more personal experiences among the women. Echoing the intrigue techniques of reality TV, women tell the camera what they "really" think of each other. Initially these interviews highlight disparities and conflicts. Women describe their diverse backgrounds of privilege or struggle. They seem to have lived in two different Americas. In one version of the United States, you might grow up with two professional parents, your own room in a two-story house, a car, vacations, and big dreams; in the other you might have lived on the street in middle school after being kicked out or abandoned, you didn't have time for dreams because you were struggling to stay fed, clean, and loved. When the groups come back together after these interview segments, the viewer has a deeper sense of the vast canyon that separates these women from each other.

As the narrative and the course progresses, the women begin to write scripts, plan sets, tell stories to and about each other. The shared process of intellectual and material labor leads to personal transformation for all the participants. By the end of the film, which is at once tragic and hopeful, women express how certain they are that the project either changed or saved their lives. At the post-screening discussion in Dallas, Charlotte, one of the formerly incarcerated women from the film, told the audience, "I'm proud of myself. I look forward to my future. I've never felt that way before."

It's Criminal offers a poignant contemporary example of the main characteristics of feminist documentary as these coalesced in the 1970s: observational techniques, personal interviews, narratives of transformation, and the cultivation of identification between diverse women within the film and between the filmed subjects and the audience. Read as a feminist documentary, *It's Criminal* also asks us to consider what haunts the reality captured by these cinematic strategies and how specific dynamics of power shape the experiences that the film both reveals and constructs. The reality that haunts *It's Criminal* arises from the inequalities that structure the material lives of economically disenfranchised women. The brown, white, and black women in the film index the thousands of incarcerated people who plead guilty to misdemeanors because they are financially unable to post bail. They also convey the ways that gender shapes their experience in the haunted house of prison. Not only are they structurally disenfranchised *in prison* because they are housed in a male facility and allocated a limited amount of living and leisure space; they also endured brutal experiences of sexual, physical, and emotional abuse by parents, partners, and friends before prison. As they serve sentences for crimes they never stood trial for, the state disempowers them completely; they are unable to protect their children, unable to defend their actions, and unable to imagine how their futures will be any different. The goal of her work in the prison, Pati Hernandez explains in one of the many interviews in the documentary, is to provide an opportunity for women to find their voices and tell their stories. In collaboration with the students, the women come to the realization that they are more than their sentence, more than their mistakes, and more than victims of their circumstances. Most importantly, they understand how much their stories matter to other women, and that sharing their stories potentially sparks change and hope in others. "If my story can inspire even just one other woman," implored Charlotte, "then I've done something I never dreamed I'd do."

It's Criminal does not shy away from conflict and disagreement, exposing the way that class and racial differences complicate the aspiration for feminist solidarity. In a memorable sequence, Malika, who is serving a twelve-month sentence, and Georgia, who admits to having an idyllic childhood and parents who pay full tuition, in their separate interviews with the filmmakers admit to hating one another. Lovely, white, young Georgia feels put out by Malika's stink eye and cold shoulder. Strong and vocal Malika seethes at Georgia's insensitive decision to wear expensive pearls to her first visit to the women's unit: "How dare she wear those pearls here?" she criticizes. During another moment of conflict, the incarcerated women tell Pati that they feel exploited by the project; they feel exposed and vulnerable, forced to share intimate details of their lives to the students, who share little to nothing about their own experiences. The politics of difference are central to the lives of the women in this film, and central to the vision of feminism that the film constructs.

Like so many documentaries that chart slow progress towards a shared goal, the tension builds as the group wonders if they are going to be able to pull off the big event. Numerous scenes of women setting up the stage, arranging costumes, feeling rushed and nervous, create a delicious tension in the audience. By the time we get to the performance, we are eager to see what the women wrote and developed over the course of the semester. However, the film holds back on delivering the full performance, opting instead for a swift montage of scenes from the magical evening. Instead of the performance, the film focuses on the effect of the evening on the participants and their audience. Under a summer canopy of outdoor lights, audience members from local communities, including the families of the incarcerated women, marvel at what the group has accomplished. They clap enthusiastically, shed emotional tears, and stand to tell the performers how moved they were. *It's Criminal* momentarily "tears down the walls" that initially separate the women so drastically from one another, and from the audience both within and outside the film.[9]

In the film's final scenes, everyone in the performance wears costumes, makeup, wigs. The audience of the profilmic performance cannot tell the inmates from the students. Even for the documentary audience, who by this point in the film is familiar with the women's faces, the class participants have momentarily accomplished the goal of tearing down walls and seeing each other and themselves anew through an activated feminist lens. In the Dallas audience, during the updates at the end of the film, we clapped loudly at positive news about the women's experiences after their release. Snapshots of their marriages, children, jobs, success, and setbacks felt near and dear to us in the audience. We also noticed persistent differences between the women: this Dartmouth grad works at an investment firm, that one as a real estate agent; that formerly incarcerated woman worked at a fast food restaurant or had returned to jail. The results were not uniformly positive; they too were haunted by and consistently subjected to realities beyond the scope of the documentary.

In the audience that surrounded me that night in Dallas, the walls also momentarily came down. Charlotte, Signe, and Pati shared the stage, and the audience, which included more than thirty participants from a local rehabilitation program for previously incarcerated women run by the Salvation Army, clapped and cried along with them. In their comments, the Dallas women explained how they identified deeply with the women in the film. They asked how they might become facilitators like Pati, how they might give back, share what they've lived, bring others up with them. This, too, is the power of feminist documentaries. So deeply committed to giving voice, space, and time to the faces, bodies, and experiences of women, they create intoxicating if elusive moments of identification and solidarity.

Scene Two

At the Lakewest Family YMCA in Dallas, months after the screening of *It's Criminal,* I attended a screening of Cynthia and Allen Mondell*'s Beauty in the Bricks* (1980), which had been organized by local activist Olinka Green. Much to Green's surprise, the size of the audience almost exceeded the capacity of the small space as subjects from the film, family members, community organizers, activists, and fans of the Mondells braved a cold, rainy morning to see this unique document of life in West Dallas in the late seventies. Shot almost exclusively as a vérite documentary, *Beauty in the Bricks* follows a group of young women involved in the first local Girl's Club chapter under the leadership of Audrey Hinton. With Hinton's strong and empathetic guidance, the girls experiment with filmmaking, art, life skills, sports, and more, building confidence and community as they laugh, play, and take risks toward a future outside the projects. The title captures the ambition of the documentary, which was clearly in part to show the happiness, resilience, and strength of the young girls not merely in spite of their material circumstances, but within and because of them.

The project began when in 1979, the white, Jewish filmmaking couple Cynthia Salzman Mondell and her husband Allen were invited to document a theatrical performance organized by the Girls' Club in West Dallas. Impacted by the girls and the role that the club played in their lives, the couple decided to stay and film a longer project. As Allen Mondell explained at the screening I attended, the couple spent about eight weeks among the young women, asking almost no questions but hoping to "capture a way of life and not to have any judgment on it."[10] At the time, the West Dallas housing project was notoriously defined by poverty and race, bearing the nickname "the monument to poverty."[11] In the early part of the century, West Dallas was the dusty rural outpost that gave rise to

Promotional image for *Beauty in the Bricks* by Media Projects, Inc. Pictured are Michelle Wells, Karen Morgan, Teresa Evans, and Tina Williams. (Courtesy of Media Projects, Inc.)

the legendary tale of Bonnie and Clyde. By the seventies, however, West Dallas was still poor, but also primarily black and brown. Yet community leaders and nonprofits like the Girls' Club had a strong presence within West Dallas, which has also been said to have "a rare and vibrant spirit."[12] The now-grown women in the documentary remember their lives growing up in West Dallas as safe, communal, and lively despite the challenges they faced in a deeply segregated city with visible white supremacist activity. Into this world stepped the unlikely filmmaking couple, outsiders by race, class, and religion, but welcomed in and urged to document the complex dreams, hopes, and challenges that took place there.

Now in her midforties, Olinka Green happened to watch *Beauty in the Bricks* when it screened on public television in Dallas in the early 1980s and found herself profoundly moved by the documentary, which showed a life so close to her own. As she matured, Green explained in her introduction to the screening, she consistently thought about the girls in the film. When she struggled as a survivor of domestic violence and a homeless mother of three in her early twenties, Green thought back to the determination, optimism, and grit embodied by the young women in *Beauty in the Bricks*. Prompted by a new moment of activism for racial justice today, Green decided that if the film could make such an impact on her life, surely others needed to see it, too. In her words, "*Beauty in the Bricks* changed my life. Now it will change others."[13]

The idea that documentaries can change lives is a familiar one for scholars. Although only a handful of documentaries have been known to make tangible changes to the material world, all of us know that documentaries certainly instigate and inspire participation in political, ethical, and affective change. Occasionally, a public screening like the event Green organized manifests that unique power of documentaries. In that modest space at a free screening in a local Y, where the extension cord had to be replaced and the DVD refused at first to cooperate, filmmakers, filmed subjects, community members, and families defied the traditional walls erected by race, class, and gender in the city of Dallas. Instead, matters of experience, voice, time, and reality consolidated our attention in solidarity. Songs were sung, tears were shed, friends were reunited, and new friendships were inaugurated. The thirty-minute documentary had captured a way of life, a texture of feeling, the permanence of being for a community that had so rarely seen itself represented by cinema or television. Those of us who may have been outsiders to their world were momentarily a part of its validation and celebration.

In a key scene in *Beauty in the Bricks,* a group of teenage girls fills a small bedroom. Draped over pillows and perched on furniture, the girls are giddy and performative. Bebe, an aspiring dancer and singer, takes center stage with a bravado lip-sync performance to "Sandra Dee" from the hit musical *Grease* (1978). In the film *Grease,* Olivia Newton-John plays Sandy, a delicate 1950s Pollyanna who revamps her look and her sass to win over John Travolta's bad boy, Danny. In the original "Sandra Dee" number, the other high school girls mock Sandy's naiveté and her lack of experience with cigarettes, sex, and alcohol. When the beauties of West Dallas perform the number, they drink from capped bottles and drag off fake cigarettes, upping the campiness with parody and excess. They perform their roles to a tee, effectively staging a takeover of Hollywood, if only for a moment. In their playful parody, however, they also unveil the latent racial politics of *Grease,* which, after all, is shaped around a narrative in which white kids triumph over a rival high school's band of browner, sexier, and edgier leaders. The young black girls of West Dallas may not have had the attention of Hollywood, but they certainly won the attention of issue-driven filmmakers Cynthia Salzman Mondell and Allen Mondell, who granted them the authority of documentary in the space and time of cinema.

Cynthia and Allen's legacy in social-justice documentaries resonates deeply with the overarching narrative I develop in this book about the long-standing commitments to solidarity and difference in the entwined history of visual ethnography, gender politics, and documentary. Like the Johnsons and the Flahertys before them, the Mondells' collaborative filmmaking belongs firmly within the history of women's documentary filmmaking; Cynthia's vision and commitment to matters of gender and racial equity shaped the couple's collective work for decades. Their body of work includes more than forty documentaries about slavery, domestic violence, anti-Semitism, divorce, suicide, ladies' restrooms, women comedians, and much more. Furthermore, Cynthia and Allen, along with Joyce Chopra and Amalie Rothschild, whom I discuss in chapter 3, were early members of New Day Films, a feminist distribution collective that continues to support and exhibit social-justice documentaries.

Whereas filmmaking hot spots like New York and Boston nurtured numerous filmmakers at the heart of this book, Cynthia Salzman Mondell and Allen Mondell, transplants from the East Coast city of Baltimore, built their careers in Dallas, and initially with the support of public television. In Dallas the couple found a supportive community of media makers and social-justice activists. Cynthia's participation in feminist organizations in Dallas in the 1970s led her to make a film about "displaced homemakers," middle-aged women who had been divorced by their husbands and effectively abandoned without financial or emotional resources. *Who Remembers Mama?* (1978) features a number of women's stories from across the spectrum of race and class. The documentary also features reenacted scenes set in a courtroom, which highlighted the sexism that structured divorce, custody, and child support proceedings.

Like their colleagues at New Day, Cynthia and Allen traveled with their film, showing it widely to community groups, activists, politicians, and students. They saw how the film impacted people from local audiences in Dallas to places as far away as Moscow. Early in their careers they became persuaded that film could be a "powerful tool for social change"—a conviction that has continued to drive their filmmaking.[14] Cynthia remarks that *Who Remembers Mama?* especially consolidated her filmmaking ethos, which holds fast to the idea that people care about issues, that robust audiences exist for this mode of filmmaking, and that film is a masterful tool of social change. *Who Remembers Mama?* also focused the couple's attention on distribution and inspired them to make films together. Working as a couple in fact improved their marriage, in Cynthia's opinion. They had equal commitments to the work and could balance their domestic and waged labor more equitably. Moreover, the issues they documented were pertinent to their own lives.

Who Remembers Mama? also shaped the way Cynthia would prioritize racial diversity in her feminist and collaborative work with her husband. Conversations within her feminist groups at the time often centered on matters of diversity and racial and class differences among women and how these differences structured their varied experiences in the world. Both filmmakers also point to their Jewish upbringing in Baltimore as instrumental in their commitments to social justice, especially as advocates for other disenfranchised groups. The Jewish mandate of *Tikkun Ha'Olam*, which translates as "repair of the world," became central to their artistic, professional, and personal endeavors, clearly driving their attention to social issues—racism, sexism, poverty, mental health—in need of repair.[15] Like her contemporaries Joyce Chopra, Amalie Rothschild, Claudia Weill, Barbara Kopple, Michelle Citron, and others, Cynthia Salzman Mondell and other Jewish women vitally shaped both second-wave feminism and the recent history of feminist documentary filmmaking.[16] Revisiting the contributions of these women as emblems of the entwined history of documentary, ethnography, and feminism as I do in *Subject to Reality* brings their work from the margins of documentary history into the center, where revised narratives about gender, race, class, and ethnicity begin to emerge.

This book has argued that the subjects of reality at stake in women's documentary filmmaking are vigorously shaped by political ideologies of race, class, ethnicity, gender, and sexuality. The realist aesthetics of women's documentary filmmaking, moreover, have intersected both aggressively and constructively with the ethos of ethnographic filmmaking throughout the twentieth and twenty-first centuries. Reading women's documentary filmmaking for its ethnographic valences reveals women filmmakers' enduring willingness to engage with the political and ethical complexities of difference—which I see as the vital life force of feminist thinking, acting, and being. As feminist scholars, we have more often deployed the significant power of our critiques against misogynist media and even against feminist media that misses the mark than we have reparatively embraced feminist media that brings down walls. *Subject to Reality* investigates the contours of women's documentary aesthetics, ethics, and politics in hopes of both destabilizing and expanding the canon of women's production throughout the long history and future of documentary. The work continues; but for now, I end this book with a call urging feminist and documentary scholars to continue to pursue both recuperative and transformational forays into global archives of women's film production, where neglected, misremembered, and complex legacies surely await their turn.

Notes

Book Epigraph

1. Cherríe Moraga, "Catching Fire: Preface to the Fourth Edition," *This Bridge Called My Back: Writings by Radical Women of Color,* eds. Cherríe Moraga and Gloria Anzaldúa (Albany: State University of New York Press, 2015), xix.

Introduction

1. Barbara Martineau, "Thoughts About the Objectification of Women," *Take One* 3, no. 2 (February 1972): 15–18.

2. Estelle B. Freedman, "The New Woman: Changing Views of Women in the 1920s," *Journal of American History* 61, no. 2 (September 1974): 372–93.

3. Jan Rosenberg, *Women's Reflections: The Feminist Film Movement* (Ann Arbor, Mich.: UMI Research Press, 1983), 35. Rosenberg's interviews with filmmakers, several of whom I also discuss in this book, include valuable details about their backgrounds and education. See chapter 3 "The Filmmakers," 25–46.

4. Kristen Fallica, "Sustaining Feminist Film Cultures: An Institutional History of Women Make Movies." Doctoral dissertation, 2013, University of Pittsburgh. Also see "Looking Back and Forward: A Conversation About Women Make Movies," *Camera Obscura* 28.1.82 (2013): 147–55.

5. Paula Rabinowitz, *They Must Be Represented* (New York: Verso, 1994), 131.

6. Ibid. See chapters 6 and 7. Also see Rabinowitz, "Medium Uncool: Women Shoot Back; Feminism, Film and 1968—A Curious Documentary," *Science & Society* 65, no. 1 (Spring 2000): 72–98.

7. Rabinowitz, *They Must Be Represented,* 157.

8. Ibid.

9. Rabinowitz mentions "cinema vérite" feminist documentaries like *Janie's Jane* (Ashur et al., 1971). However, she sees them as realist attempts to "authenticate women's lives on screen" and does not explore their ethnographic valences (161). Similarly, as I discuss later in the book, Alisa Lebow's *First Person Jewish* mentions but does not investigate Jewish women filmmakers of the 1970s with the exception of Michelle Citron, whose fabulous oeuvre also challenges realist conventions in documentary.

10. Amelie Hastie, "The 'Whatness' of *Ms.* magazine and 1970s Film Criticism," *Feminist Media Histories* 1, no. 3 (Summer 2015): 5.

11. Helen Powdermaker, *Hollywood, the Dream Factory: An Anthropologist Looks at the Movie-Makers* [1950] (Los Angeles: Martino Fine Books, 2013).

12. Diane Waldman and Janet Walker, eds., *Feminism and Documentary* (Minneapolis: University of Minnesota Press, 1999).

13. Ibid., 13–19.

14. For scholarship on women and early cinema, see Jennifer M. Bean and Diane Negra, *A Feminist Reader in Early Cinema* (Durham, N.C.: Duke University Press, 2002); Karen Ward Mahar, *Women Filmmakers in Early Hollywood* (Baltimore: Johns Hopkins University Press, 2006); Vicki Callahan, *Reclaiming the Archive: Feminism and Film History* (Detroit: Wayne State University Press, 2010); Christine Gledhill and Julia Knight, *Doing Women's Film History* (Urbana: University of Illinois Press, 2015).

15. For example, my research on early women documentary filmmakers was inspired by the valuable biographic entries in the *Women Film Pioneers Project.* Jane Gaines, Radha Vatsal, and Monica Dall'Asta, eds., *Women Film Pioneers Project*, Center for Digital Research and Scholarship (New York: Columbia University Libraries, 2013). Available at https://wfpp.cdrs.columbia.edu.

16. Key exceptions include Clarissa Jacob and Kate Wieteska's recovery of the *Women & Film*, the first feminist film magazine. See Jacob, "Women & Film," *Feminist Media Histories* 1, no. 1 (2015): 153–62. Also, Alexandra Juhasz's body of work, including *Women of Vision: Histories in Feminist Film and Video* (Minneapolis: University of Minnesota Press, 2001) and "The Future Was Then: Reinvesting in Feminist Media Practice and Politics," *Camera Obscura* 21, no. 1 (2006): 53–57. Patricia White, "The Last Days of Women's Cinema," *Camera Obscura* 21, no. 3 (2006): 145–52. Amelie Hastie, "The 'Whatness' of *Ms. Magazine* and 1970s Feminist Film Criticism," *Feminist Media Histories* 1, no. 3 (Summer 2015): 4–37.

17. Barbara Evans, oral presentation at Visible Evidence XXII, Toronto, Canada, August 2015.

18. Ellen Strain, *Public Places, Private Journeys: Ethnography, Entertainment, and the Tourist* (New Brunswick, N.J.: Rutgers University Press, 2003). See also Vivian Sobchack, *Carnal Thoughts: Embodiment and Moving Image Culture* (Berkeley: University of California Press), 181.

19. Ella Shohat and Robert Stam, *Unthinking Eurocentrism: Multiculturalism and the Media* (New York: Routledge, 2013), 100.

20. Ibid., 106.

21. Ibid.

22. Strain, *Public Places,* and Heidegger, "The Age of the World Picture," in *The Question Concerning Technology and Other Essays* (New York: Harper & Row, 1977), 115–54.

23. Walter Benjamin, "Theses on the Philosophy of History," *Illuminations,* Trans. Harry Zohn (New York: Houghton Mifflin Harcourt, 1985), 257.

24. Alice Walker, "Looking for Zora," *Ms.* magazine (1975).

25. Exceptions include: Gloria Gibson, "Cinematic Foremothers: Zora Neale Hurston and Eloyce King Patrick Gist," in *Oscar Micheaux and His Circle: African-American Filmmaking and Race Cinema of the Silent Era,* edited by Pearl Bowser, Jane Gaines, and Charles Musser (Bloomington: Indiana University Press, 2001) and Elaine Charnov, "The Performative Visual Anthropology Films of Zora Neale Hurston," *Film Criticism* 23.1 (1998).

26. Maryse Holder, "First International Festival of Women's Films: In New York City," *off our backs* 3.1 (September 30, 1972).

27. See Laura Mulvey's critique of women's documentary in "Feminism and the Avant Garde," *Framework* 10 (Spring 1979): 3–10.

28. Susan Kleckner, "A Personal Decade," *Heresies* 16 (1983): 77.

29. Joan Wallach Scott, "Feminist Reverberations," *differences: A Journal of Feminist Cultural Studies* 13, no. 3 (Fall 2002): 6.

30. Sophie Mayer, *Political Animals: The New Feminist Cinema* (London and New York: IB Tauris, 2016).

31. B. Ruby Rich's *Chick Flicks* (Durham, N.C.: Duke University Press, 1998).

32. Sue Thornham, *What If I Had Been the Hero: Investigating Women's Cinema* (London: British Film Institute, 2012).

33. Belinda Smaill, "Cinema Against the Age: Feminism and Contemporary Documentary," *Screening the Past,* August 2012, http://www.screeningthepast.com/2012/08/cinema-against-the-age-feminism-and-contemporary-documentary/ Accessed July 20, 2017.

34. Ibid., np.

35. Domatilla Ovieri, "Haunted by Reality, Toward a Feminist Study of Documentary Film: Indexicality, Vision and the Artifice," Ph.D. dissertation, Utrecht University, The Netherlands, 2012.

36. Scott, "Feminist Reverberations," 6.

37. Alexandra Juhasz, "'They Said We Were Trying to Show Reality- All I Want to Show Is My Video: The Politics of the Realist Feminist Documentary," *Screen* 35:2 (Summer 1994): 171–90.

38. Diane Waldman and Janet Walker, eds. *Feminism and Documentary* (Minneapolis: University of Minnesota Press, 1999).

39. George Kouvaros, "'We Do Not Die Twice': Realism and Cinema," in *The Sage Handbook of Film Studies,* eds. James Donald and Michael Renov (London: Sage Publications, 2008), 376.

40. "Film and (as) Modernity," in Donald and Renov, eds., *Handbook of Film Studies* (London: Sage, 2008), 343. See, for example, Colin MacCabe's 1974 essay, "Realism and the Cinema," his 1976 essay, "Theory and Film: Principles of Realism and Pleasure," and Stephen Heath's 1975–1976 essay, "From Brecht to Film: Theses, Problems," and Heath, "Narrative Space" from 1976, all published in *Screen*. Also relevant is Raymond Williams's 1977, "A Lecture on Realism." *Screen* published a special issue on "Brecht and a Revolutionary Cinema" in 1974, and Dick Hebdige and Geoff Hurd summarize *Screen*'s position on realism in "Reading Realism," in a 1978 edition of *Screen Education*. Also see Christopher Williams's eclectic book, *Realism and the Cinema: A Reader* (London: Routledge and Kegan Paul, in association with the British Film Institute, 1980) for excerpts on these and a host of other texts at stake in the realist/anti-realist debates of seventies film theory.

41. Kouvaros, "We Do Not Die Twice," 378.

42. Laura Marcus, "Cinematic Realism: 'A Recreation of the World in its Own Image'," *Adventures in Realism* (Malden, Mass.: Blackwell Publishing, 2007), 189.

43. Jane Gaines, "The Real Returns," introduction, in *Collecting Visible Evidence,* eds. Jane Gaines and Michael Renov (Minneapolis: University of Minnesota Press, 1999), 10.

44. Claire Johnston, ed., *Notes on Women's Cinema,* Vol. 2. (London: Society for Education in Film and Television, 1973), 214.

45. Ibid., 215.

46. Ibid., 214. Essays that celebrate these same films include: Susan Rice, *"Three Lives"* Review, *Women & Film* 1, no. 1 (1972): 66. Ruth McCormick, "Women's Liberation Cinema," *Cineaste* 5, no. 2 (Spring 1972): 1–7.

47. Johnston, *Notes on Women's Cinema,* 215.

48. Toril Moi, *Henrik Ibsen and the Birth of Modernism: Art, Theater, Philosophy* (Oxford, U.K.: Oxford University Press, 2006), 23.

49. Moi, *Henrik Ibsen and the Birth of Modernism,* 19.

50. Ibid., 24.

51. Ibid., 31.

52. Fredric Jameson, "A Note on Literary Realism in Conclusion," *Adventures in Realism* (Malden, Mass.: Blackwell Publishing, 2007), 261. Moi's conversation with Jameson's notion of the ideology of modernism occurs through *A Singular Modernity: Essay on the Ontology of the Present* (London: Verso, 2002). Here, I evoke a separate essay by Jameson.

53. Moi, *Henrik Ibsen and the Birth of Modernism,* 31.

54. Ivone Margulies, *Rites of Realism: Essays on Corporeal Cinema* (Durham, N.C.: Duke University Press, 2003), 5.

55. For more on the Visible Evidence Series, initially published by the University of Minnesota Press and edited by Michael Renov, Faye Ginsburg, and Jane Gaines see Michael Renov's concluding essay in *Collecting Visible Evidence,* "Documentary Horizons: An Afterword." Renov comments that the books in the series indicate trends in the field of documentary studies, away from "its once single-minded focus on docu-

mentary film history, aesthetics, and ideological criticism in favor of producing a kind of *situated knowledge* in which cultural representation is linked to larger social and historical forces" (321).

56. Elizabeth Cowie, *Recording Reality: Desiring the Real* (Minneapolis: University of Minnesota Press, 2011). Belinda Smaill, *The Documentary: Politics, Emotion, Culture* (Basingstoke, U.K.: Palgrave Macmillan, 2015). Ilona Hongisto, *Soul of the Documentary: Framing, Expression, Ethics* (Amsterdam: Amsterdam University Press, 2015).

57. Alexandra Juhasz, *Women of Vision: Histories in Feminist Film and Video* (Minneapolis: University of Minnesota Press, 2001), 1.

58. Ibid., 2.

59. Hastie, The 'Whatness' of *Ms.* magazine, 18.

60. Ibid.

61. Clare Hemmings, *Why Stories Matter: The Political Grammar of Feminist Theory* (Durham, N.C.: Duke University Press, 2010).

62. Ibid., 1.

63. Ibid., 3.

64. Stamp writes, "Individual case studies—which are mounting at an impressive pace—ought to be drawn together and mobilized in the service of a new overarching narrative, a narrative that asserts the fundamental importance of women's engagement with early film culture." "Feminist Media Historiography and the Work Ahead," *Screening the Past* 40 (2015), available at http://www.screeningthepast.com/2015/08/feminist-media-historiography-and-the-work-ahead/ (accessed June 10, 2016).

65. Pam Cook, "Border Crossing: Women and Film in Context," in Pam Cook and Philip Dodd, eds., *Women and Film: A Sight and Sound Reader* (Philadelphia: Temple University Press, 1993): ix–xxiii.

66. Barbara Martineau, "Women's Film Daily," *Women and Film* 1, no. 5–6 (1974): 41.

67. Chick Strand and Irina Leimbacher, *Chick Strand: Seeing in Between* (Berkeley, Calif.: Pacific Film Archive, 1994).

68. Trinh Minh-ha's work includes: *Reassemblage* (40 mins, 1982); *Surname Viet Given Name Nam* (108 mins, 1989); and *Forgetting Vietnam* (90 mins, digital, 2015). Minh-ha has published more than twelve books, for example, *Lovecidal, Walking with the Disappeared* (New York: Fordham University Press, 2016); *D-Passage. The Digital Way* (Durham, N.C.: Duke University Press, 2013); *Cinema Interval* (New York and London: Routledge, 1999); *Framer Framed* (New York and London: Routledge 1992); and *Woman, Native, Other. Writing Postcoloniality and Feminism* (Bloomington: Indiana University Press, 1989).

69. See Geyla Frank, "The Ethnographic Films of Barbara G. Myerhoff: Anthropology, Feminism, and the Politics of Jewish Identity," *Women Writing Culture,* eds. Ruth Behar and Deborah A. Gordon (Berkeley: University of California Press, 1995), 207–32.

70. Scott MacDonald, *American Ethnographic Film and Personal Documentary: The Cambridge Turn* (Berkeley: University of California Press, 2013).

Chapter 1. Filming Among Others:
Frances Flaherty and Osa Johnson

1. The term "contact zone" was first used by Mary Louise Pratt in "Arts of the Contact Zone" (1991) and developed further in *Imperial Eyes: Travel Writing and Transculturation,* 2nd ed. (New York: Routledge, 2007).

2. Fatimah Tobing Rony, *The Third Eye: Race, Cinema, and Ethnographic Spectacle* (Durham, N.C.: Duke University Press, 1996), 84.

3. Ellen Strain, *Public Places, Private Journeys: Ethnography, Entertainment, and the Tourist Gaze* (New Brunswick, N.J.: Rutgers University Press, 2003).

4. See Robert Christopher's *Robert and Frances Flaherty: A Documentary Life, 1883–1922* (Montreal and Kingston: McGill Queen's University Press, 2005), which includes Frances's original diary entries and letters.

5. Lewis Jacobs, *The Documentary Tradition* [1971] (New York: W.W. Norton, 1979), 7.

6. Patricia Aufderheide, *Documentary Film: A Very Short Introduction* (Oxford, U.K.: Oxford University Press, 2007), 2.

7. Lucien Taylor and Ilisa Barbash, *Cross Cultural Filmmaking: A Handbook for Making Documentary and Ethnographic Films and Videos* (Berkeley: University of California Press, 1997), 24.

8. Christopher, *Robert and Frances Flaherty,* 382.

9. Frances Flaherty, *The Odyssey of a Film-Maker* (Urbana, Ill.: Beta Phi Mu Chapbook, Number Four, 1960), 17.

10. *Nanook of the North.* Advertisement. Pathépicture, 1922.

11. Rony, *The Third Eye,* 101.

12. Ibid., 15.

13. John Grierson, "Flaherty's Poetic *Moana,*" *New York Sun,* February 8, 1926. Reprinted in Lewis Jacobs, ed., *The Documentary Tradition,* 2nd ed. (New York: W.W. Norton, 1979), 25.

14. Ibid, 25. My emphasis.

15. A very recent exception is Jonathan Rosenbaum, "Robert J. Flaherty's *Moana with Sound,*" *Artforum,* March 2016.

16. Christopher, *Robert and Frances Flaherty,* 202.

17. Ibid., 269.

18. Ibid., 269–70.

19. Ibid., xvi.

20. Ibid., 230.

21. I have Kimberly Lamm to thank for the term "emotional translator."

22. Frances Flaherty, *The Odyssey of a Film-maker: Robert Flaherty's Story* (Urbana, Ill.: Beta Phi Mu, 1960), 19.

23. Flaherty, *Odyssey of a Film-maker,* 19. Frederick O'Brien's *White Shadows in the South Seas* (New York: Garden City Publishing, 1919) was also made into an award-winning film in 1928 (W.S. Van Dyke).

24. Flaherty, *Odyssey of a Filmmaker,* 19.

25. Frances Flaherty, interview with Robert Gardner on *The Screening Room* (1960). On his unique broadcast television program, Gardner, an influential ethnographic filmmaker and founder and director of the Film Study Center at Harvard University (1957–1997), interviewed filmmakers and showed excerpts of their work. This interview is a stark example of Frances's labor as the emotional translator of her husband's work.

26. Flaherty, *Odyssey of a Filmmaker*, 27. Frances Flaherty read excerpts of her manuscript in *The Screening Room* interview with Robert Gardner later reproduced in *Restoration of Moana with Sound* (Kino Lorber, 2014).

27. Pascal James Imperato and Eleanor M. Imperato, *They Married Adventure: The Wandering Lives of Martin & Osa Johnson* (New Brunswick, N.J.: Rutgers University Press, 1992), 55.

28. One of the few profiles of her work as a woman in documentary is Laura Horak, "Osa Johnson," *Women Film Pioneers Project*, available at https://wfpp.cdrs.columbia.edu/pioneer/ccp-osa-johnson/.

29. Osa Johnson, "A Wife in Africa," *Photoplay* (June 1923): 32–34, 109.

30. Ibid.

31. Ibid.

32. Alison Griffiths, *Wondrous Difference: Cinema, Anthropology, and Turn-of-the-Century Visual Culture* (New York: Columbia University Press, 2002), 55.

33. The 1917 expedition was funded by Massachusetts investors, who raised $7,000 after receiving a letter of recommendation on Martin's behalf from Charmian London. With the financial backing Martin was able to form The Martin Johnson Film Co.

34. Imperato and Imperato, *They Married Adventure*, 68.

35. Not only did European colonial authorities host and transport the Johnsons around the South Pacific, but the Johnsons also agreed to not film brutal labor practices on colonial plantations. See Imperato and Imperato, *They Married Adventure*, 68.

36. The entire film is available at the Library of Congress, but an excerpt can be seen here: http://goo.gl/jOsDT1, accessed November 17, 2015.

37. Imperato and Imperato cite glowing reviews in *Variety*, the *New York Times*, and *Motion Picture News*, 74–75.

38. Imperato and Imperato, *They Married Adventure*, 11.

39. Remarkably, that second South Pacific film contains footage of the Tomman Islanders watching themselves in *Cannibals of the South Seas*, an event that marks one of the first times in film history that filmmakers filmed their subjects viewing their work.

40. Cynthia Chris, *Watching Wildlife* (Minneapolis: University of Minnesota Press, 2006), 3.

41. Imperato and Imperato, *They Married Adventure*, 70.

42. Osa's book was the number-one national bestseller in nonfiction for 1940 and sold more than 500,000 copies within its first year of publication (Imperato and Imperato, *They Married Adventure*, 209).

43. In "A Wife in Africa," for example, Osa describes her interactions with native women. "They tried to be wellbred and polite and they didn't laugh at me when they thought I could see them. Some of them were real true friends, too." "The African women are really very decent folks."

44. Imperato and Imperato, *They Married Adventure,* 212.

45. Shelley Stamp, "Feminist Media Historiography and the Work Ahead," *Screening the Past* 40 (2015): np, available at http://www.screeningthepast.com/2015/08/feminist-media-historiography-and-the-work-ahead/, accessed March 4, 2018.

46. Ibid.

Chapter 2. Anthropological Visions Inside and Out: Zora Neale Hurston and Margaret Mead

1. Kamala Visweswaran, "Histories of Feminist Ethnography," *Annual Review of Anthropology* 26 (1997): 594.

2. Nancy Lutkehaus, *Margaret Mead: The Making of an American Icon* (Princeton, N.J. and Oxford, U.K.: Princeton University Press, 2008), 153.

3. Gloria Gibson, "Cinematic Foremothers: Zora Neale Hurston and Eloyce King Patrick Gist," in *Oscar Micheaux and His Circle: African-American Filmmaking and Race Cinema of the Silent Era,* edited by Pearl Bowser, Jane Gaines, and Charles Musser (Bloomington: Indiana University Press, 2001), 196.

4. Zora Neale Hurston was born in 1891 and died in 1960. Carla Kaplan established Hurston's birthday (long under debate) in *Zora Neale Hurston: A Life in Letters* (New York: Anchor Books, 2003), 37.

5. For a thorough history of the use of the motion picture camera by anthropologists, see Alison Griffiths, *Wondrous Difference: Cinema, Anthropology, and Turn-of-the-Century Visual Culture* (New York: Columbia University Press, 2002), 309.

6. Elaine Charnov, "The Performative Visual Anthropology Films of Zora Neale Hurston," *Film Criticism* 23.1 (1998): 39.

7. Robert E. Hemenway, *Zora Neale Hurston: A Literary Biography* (Urbana: University of Illinois Press, 1980), 115.

8. In fact, Hurston submitted four works to the *Opportunity* literary contest organized by Charles Johnson in 1925. Her short story "Spunk" and her play *Color Struck* both won second place in their categories. Her other two works of fiction, "Black Death" and *Spears,* won honorable mentions.

9. Hazel V. Carby, "The Politics of Fiction, Anthropology, and the Folk," in *New Essays on Their Eyes Were Watching God,* edited by Michael Awkward (Cambridge, U.K.: University of Cambridge Press, 1990), 81.

10. Hurston describes her own interest in anthropology in *Mules and Men* (1935): "It was only when I was off in college, away from my native surroundings that I could see myself like somebody else and stand off and look at my garment. Then I had to have the spy-glass of Anthropology to look through at that" (204).

11. Carla Kaplan repeats this line from "Characteristics of Negro Expression," which Hurston published in 1934 in the voice-over commentary on the DVD version of Hurston's footage. In *Sweat,* edited by Cheryl Wall (New Brunswick, N.J.: Rutgers University Press, 1997), 55–71.

12. Hemenway cites William Wells Brown's collection of folksongs in *My Southern Home* (1880), Charles Chesnutt's rendition of hoodoo practices, the Hampton Institute, which founded the first black folklore society, and Arthur Huff Fauset of Philadelphia, who collected animal tales in the Mississippi Delta, for example, and refuted the notion that the Uncle Remus stories were proper folklore (Hemenway 86, 90). White folklorists of black culture were obviously more prominent. In the 1920s, the most celebrated among these included Guy Johnson and Howard Odum.

13. Carla Kaplan, *Zora Neale Hurston: A Life in Letters* (New York: Knopf Doubleday, 2007), 49.

14. Hemenway, *Zora Neale Hurston,* 87.

15. Ibid., 21.

16. Ibid., 21.

17. Ibid., 63.

18. Charnov, "Performative Visual Anthropology Films," 39.

19. Gwendolyn Mikell, "The Anthropological Imagination of Zora Neale Hurston," *Western Journal of Black Studies* (Spring 1983): 27.

20. Hurston, *Mules and Men,* 17.

21. Griffiths, *Wondrous Difference,* 309.

22. Ibid., 304–5.

23. Ibid., 306.

24. Graciela Hernandez, "Multiple Subjectivities and Strategic Positionality: Zora Neale Hurston's Experimental Ethnographies," in *Women Writing Culture,* edited by Ruth Behar and Deborah A. Gordon (Berkeley and Los Angeles: University of California Press, 1995), 159.

25. Ibid., 151.

26. Hemenway, *Zora Neale Hurston,* 84, 89.

27. An exception here was her collection of conjure and hoodoo practices, which fascinated Hurston, who would go on to study them in Haiti and Jamaica.

28. Hemenway, *Zora Neale Hurston,* 109.

29. A selection of these films is also distributed by the National Film Preservation. Library of Congress: "Eight 16mm rolls of footage taken in Florida between 1927 and 1929 were identified as Hurston material . . . seven 16mm rolls taken in South Carolina in April and May 1940 are also Hurston films." http://www.loc.gov/folklife/guides/ Hurston.html. Rony also mentions the films Hurston made in 1940 in Beaufort, South Carolina. These were financed by Jane Belo and were made with the help of filmmaking professionals. Hurston herself appears in the films as worshipper.

30. Carla Kaplan's voice-over on the DVD.

31. Hemenway, *Zora Neale Hurston*, 110.

32. Ibid., 116.

33. Ibid., 112.

34. Charnov, "Performative Visual Anthropology Films," 39.

35. In her voice-over commentary on the DVD, Carla Kaplan observes that women were rarely present at work-sites like these, and so Hurston was undoubtedly interested in the effect of her presence on the other workers.

36. Fatimah Tobing Rony, *The Third Eye: Race, Cinema, and Ethnographic Spectacle* (Durham, N.C.: Duke University Press, 1996), 111.

37. Ibid., 111.

38. Mikell, "Anthropological Imagination," 32.

39. Richard Wright, review *Their Eyes Were Watching God, New Masses* October 5, 1937, 22–23.

40. Carby, "Politics of Fiction," 80.

41. Kaplan, *A Life in Letters*, 29.

42. Gibson, "Cinematic Foremothers."

43. Gibson, "Identities Unmasked/Empowerment Unleashed: The Documentary Style of Michelle Parkerson," *Feminism and Documentary*, eds. Diane Waldman and Janet Walker (Minneapolis: University of Minnesota Press, 1999), 140.

44. Bobo, "Black Women's Films: Genesis of a Tradition," in *Black Women Film and Video Artists*, ed. Jacqueline Bobo (New York: Routledge, 1988), 9.

45. In Anderson's film, Bobo detects a trend of highlighting black women as "human beings" (8) in a way that resonates with post–civil rights documentaries about African Americans. Other important 1970s films by black women were: *Valerie: A Woman, An Artist, a Philosophy of Life* (1975) by Monica Freeman, and Jacqueline Shearer's *A Minor Altercation* (1977).

46. Dolores Janiewski and Lois W. Banner, *Reading Benedict/Reading Mead: Feminism, Race, and Imperial Visions* (Baltimore and London: Johns Hopkins University Press, 2004), xiv.

47. Louise Lamphere, "Feminist Anthropology: The Legacy of Elsie Clews Parsons," *Women Writing Culture*, eds. Ruth Behar and Deborah A. Gordon (Berkeley and Los Angeles: University of California Press, 1995), 95.

48. It wasn't until 1984 that Catherine Bateson revealed these details about her mother's life.

49. For an examination of the precise differences between Benedict and Mead, see Barbara Babcock, "'Not in the Absolute Singular': Rereading Ruth Benedict," *Women Writing Culture*, 104–30 and Janiewski and Banner's *Reading Benedict/Reading Mead*.

50. See Babcock, "Not in the Absolute Singular," on the shift between empirical anthropology and "culture and personality students in anthropology," 114. The shift was inspired in part by new studies in psychology and psychiatry.

51. Behar, "Introduction: Out of Exile," in *Women Writing Culture*, 9.

52. Lutkehaus, *Margaret Mead*, xiii.

53. Ibid., 98.

54. Ibid., 98.

55. Behar, "Introduction: Out of Exile," in *Women Writing Culture*, 8.

56. Mead's "now famous formulation (1935, p. 280): 'many, if not all, of the personality traits which we have called masculine or feminine are as lightly linked to sex as are the clothing, the manners, and the form of head-dress that a society at a given period assigns to either sex.'" Kamala Visweswaran, "Histories of Feminist Ethnography," *Annual Review of Anthropology* 26 (1997), 601.

57. Visweswaran, "Histories of Feminist Ethnography," 607.

58. Lutkehaus, *Margaret Mead*, 111.

59. Griffiths, *Wondrous Difference*, 283.

60. Mead, "Visual Anthropology in a Discipline of Words," *Principles of Visual Anthropology*, 3rd ed., ed. Paul Hockings (Berlin: Mouton de Gruyter, 2003), 7.

61. Ira Jacknis, "Margaret Mead and Gregory Bateson in Bali: Their Use of Photography and Film," *Cultural Anthropology* 3, no. 2 (May 1988): 160.

62. Jacknis writes, "All of their images were in black and white—the stills taken with a 35 mm Leica camera, mostly with a 50 mm lens, supplemented with 35, 73, and 200 mm lenses, and the films made with a 16 mm Movikon, with a hand-winder. Most of the film appears to have been shot at 16 frames per second. There was no means of recording sound. Bateson developed the stills himself, while the films were processed in Java," Note 9, p. 174. According to the archivists at the Library of Congress: "These materials consist primarily of the Bali Field Footage (22,600 feet) shot in Bali between 1936–39 and the Papua New Guinea: Iatmul People Field Footage (ca. 11,500 feet) recorded by Mead and Bateson in 1938. Much of this material is not yet available for public viewing because of the organizational and preservation challenges peculiar to this sub-set of the collection," "Preserving the Margaret Mead and Gregory Bateson Legacy: A Progress Report from the Library of Congress," by Patrick Loughney, Ph.D., M/B/RS Division, Library of Congress.

63. *Balinese Character: A Photographic Analysis* (1942), *Growth and Culture: A Photographic Study of Balinese Childhood* (1951). Both Bateson and Mead used their film footage primarily for teaching in the 1940s. In the 1950s Mead worked as editor, scriptwriter, and narrator with film editor Josef Bohmer on the production of a series of six films under the series title "Character Formation in Different Cultures." In 1979 she released their most famous film, *Learning to Dance in Bali*. See Jacknis, "Margaret Mead and Gregory Bateson in Bali," 170.

64. Jacknis, "Margaret Mead and Gregory Bateson in Bali," 160.

65. Though most refer to the films as the Bateson/Mead films, Henley goes straight for Mead because: "Not only was Mead the final author of the edited films but it is also arguable, as I shall discuss here, that both the original methodology on which they were based and the theoretical inspiration lying behind them came predominantly from Mead" (76).

66. Sol Worth, "Margaret Mead and the Shift from 'Visual Anthropology' to the 'Anthropology of Visual Communication,'" *Studies in Visual Communication* 6, no. 1 (1980): 15.

67. Mead, "As Significant as the Invention of Drama or the Novel," *TV Guide,* January 6, 1973, A61-A63.

68. Ibid., A61.

69. Mead, "Visual Anthropology in a Discipline of Words," 8.

70. Ibid., 6.

71. Ibid., 8–9.

72. Paul Henley, "From Documentation to Representation: Recovering the Films of Margaret Mead and Gregory Bateson," *Visual Anthropology* 26 (2013): 77.

73. Ibid., 33.

74. It's unclear why Mead and Bateson chose to record images without sound. Henley speculates that convenience and cost likely prevented the pair from using newer technology, although conceivably, the choice may also indicate Mead's general preference for vision over voice, especially considering the tendencies of the voice-over, which neglects any mention of the native subject's words. Henley, "From Documentation to Representation," 104.

75. Faye Ginsburg, "'Now Watch this Very Carefully . . .': The Ironies and Afterlife of Margaret Mead's Visual Anthropology," *The Scholar and Feminist Online*, published by the Barnard Center for Research on Women, vol. 1, no. 3 (2003). Available at http://sfonline.barnard.edu/mead/ginsbur3.htm. Accessed September 20, 2018.

76. Margaret Mead and Gregory Bateson, "On the use of the Camera in Anthropology," *Studies in the Anthropology of Visual Communication* 4, no. 2 (1977): 78.

77. Mead, "Visual Anthropology in a Discipline of Words," 9.

78. Mead and Bateson, "Camera in Anthropology," 78–80.

Chapter 3. Strangely Familiar: Autoethnography and Whiteness in Personal Documentaries

1. Laura Rascaroli, *The Personal Camera: Subjective Cinema and the Essay Film* (London and New York: Wallflower Press, 2009), 2.

2. Victoria Hesford, *Feeling Women's Liberation* (Durham, N.C. and London: Duke University Press, 2013), 130.

3. Carla Kaplan repeats this line from "Characteristics of Negro Expression," which Hurston published in 1934 in the voice-over commentary on the DVD version of Hurston's footage. In *Sweat,* edited by Cheryl Wall (New Brunswick, N.J.: Rutgers University Press, 1997), 55–71.

4. Mead's anthropological documentaries from the 1930s were collected under the title "Character Formation in Different Cultures." See Ira Jacknis, "Margaret Mead and Gregory Bateson in Bali: Their Use of Photography and Film," *Cultural Anthropology* 3, no. 2 (May 1988): 170.

5. See, for example, Alisa Lebow, *First Person Jewish* (Minneapolis and London: University of Minnesota Press, 2008) and Michael Renov, *The Subject of Documentary* (Minneapolis: University of Minnesota Press, 2004).

6. Scott MacDonald, *American Ethnographic Film and Personal Documentary: The Cambridge Turn* (Berkeley, Los Angeles, and London: University of California Press, 2013), 128.

7. Ibid., 4.

8. Ibid., 9.

9. Ibid., 134.

10. Kimberly Lamm, "On the Other Side of the Icon: Making Images of Women with Mary Harron," unpublished manuscript, 2017.

11. Lucy Fischer, *Cine-maternity: Film, Motherhood, Genre* (Princeton, N.J.: Princeton University Press, 1996), 188. Though Fischer mentions the films at stake in this chapter, she writes, "the seminal text was Michelle Citron's *Daughter Rite* (1978)," which "forged an experimental style" and, according to Fischer, birthed a "cinema of matrilineage" (189).

12. William Rothman, "Looking Back and Turning Inward: American Documentary Film of the Seventies," in *Lost Illusions: American Cinema in the Shadow of Watergate and Vietnam 1970–1979,* ed. David A. Cook (Berkeley and Los Angeles: University of California Press, 2000), 417–52.

13. Amelie Hastie, "The 'Whatness' of *Ms.* magazine and 1970s Film Criticism," *Feminist Media Histories* 1, no. 3 (Summer 2015): 20.

14. Lauren Rabinowitz observes that the Whitney's decision to program more than fifty new documentary and experimental films by women in 1973 was a result of demonstrations and lawsuits filed against the museum for its exclusion of women artists. See *Points of Resistance: Women, Power & Politics in the New York Avant-garde Cinema, 1943–71* (Champaign: University of Illinois Press, 1991), 191.

15. *Joyce at 34* was one of three documentaries about women with professions in the arts that screened in a program of shorts at the Whitney Museum of Art titled, "A New Consciousness," in February 1973. Roger Greenspun, "Documentaries About and by Women Are Shown," *New York Times,* February 16, 1973.

16. Personal communication with Joyce Chopra, October 29, 2016.

17. Chopra recounts that once the group of women began answering her question, they couldn't stop. When she and Weill later showed them the footage of the conversation, they apparently launched into it again, commenting on each other's responses. For Joyce, it was as if the filmmakers had "opened a floodgate," as if those women had never had an opportunity to reflect on the issues before (phone interview with the author, February 17, 2010).

18. Ironically, of course, Joyce's film takes place at a school full of children. As the filmmakers work to prepare the room for the shoot, setting up lights and sound, children cry, shout, and complain in the background.

19. Chopra confirmed that her intention was not to make a "feminist" film about motherhood per se. Rather, she describes her motivation to make the film as "selfish artistry." That is, after working on many films with the founding figures of direct

cinema (including Richard Leacock and the Maysles brothers), Chopra wanted to make her own film. When she was in her eighth month of pregnancy, a friend first suggested that she make a film about herself and her baby. Joyce initially scoffed at the idea. "It seemed too narcissistic." It was the viability of the topic that eventually attracted Chopra to the idea of making a personal documentary (phone interview with the author, February 17, 2010).

20. Mary Ann Doane elaborates on the use of voice-off and voice-over in cinema with a short section on documentary in "The Voice in Cinema," *Yale French Studies* no. 60 (1980): 33–50. She writes, "In the history of documentary, this voice has been for the most part that of the male, and its power resides in the possession of knowledge and in the privileged, unquestioned activity of interpretation," 42.

21. Chopra remembered that when the film first screened in New York City in a double booking with *I.F. Stone's Weekly* (Jerry Bruck Jr., 1973), theatergoers assumed that the film would be about James Joyce (phone interview, February 17, 2010). As Alisa Lebow remarks in her review of Jennifer Fox's *Flying: Confessions of a Free Woman* (2007), "Indeed there have been numerous feminist first person films as well, most of which raise at least some aspects detailed in Fox's project, having to do with gender roles of the "modern" woman. The very first film of this type was *Joyce at 34* (1972), which attempted to reconcile the roles of mother, wife, and filmmaker," *The Cinema of Me: The Self and Subjectivity in First Person Documentary* (New York: Columbia University Press, 2012), 442.

22. Lebow, *First Person Jewish.*

23. Ibid., xi.

24. Rascaroli, *Personal Camera,* 3.

25. Jan Rosenberg, *Women's Reflections: The Feminist Film Movement* (Ann Arbor: Umi Research Press, 1983), Alexandra Juhasz, "'They Said We Were Trying to Show Reality-All I Want to Show Is My Video: The Politics of the Realist Feminist Documentary," *Screen* 35:2 (Summer 1994): 171–90, and also Alexandra Juhasz, "Our Auto-Bodies Ourselves: Representing Real Women in Feminist Video," *Afterimage* 21, no. 7 (February 1997): 10–14. Jim Lane, *The Autobiographical Documentary in America* (Madison: University of Wisconsin Press, 2002).

26. Mazyar Lotfalian, "Autoethnography as Documentary in Iranian Films and Videos," *Anthropology of Contemporary Middle East and Central Eurasia* 1, no. 2 (Winter 2013): 126–42.

27. Catherine Russell, *Experimental Ethnography: The Work of Film in the Age of Video* (Durham, N.C.: and London: Duke University Press, 1999), 5.

28. Thommy Eriksson, "Being Native—Distance, Closeness and Doing Auto/Self-Ethnography," *ArtMonitor* 8 (2010): 91–100.

29. Barbara Applebaum, "Critical Whiteness Studies," in *Oxford Research Encyclopedia of Education* (Oxford, U.K.: Oxford University Press, 2016).

30. Chris McDonald, "Open Secrets: Individualism and Middle-Class Identity in the Songs of Rush," *Popular Music and Society* 31, no. 3 (July 2008): 313–28.

31. Jennifer Hurtsfield, "'Internal' Colonialism: White, Black and Chicano Self-Conceptions," *Ethnic and Racial Studies* 1, no. 1 (1978): 60–79.

32. Ibid., 69.

33. Ruth Frankenberg, *White Women, Race Matters: The Social Construction of Whiteness* (Minneapolis: University of Minnesota Press, 1993) and Richard Dyer, *White* (London and New York: Routledge, 1997).

34. Dyer, *White,* 4.

35. Ibid., 14.

36. Vicki Hesford, *Feeling Women's Liberation* (Durham, N.C.: Duke University Press, 2013), 1.

37. Ibid., 2.

38. Ibid.

39. Ibid., 5.

40. Ibid., 2.

41. Daniel Bernardi, "The Voice of Whiteness: D. W. Griffith's Biograph Films," in *The Birth of Whiteness: Race and the Emergence of United States Cinema,* ed. Daniel Bernardi (New Brunswick, N.J.: Rutgers University Press, 1996).

42. Linda Martín Alcoff, *The Future of Whiteness* (Malden, Mass.: Polity Press, 2015), 7.

43. Ibid., 9.

44. Lebow, *First Person Jewish,* xxv.

45. Ibid., xxvii.

46. Lebow, *First Person Jewish,* 151.

47. Curiously, Lebow takes up Michelle Citron's *Daughter Rite* (1978) film as the paradigmatic Jewish women's feminist documentary of the 1970s—a telling move that tacitly continues to prioritize experimental aesthetics in the archive of women's documentary filmmaking.

48. Lebow, *First Person Jewish,* 36.

49. Ibid., 36–37.

50. Alcoff, *Future of Whiteness,* 51.

51. Ibid., 55.

52. Ibid., 55.

53. Ibid., 60.

54. Rothschild, email correspondence, June 7, 2018. Rothschild adds, "My grandfather had many business setbacks, including being ruined by Henry Ford because he was Jewish. When he died at 49 she had to take in boarders to continue to stay in the house."

55. Saba Mahmood, *Politics of Piety: The Islamic Revival and the Feminist Subject* (Princeton, N.J.: Princeton University Press, 2011), 13.

56. Ibid.

57. See, for example, E. Ann Kaplan, *Women and Film: Both Sides of the Camera* (New York: Routledge, 1983).

Chapter 4. Native Ethnographers and Feminist Solidarity

1. Alisa Lebow, *First Person Jewish* (Minneapolis and London: University of Minnesota Press, 2008).

2. Zakiya Luna, "'Truly a Women of Color Organization': Negotiating Sameness and Difference in Pursuit of Intersectionality," *Gender & Society* 30, no 5 (October 2016): 769–90.

3. Ibid., 771.

4. Nancy N. Chen, "Speaking Nearby: A Conversation with Trinh T. Minh-ha," *Visual Anthropology Review* 8, no. 1 (Spring 1992): 82- 91. In this conversation between Nancy N. Chen and Trinh T. Minh-ha, the latter defines the concept of speaking nearby as "A speaking that reflects on itself and can come really close to a subject without, however, seizing or claiming it" (87).

5. Caroline Gil-Rodríguez, "Towards Archiving: Third World Newsreel's Media Collection," master's thesis, New York University, 2016, available at http://www.nyu.edu/tisch/preservation/program/student_work/2016spring/16s_Gil_Thesis_07152016_final.pdf.

6. Joan McKinney, "The 'Quiet Women' Speak Out," *Oakland Tribune,* February 24, 1971. Frances Mulhall Achilles Library, Archives. Whitney Museum of American Art, New York.

7. Sherry Millner, "Third World Newsreel: Interview with Christine Choy," *Jump Cut* 27 (July 1982): 21–22, available at https://www.ejumpcut.org/archive/onlinessays/JC27folder/ChrisChoyInt.html.

8. "History," *Third World Newsreel,* available at https://www.twn.org/twnpages/about/history.aspx.

9. Kristen Hogan, *The Feminist Bookstore Movement* (Durham, N.C.: Duke University Press, 2016).

10. Ibid., 71.

11. "Interview with Judy Smith/S.F. Newsreel," *Women and Film* 1 (1972): 33.

12. Combahee River Collective, "A Black Feminist Statement," in *Words of Fire,* ed. Beverly Guy-Sheftall (New York: The New Press, 1995), 232–40.

13. "'Woman's Film': A Look at Poverty," *San Francisco Chronicle,* February 26, 1971.

14. For example, a Newsreel press release advertises screenings in February 1971 at American Zoetrope, Surf Interplayers, and the University of California, Berkeley, Museum of Modern Art (MOMA) Archives, New York.

15. Museum of Modern Art press release draft, MOMA Archives. Sharon Smith describes the screening to telephone company employees in the *Women & Film* interview (31).

16. Press reviews of the film include: Joan McKinney, "The 'Quiet Women' Speak Out," *Oakland Tribune;* Beverly Koch, "Liberated Women Take Up the Arts," *San Francisco Chronicle;* Jonas Mekas, "Movie Journal," *Village Voice;* Molly Haskell, "Women Without Men," *Village Voice;* "Femmes Fatales," *Women's Wear Daily;* Irwin Silber, "The Woman's Film," *Guardian,* all 1971.

17. Redstockings, "Redstockings Manifesto," in *Radical Feminism: A Documentary Reader,* ed. Barbara A. Crow (New York and London: New York University Press, 2000), 224.

18. Ibid.

19. Clare Hemmings, "Telling Feminist Stories," *Feminist Theory* 6, no. 2 (August 2005): 115–16.

20. See Clare Hemmings, *Why Stories Matter* (Durham, N.C.: Duke University Press, 2010) for a thorough summary of the dominant narratives of feminist theory.

21. The "Redstockings Manifesto" reads: "Male supremacy is the oldest, most basic form of domination. All other forms of exploitation and oppression (racism, capitalism, imperialism, etc.) are extensions of male supremacy: men dominate women, a few men dominate the rest. All power-structures throughout history have been male-dominated and male-oriented" (223).

22. Victoria Hesford, *Feeling Women's Liberation* (Durham, N.C. and London: Duke University Press, 2013), 63–64.

23. Ibid., 65.

24. Ginny Berson for The Furies, "Beyond Male Power," in Crow, ed., *Radical Feminism,* 163.

25. Beverly Jones and Judith Brown, "Toward a Female Liberation Movement," in Crow, ed., *Radical Feminism,* 36.

26. Ibid.

27. Marlene Dixon, "Why Women's Liberation?" in Crow, ed., *Radical Feminism,* 71.

28. Dixon, for example, writes, "What most people do not know is that in certain respects, women suffer more than do non-white men," but she goes on to distinguish between non-white men and non-white women: "and that black and third world women suffer most of all" (79).

29. Combahee River Collective, "A Black Feminist Statement," in *Words of Fire,* ed. Beverly Guy-Sheftall (New York: The New Press, 1995), 232.

30. Carol Hanisch and Elizabeth Sutherland, "Women of the World Unite—We Have Nothing to Lose but Our Men!" *Notes from the First Year,* ed. New York Radical Women (New York: New York Radical Women, 1968), 12–16.

31. Ibid., 12.

32. Cellestine Ware, "The Relationship of Black Women to the Women's Liberation Movement," in Crow, ed., *Radical Feminism,* 100.

33. Hanisch and Sutherland, "Women of the World Unite," 12.

34. Ibid. The "Radical Women Manifesto, Seattle" contains a similar emphasis on an imagined pluralistic future for the women's movement: "The current leadership of the women's movement is largely student, professional, middle-class and white. But its future leadership will emerge from the vast ranks of militant women from the working class and from ethnic and sexual minorities," 269. In this 1974 manifesto, the Seattle women demonstrate a complex understanding of differential oppression: "These women come into direct and daily conflict with bosses on the job, and with racists and sexists on every level of life. They develop a keener awareness and

consciousness of the triple nature of oppression—class, race, and sex—than is possible for most white, non-working, middle-class women," Seattle Radical Women, "Radical Women Manifesto, Seattle," in Crow, ed., *Radical Feminism,* 269.

35. *The Woman's Film* Notes. MOMA Archives.

36. Alice Echols, *Daring to Be Bad: Radical Feminism in America, 1967–1975* (Minneapolis: University of Minnesota Press, 1989), 203.

37. Combahee River Collective, "A Black Feminist Statement," in Guy-Sheftall, ed., *Words of Fire,* 232–40.

38. Toni Morrison, "What the Black Woman Thinks About Women's Lib," *New York Times Magazine* 22 (August 1971): 14.

39. Ibid.

40. Ibid.

41. Ibid.

42. Ibid.

43. Maine Williams, "Black Women and the Struggle for Liberation," *Documents from the Women's Liberation Movement.* An On-line Archival Collection Special Collections Library. December 16, 2008. Duke University, available at http://library.duke.edu/digitalcollections/wlmpc_wlmms01004/.

44. Cynthia Young, "Third World Newsreel: Third Cinema Practice in the United States," in *Global Migration, Social Change, and Cultural Transformation,* ed. Emory Elliott, Jasmine Payne, and Patricia Ploesch (Basingstoke, U.K.: Palgrave Macmillan, 2008).

45. Gil-Rodríguez, "Towards Archiving," 12.

46. Diana Agosta and Barbara Osborn, "If I Ever Stop Believing . . ." *Heresies* 16 (Fall 1983): 68.

47. Young, "Third World Newsreel," 78.

48. Gil-Rodríguez, "Towards Archiving," 16.

49. Young, "Third World Newsreel," 80.

50. David James, *The Most Typical Avant-garde: History and Geography of Minor Cinemas in Los Angeles* (Berkeley: University of California Press, 2005), 297.

51. Young, "Third World Newsreel," 94.

52. Sherry Millner, "Third World Newsreel: Interview with Christine Choy," *Jump Cut* 27 (July 1982): 21–22, available at https://www.ejumpcut.org/archive/onlinessays/JC27folder/ChrisChoyInt.html.

53. John Jackson, "An Ethnographic Filmflam: Giving Gifts, Doing Research, and Videotaping the Native Subject/Object," *American Anthropologist* 106, no.1 (March 2004): 34.

54. Ibid.

55. Natalie Havlin, "'To Live a Humanity under the Skin': Revolutionary Love and Third World Praxis in 1970s Chicana Feminism," *WSQ: Women's Studies Quarterly* 43, no. 3 and 4 (Fall/Winter 2015): 95.

56. Cherríe Moraga, "Catching Fire: Preface to the Fourth Edition," in *This Bridge Called My Back: Writings by Radical Women of Color,* ed. Cherríe Moraga and Gloría Anzaldúa (Albany: State University of New York Press, 2015), xxi.

57. Ibid., xxi–xxii.

58. Ibid., xvi.

59. All-caps in subtitles.

60. Michael M. J. Fischer, "Ethnicity and the Post-Modern Arts of Memory," in *Writing Culture,* eds. J. Clifford and G. E. Marcus (Berkeley: University of California Press, 1986).

61. Ibid., 199.

62. Ibid.

63. Moraga, "Catching Fire," xxi.

64. Leon Fink and Brian Greenberg, *Upheaval in the Quiet Zone: A History of Hospital Workers' Union, Local 1199* (Working Class in American History series) (Champaign: University of Illinois Press, 1989), 130.

65. Madeline Anderson, "An Interview with Madeline Anderson on the Making of *I Am Somebody*," *Film Library Quarterly* 5, no. 1 (1972): 39–41.

66. Ibid., 41.

67. Nancy Fraser, "From Re-distribution to Recognition: Dilemmas of Justice in a 'Post-Socialist' Age," *New Left Review* 212 (1995): 68–93.

68. Ibid.

69. Ibid., 71.

70. Ibid., 73.

71. See, e.g., Jeanne Betancourt, *Women in Focus* (Dayton, Ohio: Pflaum, 1974). Julia Lesage also mentions *I Am Somebody* in her landmark essay, "The Political Aesthetics of the Documentary Film," *Quarterly Review of Film Studies* 3.4 (1978): 507–23.

72. Hogan, *Feminist Bookstore Movement,* 4.

73. Hesford, *Feeling Women's Liberation,* 2.

74. On the history of the term, see: Kimberle Crenshaw, "Mapping the Margins: Intersectionality, Identity Politics, and Violence against Women of Color," *Stanford Law Review* 43, no. 6 (July 1991): 1241–99; Margaret L. Andersen and Patricia Hill Collins, *Race, Class, and Gender: An Anthology* (Belmont, Calif.: Wadsworth, 1992); Avtar Brah and Ann Phoenix, "Ain't I a Woman? Revisiting Intersectionality," *Journal of International Women's Studies* 5, no. 3 (2004): 75–86; Jennifer C. Nash, "Intersectionality and Its Discontents," *American Quarterly* 69, no. 1 (March 2017): 117–29; Toril Moi, *Revolution of the Ordinary: Literary Studies after Wittgenstein, Austin, and Cavell* (Chicago: University of Chicago Press, 2017).

75. "The Real 'Shy Trump' Vote—How 53% of White Women Pushed Him to Victory," *The Guardian.* Last modified November 10, 2016, available at https://www.theguardian.com/us-news/2016/nov/10/white-women-donald-trump-victory.

76. For example, Farah Stockman, "Women's March on Washington Opens Contentious Dialogues About Race," *New York Times,* last modified January 9, 2017, available at https://www.nytimes.com/2017/01/09/us/womens-march-on-washington-opens-contentious-dialogues-about-race.html; Jia Tolentino, "The Somehow Controversial Women's March on Washington," *New Yorker,* last modified January 18, 2017, available at http://www.newyorker.com/culture/jia-tolentino/the-somehow-controversial

-womens-march-on-washington; Karen Grigsby Bates, "Race and Feminism: Women's March Recalls The Touchy History," *NPR,* last modified January 21, 2017, available at http://www.npr.org/sections/codeswitch/2017/01/21/510859909/race-and -feminism-womens-march-recalls-the-touchy-history; Heather Wilhelm, "'Women's March' Morphs into Intersectional Torture Chamber," *Chicago Tribune,* last modified January 12, 2017, available at http://www.chicagotribune.com/news/opinion/ commentary/ct-womens-march-washington-white-black-perspec-0113-20170112 -story.html.

Conclusion

1. Anita Little, "Top 10 Feminist Documentaries Streaming on Netflix," *Ms.* magazine blog, November 24, 2014, available at http://msmagazine.com/blog/2014/11/24/ top-10-feminist-documentaries-streaming-on-netflix/.

2. Olivia Truffaut-Wong, "13 Feminist Documentaries on Netflix all Women Should See," *Bustle,* January 30, 2017, available at https://www.bustle.com/p/13-feminist -documentaries-on-netflix-all-women-should-see-34176; Lacy Wright, "5 Empowering Feminist Documentaries That'll Rock Your Next Movie Night," *HelloFlo,* January 20, 2016, available at http://helloflo.com/5-empowering-feminist-documentaries-thatll -rock-your-next-movie-night/.

3. Sophie Mayer, *Political Animals: The New Feminist Cinema* (London and New York: IB Tauris, 2016).

4. Rebecca Traister and Sally Edelstein, "Let's Go Full Crocodile, Ladies (1970s Feminist Political Documentary Year of the Woman Available Now)," *Highline HuffPost,* July 29, 2015, available at http://highline.huffingtonpost.com/articles/en/lets-go-full -crocodile-ladies/. Also see Traister, *Good and Mad: The Revolutionary Power of Women's Anger* (New York: Simon & Schuster, 2018).

5. Ibid.

6. See Patricia White's eloquent discussion of cultural discourse surrounding the notion of the woman filmmaker in *Women's Cinema, World Cinema: Projecting Contemporary Feminisms* (Durham, N.C.: Duke University Press, 2015). As I was writing this book, the #metoo movement brought the entrenched and often violent misogyny of the film industry into public view.

7. Lucas Hilderbrand, ed. "The Big Picture: On the Expansiveness of Cinema and Media Studies," *Cinema Journal In Focus: The 'C' and 'M' in SCMS* 57.2 (Winter 2018): 113–16.

8. Sangita Gopal, "Feminism and the Big Picture: Conversations," *Cinema Journal In Focus: The 'C' and 'M' in SCMS* 57.2 (Winter 2018): 131–36.

9. "To tear down the walls that separate us from each other," is how Pati Hernandez described the purpose of the work she performs with incarcerated women at the post-screening Q&A in Dallas on August 19, 2017.

10. Screening organized by Olinka Green on Saturday, February 17, 2018.

11. Courtney Collins, "The Story of West Dallas From Bonnie and Clyde to Margaret

Hunt Hill," *KERA,* available at http://stories.kera.org/no-place/2017/04/23/the-story -of-the-place-on-the-other-side-of-the-trinity/. Accessed on February 18, 2018.

12. Ibid.

13. Quoted in a promotional email by Media Projects, Inc., Cynthia and Allen's production and distribution company.

14. Interview with Cynthia and Allen in Dallas, Texas, June 2017.

15. Alisa Lebow explores how the mandate to Tikkun Ha'Olam shapes the autobiographical documentaries of a number of filmmakers in *First Person Jewish* (Minneapolis and London: University of Minnesota Press, 2008). Despite her valuable attention to both Jewish values and personal documentaries, however, Lebow mentions only a couple of Jewish women filmmakers, such as Joyce Chopra and Michelle Citron (xxiv–xxv). A similar gloss over women documentary filmmakers occurs in Lebow's otherwise valuable introduction to *Cinema of Me: The Self and Subjectivity in First Person Documentary Film* (London and New York: Wallflower Press, 2012).

16. See Joyce Antler, *Jewish Radical Feminism: Voices from the Women's Liberation Movement* (New York: New York University Press, 2018).

Index

SHILYH WARREN is an associate professor of film and aesthetic studies at the University of Texas at Dallas.

WOMEN AND FILM HISTORY INTERNATIONAL

The University of Illinois Press
is a founding member of the
Association of University Presses.

Composed in 10.25/13 Marat Pro
with ITC Avant Garde Gothic display
by Lisa Connery
at the University of Illinois Press
Cover designed by Faceout Studios, Lindy Martin

University of Illinois Press
1325 South Oak Street
Champaign, IL 61820-6903
www.press.uillinois.edu